THE LOCUS OF CARE

Much recent debate among historians, sociologists, and specialists in welfare policy has been based on the assumption that the quite recent past has seen an evolutionary shift from the family to the state as the chief provider of health care. This is a shift which 'community care' is supposedly beginning to reverse. *The Locus of Care* challenges simple linear narratives, making it difficult for future policy decisions in this area to be justified by appeals to history.

Focusing on such themes as the limitations of household care, the pervasiveness of institutions, support for the mentally ill, and child care, eleven international contributors show how various the 'locus of care' has been in Europe and the Mediterranean world since antiquity, and also how various it continues to be in other parts of the globe such as China and South Africa. More wide-ranging in time and space than previous studies of the connections between informal and institutional care, this volume reveals that there is nothing new about the 'mixed economy' of welfare provision. Families, wider communities and institutions of many kinds have interacted and complemented one another in complex ways through the ages.

Peregrine Horden is Wellcome Trust Research Lecturer in the History of Medicine, Royal Holloway and Bedford New College, University of London. **Richard Smith** is Director of the Cambridge Group for the History of Population and Social Structure, University of Cambridge.

STUDIES IN THE SOCIAL HISTORY OF MEDICINE
Series Editors: Jonathan Barry and Bernard Harris

In recent years, the social history of medicine has become recognized as a major field of historical enquiry. Aspects of health, disease, and medical care now attract the attention not only of social historians but also of researchers in a broad spectrum of historical and social science disciplines. The Society for the Social History of Medicine, founded in 1969, is an interdisciplinary body, based in Great Britain but international in membership. It exists to forward a wide-ranging view of the history of medicine, concerned equally with biological aspects of normal life, experience of and attitudes to illness, medical thought and treatment, and systems of medical care. Although frequently bearing on current issues, this interpretation of the subject makes primary reference to historical context and contemporary priorities. The intention is not to promote a sub-specialism but to conduct research according to the standards and intelligibility required of history in general. The Society publishes a journal, *Social History of Medicine*, and holds at least three conferences a year. Its series, Studies in the Social History of Medicine, does not represent publication of its proceedings, but comprises volumes on selected themes, often arising out of conferences but subsequently developed by the editors.

THE LOCUS OF CARE

Families, communities, institutions,
and the provision of welfare
since antiquity

*Edited by Peregrine Horden
and Richard Smith*

London and New York

First published 1998
by Routledge
11 New Fetter Lane, London EC4P 4EE

Simultaneously published in the USA and Canada
by Routledge
29 West 35th Street, New York, NY 10001

Typeset in New Baskerville by Keystroke, Jacaranda Lodge,
Wolverhampton
Printed and bound in Great Britain by
T. J. International Ltd., Padstow, Cornwall

British Library Cataloguing in Publication Data
A catalogue record for this book is available from the British Library.

Library of Congress Cataloguing in Publication Data
The locus of care : families, communities, institutions, and the
provision of welfare since antiquity / edited by Peregrine Horden
and Richard Smith.
p. cm. — (Social studies in the history of medicine)
Includes bibliographical references and index.
1. Public welfare—History. 2. Social service—History.
3. Public welfare—History. 4. Welfare state—History. 5. Human
services—History. 6. Institutional care. I. Horden, Peregrine.
II. Smith, Richard. III. Series: Studies in the social history of
medicine.
HV51.L63   1998
361′.009—dc21   97–15177
CIP

ISBN 0–415–11216–8

CONTENTS

FIGURES AND TABLES

FIGURES

TABLES

CONTRIBUTORS

Amanda Berry, Wellcome Unit for the History of Medicine, University of Oxford.

Sandra Burman, Centre for Socio-Legal Research, University of Cape Town, South Africa.

Sandra Cavallo, Department of History, Royal Holloway and Bedford New College, University of London.

Martin Dinges, Institut für Geschichte der Medizin der Robert Bosch Stiftung, Stuttgart.

Peregrine Horden, Department of History, Royal Holloway and Bedford New College, University of London.

Lara Marks, Imperial College, University of London.

Marjorie K. McIntosh, Department of History, University of Colorado at Boulder, USA.

Richard Smith, Cambridge Group for the History of Population and Social Structure, University of Cambridge.

Akihito Suzuki, School of Economics, Keio University, Japan.

Mathew Thomson, Department of History, University of Sheffield.

Patricia van der Spuy, Centre for Socio-Legal Research, University of Cape Town, South Africa.

David Wright, School of Nursing, Postgraduate Division, University of Nottingham.

Zhongwei Zhao, Graduate School of Demography, Australian National University, Canberra.

ACKNOWLEDGEMENTS

The editors are greatly indebted to the participants in the conference in which this volume originates; to the contributors, for their responsiveness and forbearance during the collection's long gestation; to Bernard Harris, the immensely painstaking editor of the series in which it appears; to two anonymous referees; to Laura Lamont for preliminary editorial assistance; to Eilidh Garrett and Jim Oeppen for help with graphics; to Samantha Williams for compiling the index and Judy Winchester for invaluable help with proofs; to Heather McCallum and Ian Critchley of Routledge for making the volume a locus of their care; and to Humaira Erfan Ahmed for her customary prestidigitation with all aspects of the preparation of final copy.

INTRODUCTION

Peregrine Horden and Richard Smith

The difference between Social Security and earlier
arrangements is that Social Security is compulsory and
impersonal – earlier arrangements were voluntary and
personal . . . Children helped their parents out of love or
duty. They now contribute to the support of someone else's
parents out of compulsion and fear. The earlier transfers
strengthened the bonds of the family; the compulsory
transfers weaken them.[1]

I

What has the 'locus of care' been? That is: where has care of the
needy, and especially the sick, been delivered, and by whom? In
any given period and area, have the main providers of welfare been
members of the immediate family, the wider community, an
institution – or some combination of the three? How far have their
respective roles changed over time?

Those are the questions that this volume addresses, perhaps in a
more wide-ranging way than has so far been attempted, particularly
with respect to the European past. The answers provided by the
eleven chapters that follow – inevitably partial and preliminary
answers – are complex. But their starting point was a simple one. It
was a conception of the history of welfare espoused, whether
consciously or not, by many modern historians, sociologists, and
policy-makers and, as our epigraph is intended to indicate, by
economists too. This conception, put starkly, is that the quite
recent past has witnessed an evolutionary shift – from informal
provision, dominated by the extended family and the immediate
neighbourhood, to institutional care directed and funded by the

1

state.[2] An underlying value judgement is also frequently detectable: that families are to be preferred to institutions as care-providers, and that in the approach to the third millennium there can and should be strenuous efforts to revert to a past and supposedly golden age of kin-based welfare provision.[3] It is to the reconsideration, indeed the refutation, of such ideas that this volume is dedicated. A clear example of them, which will help bring the target into focus, is provided by the debate surrounding 'community care' in Britain. This debate illustrates both the preferred view of the past to which we are hostile and the mythmaking that attends it.

In 1990 the National Health Service and Community Care Act was passed, and on 1 April 1993 a new system for delivering care to millions of elderly, mentally ill, disabled, and other vulnerable individuals came into being. The purpose of this radical change was supposedly to provide the services and support that would enable the vulnerable to live as independently as possible in their own homes, in nursing or residential care, or with their families, rather than in institutions. The conventional account of the emergence of community care policies in Britain dates the process from the late 1950s.[4] Those years and the early 1960s witnessed a growing awareness of the negative consequences of hospitalizing mental patients for long periods. The awareness was reflected in the 1962 Hospital Plan to halve the number of beds in large establishments within fifteen years, and to discharge the ex-patients into 'the community'.[5] The idea that large residential institutions should be replaced by small-scale, localized forms of care subsequently spread into the discussion of the appropriate locus of provision for the whole range of physically and mentally handicapped and elderly people.[6] During the 1970s, the emphasis tended to be placed rather more on care *in* than care *by* the community. The care was to be located in the community but its provision was a public responsibility.[7] In the 1980s, a noteworthy shift of emphasis to care *by* the community occurred. Certain individuals conceived as 'the community' were to be providers for the dependant. Their care would be voluntary rather than statutory, informal rather than formal, unpaid rather than paid. And such services should spring from the personal ties of kinship, friendship, and neighbourhood. The principal causes of the change of policy were, first, an economy in which public expenditure was generally being reduced and, second, a fear of the rising costs of residential care that would be created by an ageing population.[8] The designation of who should principally assume responsibility for 'front-line' care was vague. Feminist commentators have been quick to assume that this particular notion of the community appealed to a false sense of family and of the warmth and intimacy that familial bonds are supposed to foster.[9]

The policy developments sketched above were predicated upon a set of historical assumptions: first, that the decline of the family as the chief provider of care had been very recent; second, that the extra-familial community had, until the emergence of so-called welfare states, been of minimal importance in the field of welfare; third, that the roles of family and state had been inversely related such that as one declined the other expanded; fourth, that the terms of the debate were historically invariant, and consequently that 'family' and 'state' – or 'informal' and 'formal' – were unproblematic pairs of categories; fifth, that the change from family to state provision had been peculiar to developed or westernized economies – the contemporary developing world no less than the pre-modern western past being seen as, essentially, all of a piece.

Somewhat like the tenets of Freudian analysis, this interpretative framework, supposedly universal in its application, has in fact been the product of a highly specific set of historical circumstances. Among these were: unprecedented economic growth in the aftermath of World War II; governments' subsequent disenchantment with Keynesian economic management; and the supposed threat from what has sometimes been termed the demographic 'time bomb' of ageing. The interpretation is akin to psychoanalysis in another respect too. Its analytical tools were forged in the later nineteenth century. Particularly prominent among them is a conception of change in terms of a clear sequence of stages, with some parts of the world progressing through the stages more rapidly than others.

An unusual correlate of this evolutionary diagnosis has been the conviction that trends can be reversed – that it is possible to effect a return to a previous stage. The ideal caring families of the late nineteenth and late twentieth centuries are therefore construed as fundamentally identical.[10] No allowance is made for intervening changes in fertility, gender roles, divorce rates, or rising life expectancies in the higher age groups. Yet such changes make it impossible to recreate the family environments of the late

3

nineteenth century. For instance, as Michael Anderson has trenchantly noted, the 1921 birth cohort now well into old age had, on average, slightly more than two children who reached age 25. Women in that cohort could look forward to on average at least twenty years of further life after age 60. This yields a ratio of survival years to children alive of approximately ten. The 1831 birth cohort, in contrast, had on average between three and four children who reached at least 25 years and a median life expectancy of only eight years. For a female reaching 60 years of age, the comparable ratio of surviving years to children alive was just over two. The 'burden of care' for individual daughters, if expressed in these crude demographic terms, has evidently increased. Furthermore, claims on the daughter's time may have risen significantly if she has entered the labour force with the intention of sustaining a career of her own. A role as family carer now carries many more opportunity costs for the adult female of working age.[11]

Proponents of the conventional evolutionary account are distinguished not only for their assumption that trends can be reversed, but still more for their conviction that these trends are easy to summarize. Alternatives to familial support – for the elderly for example[12] – have clearly been desirable. But it would be unwise to assume that simple trends are discernible in the development of non-familial forms of welfare provision.[13] In England, indoor relief – almshouses, hospitals, and the like – did not grow steadily at the expense of outdoor relief, rising to a climax in the large Poor Law Union workhouses of the nineteenth century.[14] Indeed it was during the *early* years of the Old Poor Law that, at least in the intentions of the legislators of 1598 and 1600, a large role was given to 'bricks-and-mortar' institutions offering people care away from their own hearths.[15] This emphasis soon diminished, so it seems, after *c.* 1640. Moves were, however, made during the early eighteenth century, possibly in the wake of burgeoning expenditure on outdoor relief, to promote workhouses. In the particularly stringent circumstances of the late eighteenth century, this initiative may in many places have led to a growth in relief to elderly females, the most expensive category of rate-supported beneficiary. And much of that relief would have been supplied in institutions that detached them from their communities and their kin.[16] Similar consequences may have flowed from the campaign to reduce outdoor relief during the late nineteenth century, before the establishment of state-funded old age pensions in 1908.

Any attempt to contain these developments within a linear model of change would be to impose on them a decidedly inappropriate conceptual framework. To reinforce the point with the specific example of the elderly: institutionalized care for them has not grown steadily over the last hundred years as a result of greater public involvement in meeting their needs.[17] David Thomson has demonstrated that, as recently as 1971, the proportion of elderly persons housed in institutions was substantially below levels reached between 1891 and 1911.[18] As Paul Johnson remarks, 'it is ironic, in the light of some recent political rhetoric, that the high point of the caring, sharing Victorian family coincided with an institutionalisation of the elderly never reached before or [until 1971] since'.[19] Certainly the proportion of the elderly over 75 years of age and in residential care has in recent years risen to exceed late Victorian and Edwardian levels. Yet it should also be noted that there has simultaneously been an enormous increase in the proportions, especially of females, who live alone in their own homes.[20]

It might at least be supposed that, as demographic conditions have improved, so nowadays those in need have more surviving kin potentially available as domestic carers. Yet here too developments have been far from straightforward. In antiquity there was perhaps a 98 per cent chance that a child aged 11 would have no living grandparents. In England *c.* 1800 such a probability would have fallen somewhat to 77 per cent. In the 1990s, grandparents' longevity is taken for granted, and for a child of 11 there is only a 31 per cent chance that no grandparent survives. The proportion in England of individuals without paternal uncles, however, is now higher at every age than it was during the second half of the eighteenth century. Likewise, at all ages an individual is more likely to lack cousins than would have been the case in the eighteenth and nineteenth centuries – a change that primarily reflects sharp twentieth-century reductions in fertility. Notwithstanding the great decline in infant and child mortality which has taken place over the last century, an individual reaching age 77 today is less likely to have at least one surviving child than was an individual of the same age in 1797, even though the eighteenth-century septenarian would have had more offspring. The counteracting movements of mortality and fertility levels in England play havoc with any attempt to tell a simple story of progress regarding the survivorship of kin and their availability as carers.[21]

Any specification of the state's role in the provision of care will be equally misleading if presented in terms of a whiggish chronology. The substitutability of state for family as care-provider should not be taken for granted. Some students of the English Old Poor Law legislation of the late sixteenth century have none the less assumed that the parish replaced the peasant family as protector against risk, adversity, and decrepitude. They have thus failed to realize that, in offering welfare payments and services, seventeenth- or eighteenth-century overseers of the poor were not undermining inter-generational support within the family but rather, in certain crucial respects, were attempting to preserve or foster it.[22] Similarly, as Jane Lewis notes, Conservative governments of the 1980s and 1990s have spoken not of relieving the family of its burdens but of helping it to perform its tasks.[23] Their declaration paradoxically aligns the 'contracting' late twentieth-century state with the 'burgeoning' late Tudor regime.

II

Enough has been said, by way of opening example, to suggest the difficulty of the subject. Recent developments in health care policy have to be seen against a background that is far more complex, that involves familial, community, and institutional support in more intricate combinations, and that reaches further back into the past, than can be conveyed by any quasi-historical tableau of 'before the Welfare State'.[24] Yet this opening example has been cursory; it concerns only England; and it invokes only four centuries. What if more detail – and more distant horizons – be sought?

With that enquiry in mind, the Society for the Social History of Medicine held its 1992 annual conference on the theme of 'Communities, Caring and Institutions'. The present volume comprises the revised versions of ten papers selected from those given at the conference, together with one commissioned essay. Quite obviously, no single collection of papers – at least none of feasible length and cost – could adequately encompass the history of this subject since antiquity and in every part of the globe. What we present must therefore be taken as soundings, hints of what is to be found elsewhere in a field that is still, for reasons already hinted at, very unevenly charted. Sometimes the individual contributions reflect the preoccupations of contemporary scholarship, as in Part III on mental health, which can build on a substantial number of earlier studies while yet revising their conclusions. At other points – as with Parts I and II on the history of *non*-institutional relief in Europe, or with the very recent history (and indeed futurology) of China and South Africa offered in Part IV – there is relatively little previous work to draw on, and approaches are perhaps being tried out rather than reflected.

Just as the collective scope of the papers cannot aspire to completeness of coverage, so, equally obviously, for reasons of space and (still more) availability of evidence, no single paper can be expected to give even-handed treatment to all three of the principal terms of our subtitle – families, communities, institutions. Contributors have been encouraged to focus. They should be seen as each seeking to illuminate a part, albeit often a substantial one, of the spectrum of possible sources of welfare provision – domestic or communal, formal or informal.

It is in keeping with that brief that the editors have deliberately avoided proposing – or imposing – any trans-historical definitions of 'care', 'family', 'community', 'institution', or 'welfare'. The variety of constructions that has been put on some of these and their equivalents in other languages, by modern scholarship as much as in the past, is touched on in chapter 1. Each term has in our own time generated a copious literature, driven, not always to advantage, by extreme feminism, the conservative New Right, and every ideological station in between. Each term has undergone major changes of connotation since antiquity.[25] In the following papers, *family* for instance is now the nuclear family, now the household (itself a hardly less elusive category), now the functionally extended kin group embracing relatives (agnatic, cognatic, or fictive) who do not live under the same roof. The *community* is local society (without prejudice as to its coherence or unanimity), the parish, the voluntary association, the borough, the work place, the ethnic category; and it is the community either as imaged at the time or as a convenient analytic tool – for which, despite much searching, no decent substitute has been found. *Institutions* are buildings such as the hospital or workhouse; but they are also procedures and practices, such as the operation of the Poor Law or the formalities of incarceration. Each term is shorthand for a cluster of concepts. There is nothing obvious or natural about any of them: their mutable characters should emerge from the discussion. Nothing of value is to be gained by stipulative editorial definition. As James Casey writes in essaying the most protean of the topics in question, the history of the family, '"definition" is what all family history is really about, the last chapter of the book rather than the first'.[26] Students of the history of welfare are not yet in a position to write any 'last chapters'.

Of course, to the extent that the crucial terms of the analysis are 'relativized' to particular social, demographic, and cultural contexts, so drawing comparisons across time and space becomes all the more daunting. We seek neither to underestimate the difficulty nor to diminish it. Indeed, we have already stressed that one of our purposes is to render suspect all simple narratives of the rise of institutions or the expansion of community care. And if those linear narratives so often told of nineteenth- to twentieth-century England are misleading, how much more so will be any that attempt to encompass a longer time-span.

The eleven papers in this volume are, then, various in period, in particular subject matter, and in conceptual armoury. They do none the less constitute an integrated set of reflections, not only on families, communities, and institutions (however construed) but also on several subordinate themes. The appearances of these themes, several of which are elaborated in chapter 1, are sometimes centuries and even continents apart. That is why a number of different chapter arrangements, both thematic and chronological, might have been equally helpful or attractive. To take three examples: A section on the history of child care could have been created, bringing together the chapters by McIntosh, Cavallo, Wright, Marks, and Burman and van der Spuy, and complementing another book on that topic edited by John Henderson and Richard Wall.[27] Or again, it would have been easy to devise a subdivision of the book that focused on the parish as welfare provider: McIntosh, Dinges, Suzuki, and Berry all deal with this. Another gathering of chapters – those by McIntosh, Cavallo, Dinges, Thomson, and Burman and van der Spuy – could have been advertised as a debate on the coercive character of institutions and of welfare policies more generally. The sequence of individual chapters and group titles that we did eventually choose is to that extent arbitrary: one among several possible ways of sign-posting the contents.

Part I, which focuses almost exclusively on the history of informal care, contains only a single, extended, chapter. Peregrine Horden sets himself three related tasks. One of these is to draw out certain themes in the contributions following his which have a broad bearing on the comparative history of informal care and its connections with other 'sectors' of welfare provision. In that sense his chapter is, in part, the present Introduction continued by other means. His purpose is, however, less to summarize other chapters than to apply some of their conclusions beyond their original purview. The second of his tasks is to supplement the evidence of those chapters by rehearsing discussions by both ethnographers and historians that best reveal informal networks of household, kin, and neighbourhood support – and that reveal them in action from day to day, and not just at their moments of breakdown. The third task is to relate the implications of that material to evidence from earlier periods, ancient and medieval. The tentative proposal is that, although such informal networks have doubtless undergone immense changes over time, their limitations, fragility, and necessary intersection with other sources of support for the sick and needy have *not* changed so dramatically. To that extent, and whatever else may eventually be said about it, the long-term history of the subject is one of continuity.

The overall argument is thus (a) that no 'golden age' of family care can be found when (among the poor) large households or coresident kin groups did almost all the caring work required by the ill, handicapped, or impoverished. No such age is to be found in Mediterranean antiquity or the European Middle Ages. Nor, Horden suggests in brief asides on other parts of the globe, is it likely to be found elsewhere. Since there has been no golden age of the self-sufficient family or household, then (b) networks *linking* households, and indeed often making a nonsense of modern attempts to define them, have almost always been extremely important welfare agencies. But (c) networks too have their limitations: wherever we catch a glimpse of them they seem rather less cosy and supportive than stereotypes of pauper solidarity might lead us to expect. Hence, in antiquity as later, 'vertical' ties such as those linking patrons and clients, benefactors and the poor, have always been intimately bound up with 'horizontal' ones of mutual support. In all this, to repeat, no simple secular rise of institutions, no decline of the family that can be allocated to a particular period. Instead, what emerges is a complicated and shifting 'mixed economy' of care, in which the role of the *immediate* family may have been overestimated – a mixed economy discernible as far back in time as there is evidence of welfare provision.

Part I, 'Informal care: from ethnography to ancient history', functions as prologue to later parts, in that it deals with earlier periods than they do. By focusing on informal support systems, which they confront as only one topic among several, it also sets the scene for their more detailed, and chronologically more specific, explorations. Part II, 'Networks and institutions in Western Europe *c.* 1500–*c.*1800', presents four geographically distinct studies of the interpenetration of informal and institutional sectors in western Europe between the Reformation and the French Revolution.

In chapter 2, Marjorie McIntosh places under the microscope a part of that much larger canvas of the history of poor relief in later medieval to early modern England that she has outlined in a previous article.[28] In the background to her discussion of arrangements in Hadleigh, Suffolk, is a blend of informal relief from friends, neighbours, and wealthier households and the more formalized support provided by parishes, confraternities, and town governments – a truly mixed economy, 'flexible and diverse, marked by complementarity and a lack of rigid definition'. Indeed, the one clear contrast that McIntosh allows is that between voluntary and compulsory assistance. Her period, the later sixteenth century, is one in which the second was superimposed on the first. Private voluntary assistance was no longer adequate to the much-increased demand that resulted from the cluster of economic and demographic changes that Tudor England had been undergoing. Major English towns increasingly experimented with local taxes levied on more prosperous citizens for the benefit of the poor, a system of redistribution that would of course eventually become national in scope following the passage of the Old Poor Law. Towns such as Hadleigh had to use their poor rates to supplement, though never replace, informal care – through grants-in-aid, 'boarding out' those in need with other families, or indoor relief from residential institutions. There survives from Hadleigh a long run of accounts kept by those in charge of its charitable disbursement and a parish register which spans the whole Elizabethan age. Thanks to these, McIntosh is able to provide a uniquely full and precise picture of the domestic circumstances and particular requirements of those whom the town variously supported – including, unusually for the period and place, children and adolescents.

The next two chapters take us to Italy and France, the countries with whose systems of poor relief in the early modern period English developments have most often been compared and contrasted.

Sandra Cavallo's study of Turin begins by calling into question two connected ways in which England, as representative of north-western Europe, and Italy, as an example of the south, have often been distinguished in this context. The first involves the presumed contrast between English relief – typically of the 'outdoor' kind, parish-based, comprehensive, and funded by the Poor Rate – and 'continental' relief – supposedly haphazard and limited in its finances and scope, and based on 'indoor' relief provided in large hospitals. Underlying this contrast, it is held, and indeed perhaps one of its causes, is a distinction between demographic regimes and types of household organization. In early modern England, families were predominantly nuclear, their members were individualistic in outlook and the idea that they might look after their needy relatives was an alien one; responsibility for such people therefore fell upon the wider collectivity, beyond the household, and was met by public welfare measures such as the Poor Law. In contemporary southern Europe, on the other hand, families were allegedly larger and exhibited greater solidarity; hence outdoor relief was rarer and other institutions less widespread and sophisticated. The demographic argument is discussed in general terms from both conceptual and historical points of view by Horden in chapter 1. Cavallo's paper continues and focuses that critique. She shows, first, that the Italian families revealed in requests for admission to the Ospedale di Carità in Turin were, on the whole, no more ready to shoulder the burden of their dependants than were their English counterparts, and second, that the welfare system of her area was far from exclusively indoor in its application. The contrast with England seems at least to have been exaggerated.

Indeed, Cavallo's analysis echoes that of McIntosh in a surprising number of ways. The hospital in Turin supplemented domiciliary care in a manner strikingly reminiscent of the aims of the administrators of Hadleigh's nascent Poor Law. Its ethos was more of a contractualist than a coercive kind, so that the distinctive, threatening stereotype of the European hospital is also shown to be in need of modification. Torinese institutions emerge as less removed in spirit from their English counterparts than we had supposed. Finally, Cavallo shows that, in Piedmont as much as in Elizabethan England, we have to envisage a whole range of ways in which external agencies, formal and informal, complemented family care. The hospital was not the only fount of relief.

Employers of those in domestic service were one other potential source, and McIntosh and Cavallo both consider them in some detail.

Themes emerging in these two contributions are developed in chapter 4, by Martin Dinges. He establishes a subtle conceptual framework for his analysis, which enables him to separate out the varieties of self-help expected of the needy and the overlapping ties of reciprocity involved in all forms of welfare provision. (On that latter point, he implicitly reinforces the suggestion made by Cavallo that the vocabulary of clientage may not always be the most advantageous way of describing such ties.) He, too, undermines any simplistic contrast between English parish-based and continental hospital-centred relief systems – through focusing on support offered, at parochial level, by the elders of the Calvinist community in Bordeaux during the 1660s to the sick, unemployed, and destitute. As in Hadleigh, such parochial support was only one of several types of welfare provision to be found in the mixed Catholic and Protestant city. There were, for instance, several residential institutions, including a (Protestant) parish sick room. Even after the Catholic general hospital had been expanded and a workhouse founded, parochial relief still accounted for a good 20 per cent of all charitable expenditure in the city. Again as in Hadleigh, the records are quite detailed. Surviving consistorial registers enable Dinges to reconstruct a number of individual case histories. Sickness and unemployment were the two main reasons why the Consistory's help was sought. Boarding a needy person with another family was one recourse that these administrators had in common with their English forerunners. But, as in Hadleigh, much was also expended on helping adolescents into apprenticeship. The aim, overall, seems to have been to supplement rather than replace the individual's or household's ability to survive periods of hardship or incapacity.

The final chapter in Part II, by Amanda Berry, returns the discussion to England, but continues to involve the parish and the ways in which it interacted with other sources of provision. Here, though, because of the nature of the evidence, the discussion is directed more to relations between institutions and communities or groups than to those between institutions and families. The institutions mainly in question are voluntary hospitals, to which subscribers could nominate patients for admission. Hospital subscriptions have conventionally been envisaged by historians as vehicles for the patronage or charity of aristocracy and middle classes in the eighteenth century – an institutionalizing of those informal initiatives from 'above', those 'vertical' ties, that appear in the background of all four opening chapters. Berry however draws our attention away from this familiar ground and onto corporate subscribers – communities (of a kind) such as parishes, commercial firms, and friendly societies.

Evidence is taken from records of three provincial voluntary hospitals, in Bristol, Exeter, and Northampton, for the period 1765–1815. Regional variations in social and economic conditions are used to suggest why each hospital developed its own particular policy toward corporate subscribers, to help explain the age and gender distribution of patients nominated by such subscribers, and to envisage why they might have found it economical to nominate their sick members to a hospital rather than meet medical costs directly. As in Dinges's account of Bordeaux some hundred years previously, a recurrent theme is the need felt by 'persons of property' to limit parochial expenditure on relief for the sick or injured, and hence reduce their contribution to its maintenance.

Part III of the collection, 'Beyond the asylum: mental health in Britain c. 1700–1939', reflects the amount of work recently undertaken on the history of the insane and mentally handicapped in England since 1600. But it pursues a less usual course by concentrating on the fate of the afflicted *outside* the institution whose rise and decline has dominated so much of the historiography: the asylum.

In chapter 6, Akihito Suzuki draws on the records of some 130 'lunatics' whose right to reside in their parish and to receive its poor relief was examined between 1735 and 1783 by the Poor Law officers of St Martin-in-the-Fields, Westminster. He supplements this material with Middlesex Quarter Sessions records, so as to explore the circumstances in which informal, domestic provision for the insane failed and the threshold of the asylum, in this case often a private madhouse, was crossed. He thus shares Berry's concern with the relationship between parishes and private institutions, but his evidence enables us to return from the relationship's institutional to its familial aspects. The principal finding is that welfare provision for lunatics from outside the sufferer's nuclear family was scarce (cf. again chapter 1). Children who had married and set up on their own often did not help their lunatic parents; generous neighbours might offer lodging, but only in the short term. In London as in Hadleigh and Turin (chapters 2, 3), servants are also worthy of attention in this context. Indeed, in relation to the likely total number of those in domestic employment, demented servants loom disproportionately large in Suzuki's sample. Their employers sometimes looked after them, yet on the whole their position was even more precarious than that of servants in full possession of their faculties.

David Wright's chapter moves us forward to Victorian England but is similarly concerned with care in the household. He reconstructs some of the 'pre-institutional' experiences of 475 families of children admitted to the National Asylum for Idiots, Earlswood. His subject is not the family at the point of breakdown as a source of welfare provision, or the factors that induced its members to seek institutional care for a mentally ill or impaired child. Instead, he concentrates on the problems that such a child presented to its household, and on the strategies devised to cope with deviant behaviour. As in Suzuki's contribution, the nuclear family, not the institution, emerges as the significant 'locus of care' for 'idiots', despite what previous historiography would entitle us to expect. Within the household, mothers and elder sisters are shown to have been the primary carers; neither the wider kin group nor neighbours seem to have helped very much – although some children were presumably 'boarded out' with other families.

In chapter 8, Mathew Thomson pursues the topic of mental deficiency by examining the care and control of adults during the inter-war years. His immediately striking argument is that it was in this period, rather than after 1945, that community care as a policy actually emerged. The term 'community care' was first used in a British official document during the 1920s, and not, as is commonly thought, thirty years later. The evolution of the relationship between community and institutional care – the precise mixture of the period's 'mixed economy' – is shown to be more complicated than has been supposed. That is true at the level of aggregate numbers in institutions and under some form of extra-institutional supervision. It is also true at the microscopic level of the individual case history, which might involve moving back and forth between the asylum and domestic care in a manner not wholly different from that evidenced centuries earlier in Turin or Bordeaux. Leaning principally on the annual reports of the Board of Control, the government department that oversaw mental deficiency policy and its administration, Thomson is able to analyse not just the perceived advantages of care in the community but, additionally, the causes of its stagnation as a policy during the later 1930s. Above all, he reinforces the lesson that community and institutional care should no more be seen as essentially antithetical in modern times than they were in the Elizabethan age. At any given moment, one locus may have been thought by the administrators of institutional welfare to be more economical than the other (compare again chapters 1, 3, and 5), but that did not entail the fundamental incompatibility of community and institution.

Our final part, 'Children and the elderly in the twentieth century', takes the scope of the collection outside western Europe for the first time since the discussion of the late antique Mediterranean world that concludes chapter 1. It is important that a volume predominantly concerned with the familiar stretches of European history should also offer at least some reminder of the point registered by Horden: there is a global history of this subject as much in need of liberation from misleading stereotypes of family care and simple evolutionary schemas as is any period of the western past. Part IV returns to the theme of child welfare, a concern of several earlier contributions. Its first chapter especially, by Lara Marks, also follows on from Thomson's paper in adding to the 'pre-history' of community care. And it complements Berry's account in that it too is looking at communities and institutions – at the local inflections of community ideologies and their effect on perceptions of neighbourhood, on voluntary services, and on official policy-making. Marks's chosen territory is the four London boroughs of Hampstead, Kensington, Stepney, and Woolwich. She uses the political, economic, and social configuration of each borough to show how notions of community were locally negotiated and translated into local government initiatives, particularly the provision of milk depots and advice on contraception.

In chapter 10, Sandra Burman and Patricia van der Spuy offer another regional study, but now from South Africa under, and after, apartheid. Were the social policies introduced by the Nationalist government new, were they effectively implemented, and what is their legacy? We may profoundly hope that apartheid can be viewed as an aberration which will vanish without trace. But Burman and van der Spuy's study of the general impact of apartheid legislation on 'non-White' households, and their particular investigation of institutional provision for 'unwanted' children in Cape Town, leave grounds for only the most cautious optimism. Families have been broken up, communities undermined; and there are still not enough institutions to cope with the increasing population of street children that has resulted.

With a discussion that again complements those of an existing collection,[29] chapter 11 does, however, sound a cheerier note – one elicited by the elderly rather than by children. If South Africa after De Klerk confronts enormous problems in implementing even a qualified return to an adequately caring society, China after Deng is, in one respect, able to fulfil an old ideal of welfare provision. The scholarship of Chinese poor relief has perhaps tended to take it for granted that support for the elderly actually came, as it was traditionally thought it should, from within the extended-family household.[30] Zhongwei Zhao employs the techniques of computer microsimulation to reconstruct the likely networks of kin available to a specified type of individual. He demonstrates that, since China's very rapid post-war demographic transition, the probability that an old person will have one or two surviving close kin with whom to reside is improving all the time. The long-cherished ideal is becoming more, not less, easy of attainment as the country continues to modernize. And with that stark reversal of expectations in the history of welfare provision the volume may suitably close.

NOTES

1 M. Friedman and R. Friedman, *Free to Choose: A Personal Statement*, Penguin edn (Harmondsworth, 1980), p. 135.
2 S. Pedersen, *Family, Dependence, and the Origins of the Welfare State* (Cambridge, 1994), brings out one strand in the history of such thinking.
3 Cf. F. Prochaska, *The Voluntary Impulse* (London, 1988).
4 Royal Commission on the Law Relating to Mental Illness and Mental Deficiency, *Report* (London, 1957). Cf. Thomson, this volume.
5 D. Allen, 'An Analysis of Factors Affecting the Development of the 1962 Hospital Plan', *Social Policy and Administration* 15 (1981), pp. 3–18.
6 J. Martin, *Hospitals in Trouble* (Oxford, 1984); N. Korman and H. Glennester, *Hospital Closure* (Buckingham, 1990).
7 P. Hall, 'The Development of Health Centres', in P. Hall, H. Land, R. Parker and A. Webb, *Change, Choice and Conflict in Social Policy* (London, 1975), pp. 299–310.
8 J. Lewis and H. Glennester, *Implementing the New Community Care* (Buckingham and Philadelphia, 1996), pp. 1–16.

9 J. Lewis and B. Meredith, *Daughters Who Care: Daughters Caring for Mothers at Home* (London, 1988).

10 M. Anderson, 'The Relevance of Family History', in C. Harris (ed.), *The Sociology of the Family: New Directions for Britain, Sociological Review Monograph* 28 (1979), pp. 49–73.

11 M. Anderson, 'The Social Implications of Demographic Change', in F. M. L. Thompson (ed.), *The Cambridge Social History of Britain 1750–1950*, vol. 2: *People and their Environments* (Cambridge, 1990), pp. 52–3.

12 M. Pelling and R.M. Smith (eds), *Life, Death, and the Elderly: Historical Perspectives* (London, 1991).

13 Cf. A. de Swaan, *In Care of the State: Health, Education and Welfare in Europe and the USA in the Modern Era* (Oxford, 1988), who sees his whole period in terms of increasing collectivization of provision. Cf. J. Barry and C. Jones (eds), *Medicine and Charity Before the Welfare State* (London, 1991).

14 D. Thomson, 'The Welfare of the Elderly in the Past: A Family or Community Responsibility?', in Pelling and Smith, *Life, Death, and the Elderly*, pp. 194–221.

15 P. Slack, *The English Poor Law 1531–1782* (London, 1990), pp. 15–16.

16 R. M. Smith, 'Charity, Self-Interest and Welfare: Reflections from Demographic and Family History', in M. Daunton (ed.), *Charity, Self-Interest and Welfare in the English Past: The Neale Colloquium in British History* (London, 1996), pp. 39–40.

17 R. M. Smith, 'Ageing and Well-Being in Early Modern England: Pension Trends and Gender Preferences under the English Old Poor Law c. 1650–1800', in P. Johnson and P. Thane (eds), *History of Old Age and Ageing* (London, 1997).

18 D. Thomson, 'Workhouse to Nursing Home: Residential Care of Elderly People in England since 1840', *Ageing and Society* 3 (1983), pp. 43–70.

19 P. Johnson, 'The Economics of Old Age in Britain: A Long-Run View 1881–1981', Centre for Economic Policy Research Discussion Paper no. 47 (1985), p. 7.

20 P. Johnson and J. Falkingham, *Ageing and Economic Welfare* (London, 1992), pp. 31–5.

21 A seminal paper on this subject is P. Laslett, 'La parenté en chiffres', *Annales: Economies, Sociétés, Civilisations* 43 (1988), pp. 5–24.

22 Smith, 'Charity, Self-Interest and Welfare', pp. 44–5.

23 J. Lewis, 'Family Provision of Health and Welfare in the Mixed Economy of Care in the late Nineteenth and Twentieth Centuries', *Social History of Medicine* 8 (1995), pp. 1–16.

24 Thomson, 'Welfare of the Elderly in the Past', pp. 194–5.

25 A few recommendations from an unmanageably vast bibliography: R. P. Saller, '*Familia, Domus,* and the Roman Conception of the Family', *Phoenix* 38 (1984), pp. 336–55; D. B. Martin, 'The Construction of the Roman Family: Methodological Considerations', *Journal of Roman Studies* 86 (1996), pp. 40–60; S. J. Yanagisako, 'Family and Household: The Analysis of Domestic Groups', *Annual Review of*

Anthropology 8 (1979), pp. 161–205; N. Tadmor, 'The Concept of the Household-Family in Eighteenth-Century England', *Past and Present* 151 (1996), pp. 111–40, with excellent opening references; M. E. Fissell, 'Individuals, Families, Institutions, Collectivities and the Locus of Care: Some Historiographical Reflections', an unpublished paper for sight of which we are indebted to the author; G. Davey, *Ideologies of Caring: Rethinking Community and Collectivism* (London, 1988); N. Barry, *Welfare* (Buckingham, 1990). See further ch. 1.

26 J. Casey, *The History of the Family* (Oxford, 1989), p. 14.

27 J. Henderson and R. Wall (eds), *Poor Women and Children in the European Past* (London and New York, 1994), Part I.

28 M. McIntosh, 'Local Responses to the Poor in Late Medieval and Tudor England', *Continuity and Change* 3 (1988), pp. 209–45.

29 Pelling and Smith, *Life, Death, and the Elderly*.

30 E.g. P. Buckley Ebrey and J. L. Watson (eds), *Kinship Organization in Late Imperial China 1000–1940* (Berkeley, Los Angeles, and London, 1986).

Part I

INFORMAL CARE: FROM ETHNOGRAPHY TO ANCIENT HISTORY

1

HOUSEHOLD CARE AND INFORMAL NETWORKS

Comparisons and continuities from antiquity to the present

Peregrine Horden

To King Ptolemy greeting from Ctesicles. I am being wronged
by Dionysius and my daughter Nike. For though I had
nurtured her . . . when I was stricken with bodily infirmity
and my eyesight became enfeebled she would not furnish
me with the necessaries of life. And when I wished to obtain
justice from her in Alexandria . . . she gave me a written
oath by the king that she would pay me twenty drachmae
every month . . . Now, however, corrupted by that bugger
Dionysius, she is not keeping any of her engagements to me,
in contempt of my old age and my present infirmity.[1]

I

What can a student of antiquity or the early Middle Ages contribute
to a volume such as this? Vignettes of broken promises will
certainly not be enough. The chapters that follow weigh the
relative significance of familial, extra-familial, and, within that
larger category, institutional care of the sick and disadvantaged.
They investigate the multiple connections between those different
support sectors. They adduce case histories, generate statistics,
date changes to within a decade. Where much earlier centuries are
concerned, none of this is possible. Tentative suggestions must
substitute for solidly buttressed arguments.

That is most acutely the case with informal care, which is the
chief focus of this opening chapter. Part of its purpose is to sketch

21

a broad historical and anthropological backdrop to the more localized concerns of subsequent contributions. The intention is also, however, to give some indication of how, under this heading of informal care, we might conceive the period preceding that covered in the next contribution (McIntosh's account of the later Middle Ages).

The present offering is thus prologue as well as scenery. It assembles and compares evidence of domiciliary care and informal networks of support in the *longue durée*, from antiquity to the recent purview of ethnographers, sociologists, and experts in social policy. It uses that evidence, by implication throughout and explicitly at the end, to lend plausibility to three linked suggestions. The first is that there is no 'golden age' of household care to be discerned in the European and Mediterranean worlds in antiquity or the Middle Ages, no period or area in which large supportive families have been efficiently responsible for the overwhelming bulk of welfare provision. The second is that networks of connections between households, not necessarily involving kin, have probably been of immense importance to the needy, but that such networks seem often to have been limited in strength and capacity. At this level of generality, it is argued, continuity in the history of households and networks is more evident than some fall from grace. Obviously enough, there have been enormous and multifarious changes in the history of welfare provision since antiquity; but they have not been of the kind that can be captured by theological analogies or simple evolutionary frameworks. The third suggestion elaborated in what follows, therefore, is that historians of the sick poor should envisage a broad spectrum of resources beyond the household and its immediate connections – patrons, formalized community organizations, institutions, and so on – as having been called upon for a very long time to supplement informal assistance. To that extent, there is nothing new or modern about the 'mixed economy of care'.[2]

Those suggestions can be proffered only tentatively because of the state of the evidence available from pre-modern times. The ancient historian or early medievalist lacks the parish registers, the wills and nationwide censuses that make it possible to discern the family structure and local connections of those in need; lacks also, beyond a few scraps, the forensic and institutional archives, the case-books and correspondence that can reveal the circumstances under which the locus of care was determined. In a field rightly dominated by the equivalent of miniaturists, the ancient historian or medievalist cannot even aspire to the detail and finish of abstract expressionism.

More daunting even than these deficiencies is the realization that, for all the relative abundance and articulacy of their documents, a number of contributors, even those involved with the apparently voluble nineteenth century, still have to confront the fact that they can study informal domestic care only through its failures (cf. Suzuki, Wright). It is the breakdown of domestic support that so often produces the written record (such as the papyrus from Hellenistic Egypt quoted on page 21). In this volume we are mostly looking at health care within the context of the wider history of poor relief, and hence at families or individuals of at best very modest means. We can therefore scarcely expect to find letters or diaries that relay in any quantity or vividness the successful routines of visiting, nursing, medication, confinement, or attending to a sick person's other 'necessaries of life'. Oral history will take us a little way back into the past but, as Wright cautions below, its witness may be coloured by nostalgia and has to be tested against what written evidence is available. In any century earlier than our own, then, family care that was adequate to its task leaves few traces.

Yet the effort to gain at least some impression of both its successes and its failures must surely be made – by students of later periods as much as by the medievalist. For self-help and domestic care constitute the great submerged ice sheets of the history of health, as also of the history of poverty in general. We perforce devote most of our attention to the visible peaks and ridges of documented medical practice and institutional support. Yet we also have to find ways of reminding ourselves how small a proportion of the whole subject is actually in view.[3] If that applies to modernists, on so many other occasions dispirited by the profusion rather than the scarcity of their sources, how much more so must it apply to historians of antiquity or the Middle Ages.

Proceeding by analogy is one remedy; a modest and partial remedy, but to be seized on none the less. And that is why the bulk of this chapter is devoted to mustering comparative material from which analogies may be drawn. The immediate comparisons are those supplied by other contributions to this collection. I shall look to them first; then cast the net more widely, to exemplary studies of informal care and household interaction; then turn, in the eighth and last section, to the period preceding that covered in later chapters, the ancient and earlier medieval worlds.

II

The following points relevant to antiquity and the Middle Ages seem to me to emerge from the papers in this collection. Each point of course has a broad bearing on the whole history of health care in modern times; but each should additionally give pause to historians involved with the less well-documented epochs. These points can be summed up, banally but accurately, under the related headings of variety or complexity.

(1) The sheer variety of what must be understood by 'care': from the arrangement of retirement facilities in a long-stay institution to the restraint of imbeciles within one room in the house; from hiring a public physician at the most medical end of the spectrum to the provision of reassuringly ordinary living or employment conditions through boarding out or apprenticeship at the other extreme – from money to company in short; from maternal and infant welfare clinics to free burial. When students of darker ages write of care, it is tempting for them to think that they can readily imagine what was involved in it. Recalling that multiplicity is a necessary corrective.

(2) The extent to which those various forms of care could be described as 'outdoor' or domiciliary relief. That the home should be a principal locus of care is to be expected in the chapters concerned with early modern England. It is somewhat more of a surprise in the contributions dealing with the mentally ill or handicapped in England during the eighteenth and nineteenth centuries. But in the historiography of that era the domination of the asylum has been ended. What is very striking, however, is the extent of outdoor relief to be found at both parochial and civic levels in Europe. In the light of Cavallo's and Dinges's chapters, and some other like-minded work, historians will have to reconsider the contrast habitually drawn between the outdoor relief sustained under the English Poor Law and the indoor relief supposedly favoured in continental welfare systems. Just as the history of the asylum is no longer taken as the whole story of the English insane in the Victorian age, but figures as one among several equally accessible resources, so the big European hospital, with its supporting policy of *renfermement*, is having to yield its centrality in

historians' agreed narrative. The great hospital may have been the focus of comprehensive poor relief measures, but it can function quite as much as the source of 'care in the community' as of campaigns to segregate.[4]

(3) The role of ideology in general, but especially religious ideology, is harder to specify than might have been expected. Types of care cannot be predicated on religious affiliation. So far as antiquity is concerned, the differences so frequently stressed in the older scholarly literature between pagan and Judaeo-Christian philanthropy may well have been overdrawn.[5] Or to take the most familiar example, no obvious and sustained divergences have emerged between Catholic and Protestant poor relief policies in the early modern period. The contrasts between two welfare communities of the same affiliation may be as significant as the similarities. It is *local* inflexions that count for most. Compare the ideals discernible at parochial level in Tudor Essex (McIntosh) with those in near-contemporaneous Bordeaux (Dinges). The latter shows how it was the hostility of the Catholic majority that strengthened informal care as a reaction to Catholic institutional provision. In Hadleigh, the animating idea behind outdoor relief had more to do with the creation of a 'godly community on earth'. In Turin, by contrast, religious notions were less important than civic patriotism in generating welfare schemes (Cavallo). Even in the utterly different context of South Africa, differences in attitude to adoption between Islam, indigenous religion, and the Dutch Reformed Church are cast emphatically into the shade by the vastly greater gulf between, on one hand, their shared ambitions for supposedly unwanted children and those underlying the government's relocation schemes on the other (Burman and van der Spuy). To judge by the present collection of essays, then, a stronger determinant of the locus of care than religion is local or regional ideology and the definitions that it brings with it: a perverted notion of community in the case of South Africa under apartheid; an ideal of motherhood variously refracted through the political cultures of four London boroughs; the personal allegiances and perceptions of the governors of voluntary hospitals; the variously engendered local initiatives of the middle-range cities of late medieval England or early modern France and Piedmont.

(4) It emerges forcefully that the different resources of care for the sick would have been conceptualized very differently in the

past from the ways in which we may now distinguish them. Even in modern times, the terminology under which policies may be enacted can change quite rapidly: as Marks and Thomson demonstrate, the *practice* of 'community care' in Britain antedates by decades its emergence as a prominent government policy. More important than changes of label is the way in which, as McIntosh is the first to point out, the 'personnel' of the various sources of care confound all analytical distinctions we might care to draw. Most obviously, it follows from the extent of outdoor relief, under both the English Poor Law and continental systems of the kind described by Cavallo, that formal and informal arrangements blur and overlap. Neighbours or relatives of the needy are paid to offer board and lodging to those whom, in other circumstances, they might have supported from their own pockets. Such formalized boarding out moreover creates, as McIntosh and Dinges note, the opportunity for the boarder to join a new informal network. Employers are encouraged by subsidies to keep on sick labourers or servants. Neighbours contribute to, or manage, local charitable institutions. Hospitals or friendly societies are patronized by leaders of the community from whom the poor might also have expected informal 'doorstep' subventions: support for the institution is an extension of private charity, not its antithesis. Parishes – publicly funded by local taxes – hire the services of private establishments to reduce their medical costs and hence the burden on tax-paying parishioners. Outdoor relief assumes the guise of its indoor variety: those boarded out together in an inn, with the landlord paid to meet their domestic needs, are virtually hospitalized. The converse also applies. A row of Tudor almshouses is modelled on, and thence becomes, a neighbourhood. More deliberately, and in a later age, homes for the mentally handicapped imitate the architecture and ethos of the village. Public and private, formal and informal, paid and voluntary – however we describe them, the sectors cannot be kept analytically distinct. They are constantly smudging any boundaries we impose on them. As Thomson suggests, modern historians come to the discussion of the past, even a past as recent as the twentieth century's inter-war period, with misleading preconceptions shaped by the categories of modern welfare states – states in which hospitals are starkly separate from other social services.

(5) The way in which the different agencies of care interact will be accordingly complex, hard to encapsulate with any simple

formula. Certainly we should not speak of any automatic *opposition* between familial, communal and institutional care. In the chapters that follow, formal support from beyond the family, however that term is glossed, is usually intended to supplement or provide a temporary replacement for domestic support (to enable, as Dinges puts it, a return to self-help).[6] Extra-familial support does not wholly take over. Nor are those who benefit from it drawn from any well-defined economic group: the beneficiaries described below are generally not the chronically destitute, for whom the workhouse, beggary or criminality are the stark alternatives to an imminent demise. Rather, it is sometimes a question of the well-to-do but vulnerable, as with Cavallo's mistresses who express their gratitude for the informal care provided by their intimate servants. More often, we are presented with the conjunctural poor, those who themselves at other stages would be supporters of the needy through the poor rate or voluntary contributions and neighbourly charity. Just as there is no automatic opposition between familial and communal support, but instead complementarity, so too institutions should not be assigned exclusively to one side of some great division. Of course some institutions were feared and avoided, a last and most desperate resort – the workhouse stereotypically, or the asylum. An important lesson to be learned from the pages that follow is, however, that we should not generalize from extreme examples. As Suzuki notes, for instance, once families had agreed on the need to consign their lunatic members to an asylum, they welcomed the relief it could bring them (if not the patient). More surprisingly, both Cavallo and Thomson reveal how far the hospital has been an institution with as it were permeable boundaries. This is evident not only in the extent of the outdoor relief for which hospitals could act as headquarters, or in the frequency with which patients might be discharged from them as, by some standard, cured (Berry), but also in their being often a temporary and even intermittent resort, with patients allowed out or returned to the community at certain times of year.[7] The hospital or similar institution is not therefore the 'end of the road' in welfare terms. Indeed, the further lesson reinforced by this collection is surely that there is no one 'road'. As we shall see, family care is not always the first resort; nor are extra-familial resources drawn upon only when that family has proved itself inadequate – and nor are institutions in question solely when all other means have been exhausted. No predictable sequence, no 'hierarchy of resort' as anthropologists call it, is evident. Any of the 'sectors' may be called upon, and in virtually any permutation.

Such dense interaction between the different possible loci of care should not be taken to show that, in any given period and place, the ensemble of resources necessarily constitutes an efficient system characterized by 'positive feedback'. For example, it may well be that (as Suzuki conjectures) the changing pattern or success rate of informal domestic care has some connection with the increasing number of private lunatic asylums in early modern England. And more generally the types of institution and community support available may correlate to some degree with economic and demographic features of the period (cf. McIntosh, Berry, Marks). But demand for extra-familial support is not inevitably perceived as such by those able to supply it. Moreover, even when it is perceived at all accurately, meeting the needs of the deserving is only one among many motives that can animate benefactors and administrators of institutional charity.[8] The different sectors may interact with the greatest complexity and subtlety, therefore. Yet they are not always functionally related, such that the decline of one tends to promote the growth of another. The causes of change in any one aspect will have to be sought more widely than simply from within 'the system'.

(6) A point relating to the previous ones about the complexity and 'open-endedness' of the different resources of the sick: there will be no simple chronology, no single evolution that can be sketched. As was emphasized in the Introduction, it is not just that there is no unilinear development in the last hundred years or so, from (in the British case) 'before the welfare state' to its seemingly imminent disintegration, yielding a simple tripartite periodizing.[9] To take this century alone, the chapter on South Africa (Burman and van der Spuy) raises the question of whether, in terms of the history of welfare, apartheid may in retrospect seem a mere episode or instead signals a permanent change in national welfare policies. Zhongwei Zhao's discussion of China during its recent and astonishingly rapid demographic transition immediately reminds us that no historiographical schema can easily be transplanted outside western Europe. As for England meanwhile, since the practice of community care is found to have antedated by decades its elevation to the forefront of policy, study of its gestation becomes the province of historians of the inter-war years (Marks, Thomson). Not only that: as Thomson in particular reveals, within

the inter-war period, implementation of the policy displays its own, relatively short-term expansion and retreat, for reasons of both ideology and economics. Cavallo, to jump back to the eighteenth century and to move to Turin, begins in a period in which (she finds) the family was only one among a variety of resources available to the needy; but she discerns in the closing decades of the eighteenth century a shift *back* to familial provision, in the rather strange form of charitable bequests to kindred.

(7) Many of the preceding paragraphs relate to the ways in which the overall 'economy of care' is 'mixed'. The last three points that I want to extract from this collection relate more particularly to informal care by household or other kin, or neighbours. The first of them registers simply an absence: in the following chapters we do not often encounter neighbours (non-kin) acting informally. Is that simply an 'optical illusion' created by the nature of the evidence, which conceals informal activities because they need no administration and hence create no records? Or does it betoken a lack of spontaneous neighbourliness in the periods under review? The argument from silence is always dangerous; but it is noteworthy that Wright for one is willing to risk a tentative version of it. Material from the ancient world with a very different emphasis will be presented below. It is far from clear how the discrepancy should be resolved.

(8) Next, the variety of means that households are shown as employing to counteract deficiencies in their capacity for support of their sick and disadvantaged. Some involve importing new members. They would include adoption and fostering,[10] remarriage, taking in lodgers or relatives from other households. Other recourses involve exporting to another household or an institution those who might constitute a burdensome surplus. Under this heading we should include apprenticeship[11] and (more commonly encountered in this volume) putting into service, as well as hospitalization and boarding out.

(9) The final point is the one most significant for the present paper. It relates to the diversity of those means and the complexity of the 'interweaving' of the various support sectors. The point is that, throughout this collection, informal domestic care by household or coresident kin is shown to be limited to a perhaps surprising degree. Granted, the 'caring' family often becomes visible in the evidence only at its moments of failure so that its limitations may receive unnatural prominence. There still seems to

be enough evidence of the 'normal' limitations of familial support. The extreme example is provided by South Africa, where many 'non-White' families were fractured and disabled as carers by apartheid legislation and its associated housing programmes. In South Africa, the incapacity is imposed on the family from the outside. Some historians have also been tempted to discern a less abhorrent and extreme, but none the less insidious, undermining of the family's supportive potential in the long-term effects of the English Poor Law, which might be seen as absolving some relatives of the supposedly traditional requirement to provide a free locus of care. The Poor Law, in other words, made many types of care not so much difficult as unnecessary.[12]

In this volume we certainly meet a contractual and seemingly unspontaneous element in the care offered by close family. From Tudor to Hanoverian England care subsidized from the poor rate is documented on numerous occasions when we might expect to find spontaneous generosity. Good reasons can often be imagined for some of this lack of the predicted nobler feelings. Those who had contributed to the poor rate could argue, not unreasonably, that in offering voluntary unpaid care as well, they were in effect paying twice over. Or perhaps the parish subsidy made possible a level of support that those involved could not otherwise have afforded: the poor rate supplemented rather than replaced family expenditure.[13] Other incentives to restraint meanwhile arose from the stage in the life cycle that the potential donor had reached. To recall the most obvious instance: parents often needed help from their children just at the stage when those children were most burdened with nurturing children of their own: the second generation can help the first or the third, but not both simultaneously.

We would, however, be wrong to assume that such considerations were everywhere responsible for apparent meanness or selfishness on the part of close kin. So much is shown by the evidence from continental Europe presented in later chapters. The lack of any clear contrast between English and continental types of institutional relief is paralleled at the level of *informal* support. Both Cavallo and Dinges show us individuals being helped by city or parish who clearly have close family available to offer support but not called upon to do so.[14] Although many early modern European cities experimented with 'voluntary' levies, there was no exact equivalent of the poor rate to act as disincentive. Nor can life-cycle problems have always been an overriding consideration.

It follows from this that the size of the family or coresident group is no accurate predictor of the 'volume' of care available from within it. Informal welfare cannot simply be read off from demographic or sociological data such as household size, as if care were automatic from those near at hand. As sociologists, and not only those of feminist persuasion, have indeed often commented, family care often means care by certain individuals, usually women. It does not actually involve the whole group. To that observation must next be added the growing conviction of some historians: that not even women's care can be taken for granted. The most powerful lesson that a student of the ancient or medieval worlds might derive from discussions by those concerned with much more recent centuries is that the household or coresident family does not, at least since late medieval times, seem to have functioned as a miniature welfare republic, caring adequately and unstintingly in proportion to its size.[15]

III

Lessons from co-contributors are not, of course, sufficient by themselves. To illuminate the *longue durée* of informal care, comparisons need to be drawn from a much wider literature even than that represented by the following chapters (and their footnotes).

Ideally there would, first of all, be a particular kind of institutional history to be noticed. This kind would look out from institutional or other forms of public charity toward the world of beneficiaries. It would reconstruct something of the domestic circumstances of patients, it would include the alternatives to the institution, and it would illustrate a little of the complex interaction between different sectors of welfare provision. Actual instances of such an approach are, however, surprisingly rare.[16] In them, moreover, informal or domestic support is not usually placed in the foreground. It comes into the picture only at its points of overlap with other types of relief. We need therefore to look further afield. We need studies that show in more than anecdotal detail how informal systems of mutual support among the sick and disadvantaged actually work. These will enable us to view such systems in the round, not just at moments of overlap. The first examples will be relayed at some length. Others can be adduced thereafter more briefly as recurrent themes begin to emerge. We can start in recent times with anthropology and sociology, move back into some useful historical studies, and thereby begin to tread gingerly into the Middle Ages.

It is the anthropology of the Americas that has produced some of the most sustained and evocative accounts[17] of informal support networks among the poor. Let us sample two of them. Larissa Adler Lomnitz's *Networks and Marginality* (1977)[18] is a translation of a study originally published under a more revealing title meaning 'How did marginals survive?'. It reports on field work carried out between 1969 and 1971 in a shantytown of about 200 dwellings in Mexico City. The inhabitants are all first- or second-generation immigrants from the countryside. They belong to the very bottom of the social scale. Many heads of household are unskilled labourers, the rest are in a variety of service occupations. None has much job security and underemployment is the norm. Indeed the average monthly earnings per residential unit are less than $100. The first strikingly pertinent feature of the discussion concerns the complexity of living arrangements. Neither family nor household is easily conceptualized. Some 81 per cent of families are described as nuclear and live in separate accommodation. Even so, a number of their households are packed very closely together in sets of one-room apartments that lead off a central court with a single entrance. Moreover, the extended or joint family could be said to prevail in the majority – 63 per cent – of households. This is because of the variety of possible residence patterns: 54 per cent of the seemingly independent nuclear families live in what Lomnitz characterizes as 'jointed' households, in which adjoining residential units not originally built for one household effectively function as an entity. Some of the extended households, a category that also includes joint ones – comprising on average 2.3 nuclear families each – live under a single roof. Others (the minority) share the same plot of land. Within the category of extended households a further subdivision is possible. It falls between those in which the included nuclear families share all expenses and those in which they do not. 'Thus . . . a cluster of seemingly independent one-room dwellings may contain a single household. Conversely, a set of rooms with a single entrance may contain several households.'[19]

The second pertinent theme to emerge from Lomnitz's study concerns the extent of cooperation and reciprocity between families and households. Of her informants she writes: 'they have literally nothing. Their only resources are of a social nature: kinship and friendship ties that generate social solidarity'. Ties between families are obviously at their closest in those 'extended' households, both under a single roof and on a single plot of land, that share cooking duties and living expenses. But among those that do not share in this way, and in the jointed-type households too, there is 'an intense reciprocal exchange including a variety of domestic functions'. And this occurs even though each co-resident or adjacent family leads a separate economic life. Of the independent nuclear families, meanwhile, the majority have relatives living in the same shantytown with whom they interact. No type of household is therefore typically isolated.[20]

Because of rigidly defined gender roles, the emotional content of marital relations is meagre. So men and women each tend to form their own circles. Men band into *cuate* (twin-brother) groups of five to ten in size. They get drunk, play games, or go to a bullfight together. But they also help each other in finding employment or building a home. It is the women who play the dominant role in cementing networks of reciprocity within and between families, networks that only a few relatively affluent families with connections outside the shantytown can afford to ignore. They lend each other money and goods; they provide food to those experiencing severe shortage and help each other with property building and maintenance, or with carrying water; they share the management of children, the burden of sitting with the sick, and funeral expenses. The resulting networks are not large, however: the majority of them link only two or three nuclear families. If their members all live under one roof or on a single plot of land, then network and household are, in a sense, coextensive. Relations of kinship dominate in the formation of networks. But some networks include close neighbours as well as kin; and a few, mostly on the smaller side, comprise neighbours only. In addition, overlapping the tight formations thus created, there are exchanges between affinal kin who are not members of the same network; there are various cross-cutting ties of godparenthood; and there are *tandas* – rotating credit groups involving companions in the work place as well as friends and neighbours – in which everyone donates a small fixed sum per month and the total is pocketed by each member in turn.

Three general aspects of the form of life that Lomnitz describes seem especially significant in the present context. First, the levels of economic security created are minimal: there is nothing cosy and readily sustaining about these networks. Second, networks can easily be diminished by friction or hostility between kin. Third, assistance is not always exchanged between those approximately equal in resources: asymmetric patron–client relations may develop out of symmetric reciprocal exchange networks. For instance, foremen become brokers between casual labourers of the shantytown and the employing builders or engineers.[21]

Another classic of American ethnography, comparable in vividness to Lomnitz's, reveals again the fluidity or permeability of boundaries between households. Carol B. Stack's *All Our Kin: Strategies for Survival in a Black Community* (1974) explores networks similar to those of the Mexican shantytown.[22] They are to be found in 'the Flats', the poorest section of a Black community in the mid-western city of 'Jackson Harbor' (both pseudonyms). Once more, the social world is not wholly sustained by symmetric transactions. Stack's informants are inevitably involved (though seldom to their lasting benefit) with landlords and the rudimentary welfare system. Her people are, none the less, so impoverished that their income – including state benefit – is exhausted by rent, 'utilities', and the purchase of food. Exchanging goods and services is the only way in which individuals can gain anything more than the barest essentials. 'Those actively involved in domestic networks swap goods and services on a daily, practically an hourly basis'. Again as in Mexico, participants are mostly kin, and the networks centre mostly on women; on the other hand, friends of either sex may be identified as virtual kin if they live up to the expected level of reciprocity.

The clearest symptom of the social and economic significance of exchange, as of the fluidity of household boundaries, is to be detected in the sharing of parental responsibility. Women residing close by one another and participating in a single network behave virtually as if they are coresident. They shop and eat together. Their children stay the night in whichever household has become the focus for that evening's visiting. Children have also to cope with less ephemeral changes of household. 'The expansion and contraction of households, and the successive recombinations of kinsmen residing together, require adults to care for the children residing in their household ... Within a network of cooperating kinsmen, there may be three or more adults with whom, in turn, a child resides.' Sometimes children circulate of their own accord.

Adolescents may be allowed the choice of residing with kin other than their biological or foster parents. But children are also in effect borrowed or loaned, even being lodged with non-kin who evince concern and a willingness to help.

Among the plurality of roles which kinsmen, and occasionally friends, perform to one another's children, 'curing' and 'grooming' seem most to the present purpose:

> Curers provide folk remedies for physical ailments. They have the right to attempt to heal rashes with a little lye or detergent in the bath water, remove warts, pull teeth, and cure stomach ailments for children with 'persnickety' – a pungent brew made from tobacco and added to the baby's milk. A groomer has the obligation to care for the children, wash clothing, and check the children's bodies for rashes and diseases.[23]

IV

The examples of Lomnitz and Stack can stand for a number of others emanating from the American continent.[24] But if we want material closer to the European home inhabited by most of the papers that follow, we should look to the British sociological tradition. Perhaps the largest and in many ways the most stimulating body of information concerning informal care has been generated in two ways: first, by the question of whether kinship retains any importance in modern British society, and secondly, by the political debate surrounding the origins, current merits, and future of the topic which has already been used to introduce this volume: 'care in the community'.

The resulting work has not surprisingly involved attempts at generalization as much as detailed case studies.[25] Efforts have for instance been made to classify the kinds of help that kin, neighbours, and friends can respectively supply. Kin, it is proposed, can make major long-term commitments; neighbours are better equipped to help in emergencies, or with less demanding chronic requirements; friends are called on for still lighter and more variable tasks, such as offering solace to the lonely.[26] Much attention has also been given to the terms 'care' and 'community', and to the differences between 'care in' and 'care by' the community – all so central to current debate, so wholly elusive in meaning. The suggestion has further been made that community be replaced

– with no manifest gain in precision but perhaps with welcome reduction in emotive connotation – by some such phrase as 'primary group'. The vocabulary of network analysis has been examined and found abstract, an adequate way of representing the *direction* of contacts between members of a group but no indicator of their *intensity* or *purpose*.[27]

More useful has been the attempt to categorize the different components or types of assistance.[28] Bulmer for example distinguishes three concentric circles of care, diminishing in intensity and in expenditure of time and energy required. First, face-to-face 'tending' (feeding, washing, cleaning – physical assistance, that is; the 'hard end' of care). Second, material and psychological support (gifts of money, visiting, and so forth). Finally, the least demanding form: general expressions of concern for others' welfare – which might issue in, say, a charitable donation, a petition, or a prayer.[29] The most extensive discussion of the content and purposes of informal caring transactions is however that of Finch.[30] Her anatomy includes economic support – money transfers, gifts in kind, inheritance, help in finding work; then the provision of accommodation for young couples, the elderly, and the divorced; personal care – nursing the chronically ill and the mentally and physically handicapped; practical support, especially with child care; and lastly emotional and moral support, not least when there is sickness in a family. She estimates whether there is a net transfer of aid from older to younger generations, and how strongly the degree of support given varies with gender and ethnicity.

The value of this kind of anatomy in the present setting is above all that it reminds us again of the sheer scope and variety of informal care. It also begins to show how much it is possible to say about it. Not that the evidence is that consistent in quality or extensive in coverage, even for recent decades: this topic has attracted less sociological attention than might have been expected, despite the frequency with which stereotyped views of it recur in political debate. But the generalizations ventured do of course rest upon some detailed local studies, comparable in many respects to the engrossing accounts by Lomnitz and Stack.

A classic in the tradition, still often cited despite its perhaps too roseate depiction of working-class solidarities, is the study of post-war Bethnal Green by Young and Willmott, *Family and Kinship in East London* (1957).[31] Here once more, particularly with respect to the relationship between mothers and daughters, the household emerges as an entity with permeable boundaries, hard to define. 'The daily lives of many women are not confined to the places where they sleep; they are spread over two or more households.' The services flowing from mothers to daughters are at their most intense in the period around childbirth, but the mother–daughter bond, together with a wider range of familial relationships, is also seen to best advantage on the very rare occasions when the daughter is so sick that she must retire to her room or go into hospital. Near residence rather than coresidence continues to be the determinant of who interacts with whom. For each of the sample couples surveyed the average number of relatives living elsewhere in Bethnal Green was thirteen, and all but four couples had some relatives in the borough. Nor were these ties of kindred antithetical to others of neighbourhood and friendship. On the contrary, they furnished the principal means by which such further ties were created.

Young and Willmott do not record in any detail the content of the goods and services exchanged within the networks. But the degree of support that these networks made possible can be gauged by recalling the reactions of families rehoused by the Borough or County Council in a new housing estate twenty miles away.[32] Their local support systems were gravely disrupted. A sick wife could no longer count so readily on the help of her mother or other relatives. Husbands had to do more than their wont, although their fear of losing wages set narrow limits to how often they could help out at home. Daughters stepped in, staying away from work; younger children absented themselves from school to lend a hand. The effects of migration are clear. Not only in crises such as illness or childbirth, but also in day-to-day affairs, kin were no longer available to any significant extent. Moreover, neighbours who were not also relatives seem to have been little relied on. Kinship really had formed the armature of social relations and informal support, and that armature had been fractured. Families had become far more isolated.

This single case study should not be taken to exemplify the modern decline of kin-based support networks. Indeed, one theme common to the studies that have followed in Young and Willmot's wake is the perhaps surprising durability of kinship in post-war Britain – despite the enormity of what might have been thought adverse social, economic, and demographic change and the growth of the welfare state.[33] Not that kin support outside the household (or within it for that matter) can ever be taken for granted. Informal care hardly emerges from the analyses of the sociologists as a sufficient alternative to the various ministrations of the welfare state. The implicit conclusion is that, at best, harmonious and productive 'interweaving' of formal and informal sectors may be possible, but that such interweaving is currently far from being adequately achieved.[34] There is no manifest comfort here for framers of social policy who appeal to 'family care' as if the state's responsibility would be unquestionably discharged if a needy person were transferred from institutional care to that of a relative.[35] It is no coincidence that one of the most influential of the more recent studies – Finch and Mason's *Negotiating Family Responsibilities* (1993) – should look critically at the processes by which the burden of caring is allocated, and should be as much concerned with the reasons why that burden is *not* shouldered as with the circumstances in which it is.[36] Domestic care, then, certainly does not demonstrate the untapped potential with which many policymakers have credited it. If, however, it is viewed without an optimism nourished more by political rhetoric than by empirical accuracy, the volume of testimony to a *certain degree* of continuity in the range of services exchanged by close kin is impressive.

That emphasis on continuity should not be taken to imply the absence of major local variation – over time as well as with place, class, ethnic group, household, and gender. Quite the contrary: it is the unpredictable waxing and waning of familial and neighbourly assistance that is continually being thrown into relief. And that has had the salutary effect of making sociologists suspicious of any grand secular narratives about informal care which posit decline from some golden age when support was more solid and less variable.[37] It has also encouraged the addition of a little history to the sociological picture. Two historical studies that sociologists commonly cite with approval also deserve notice here for their evocation of mutual support among the poor in nineteenth-century Britain.

Ellen Ross's investigation of 'survival networks' among London women in the period 1870–1914 describes remarkably homogeneous inner-city areas.[38] Almost all the inhabitants belonged to the 'labouring poor', and there was a high degree of neighbourhood endogamy. The state impinged relatively little on these enclosed worlds, at least as a provider of welfare. For most families, the 'safety net' was the neighbourhood. Landlords and landladies

– 'vertical' contacts as it were – might be sympathetic in a crisis and attentive as occasional child carers. But, for the most part, local support networks, 'horizontal' connections between the more or less equally impoverished, were crucial to survival.

As among the inhabitants of Lomnitz's Mexican shantytown, these support networks were sharply gender specific. Male co-workers would take collections to see one of their number through an illness, or pay for his funeral or subsidize his widow and orphans. Yet most day-to-day self-help involved women's networks. 'Powerful links between women and their kin and neighbours – links which often involved substantial exchanges of services and money – wove together individual conjugally-based households into the quite cohesive cockney culture which had been created by the turn of the century.' Poor women supported each other with small sums of money (a penny for the gas or a contribution to funeral expenses) and, as in Jackson Harbor, they gave each other frequent gifts of clothing or domestic equipment. Women in labour were particularly well cared for, as were battered wives or evicted families. 'Custom reserved special treatment for the sick. Neighbourhood women did their laundry, provided fuel and built their fires, prepared their meals.' Again as in the Flats, needy children became a common responsibility. In extreme circumstances such as orphanhood, informal adoption, by kin or even by unrelated neighbours, was not unusual. In most dealings reciprocity was the rule. What is striking, though, is how often the return for a service – child care, maternity nursing, sitting up with the sick, running errands – took the form of a money payment. Nor do such transfers distinguish transactions between households from those within them: 'Cash payments between family members were by no means uncommon, as all were sharply aware of the cost of their keep. Even the most loving relationships involved material obligation'. They also, it is tempting to speculate, involved a sense of the need to make an immediate return in order to continue membership of the family network and hence benefit from it in future. Compassion cannot now be disentangled from calculation in the thinking of participants. And that is perhaps not simply a by-product of the passage of time and the lack of intimate evidence. It reflects a profound confusion of motives.

A similar ethos emerges from the pages of another frequently cited study of working-class life in industrial England. Michael Anderson's *Family Structure in Nineteenth-Century Lancashire* (1971) describes the residence practices and self-help systems evolved by the poor of the cotton towns, especially Preston, around the middle of the century.[39] Families were typically nuclear: pauper households were the most likely to be extended to include kin as lodgers; newly married couples resided in a parental household for a short time before finding their own quarters; widowed or deserted parents lodged with their children in old age; unrelated elderly folk were sometimes taken in too, providing child care in exchange for accommodation.

As in previous examples, however, the household is perhaps not the appropriate unit of analysis. 'Kinship does not stop at the front door. There are few functions which can be performed by a co-residing kinsman which he cannot perform equally well if he instead lives next door, or even up the street.' And those up the street are preferable to the administrators of the workhouse, usually seen as a dreadful last resort. Immigrants mostly tried to live close to kin, naming their children after them to a significant extent. Once settled, they would find that kin assisted each other – again occasionally in return for payment – in the ways that earlier examples will now have made familiar. They did so to an extent that impressed middle-class commentators. 'Their charity is unbounded,' wrote the mayor of Clitheroe. 'Let anyone be in want from sickness or other cause – there are fifty kind Samaritans to comfort and relieve them with both food and personal services.' Certainly the crisis of illness or death in the family could be palliated only for a short time by institutions such as sick clubs or friendly societies. Money was borrowed from kin – and sometimes unrelated neighbours – to ease the family economy through the period of illness. Visiting, nursing, provision of meals and child care also seem to have been unstintingly offered. Orphans were brought up by other members of the family. Those without such support networks rapidly went to the wall.

Two strong qualifications need to be entered, though. First, anticipating Wright in this volume, Anderson notes 'some rather sketchy evidence' that help from neighbours was by no means as readily forthcoming as help from kin. In particular, newcomers without family in the area might be left to suffer illness alone. Secondly, in this fluid, economically and demographically vulnerable society, there was little of the mutual trust – or of the resources – necessary to sustain 'long-run reciprocation' among kin and neighbours. Transactions were limited to those for which a rapid return might be demanded. 'If . . . the person could make some useful immediate reciprocation either directly as with for example child care, or indirectly, by the Poor Law being willing to assist, then help was much more likely to be given to kin in need.' Relationships among the poor were, then, calculating, instrumental – and not insulated from other sources of relief. Moral imperatives and ties of affection were seemingly insufficient to generate and maintain mutual support systems. Inevitably, debate has flourished around the question of whether that grim picture can be generalized to towns other than Preston, and to rural settings, in the later Victorian and Edwardian periods.[40] But Anderson's account unmistakably resonates with those other reports from further afield summarized above.

The studies by Ross and Anderson are those most often adduced by sociologists to lend perspective and chronological depth to their discussions of family life and informal networks in British society. They could, of course, continue pressing further back into the past in search of further illustration. The returns, though rapid, would however prove meagre. The reason for that is not so much that the results would be repetitive. It is more to do with the diminishing vividness of the sources. Sufficient material to convey the quality of mutual support among the poor is hard to come by from much earlier than the nineteenth century – although a certain amount of it emerges from studies of early modern London.[41] The best that historians can do is make inferences from proxy evidence (demographic data, wills, household structure, and so on) of which the reliability is, I have already hinted, questionable. So it would seem perverse and fruitless to close this sequence of exemplary case studies, all of them urban in setting, with one pertaining to peasant society in the thirteenth and fourteenth centuries.

The ground for doing that is certainly not that nothing significant changed in the informal ties and resources characteristic of the poor between those centuries and the nineteenth and twentieth. Nor is it that rural–urban differences can be ignored. Nor, again, that the principal historiographical debates surrounding the intervening centuries have been resolved. The size of the typical pauper household in any given phase of the early modern period; the degree to which the nuclear family was a social isolate; the extent and functions of the kinship networks which can, despite much nuclearity, be detected; the degree to which the obligations to immediate family listed in the Elizabethan Poor Law were legally enforced; the apparent 'commoditization' of the care provided with Poor Law subsidy – all these continue to engender discussion; on none of them is there even temporary consensus.[42] The reasons for vaulting over such scholarly minefields are twofold: first, this chapter is hardly the place for a complete historiographical resumé; and second, whatever the vicissitudes of family care in the early modern period, the period before the Black Death never-theless returns a strong echo to several themes prominent in more recent examples. Encouragement to look to that period can even be derived from the sociological camp. Reviewing the sources of the myth of a golden age of family responsibility for the poor and sick, Janet Finch invokes Alan Macfarlane's search for the 'origins of English individualism', and thus for the beginnings of a progressive devaluation of kin beyond the nuclear family, in the thirteenth century if not earlier.[43]

Macfarlane's assertions have, however, been no more immune to revisionism than has any other aspect of the social and demographic history of the period spanning the later Middle Ages and early modernity. And what is being put in their place is a vision of social relations in which the household is once more found to be an unhelpful category. As Razi writes: 'the peasant family can be viewed not only as a co-resident unit, but also as a group of relatives living in the same village or parish'.[44] The majority of households in the west-midland manor of Halesowen that Razi investigates, chiefly through the medium of its court rolls, were nuclear; and the households of the poor were generally the smallest. But effective kinship ties were by no means confined to members of the conjugal family, even if the range of kin involved in legally registered transactions was not very wide. In pre-plague times, when the population was very high and land correspondingly scarce, parents often settled their eldest children on the family holding but under a different roof, creating *ad hoc* agglomerations of living quarters faintly reminiscent of the growth of a shantytown. Among the ways in which families found their way onto the court rolls was through their support of the poor and infirm, as well as the mentally ill and orphans. Landless poor depended on gleaning, begging, or stealing for subsistence. If they had kin with sufficient resources, they lodged with them; but they were also liable to expulsion from the manor.[45]

Here, then, as in earlier examples, there were apparently severe limits to the amount of support available. Of course we have to tread carefully when making such judgements. Court rolls afford only a narrow and slanted view of the social world.[46] The bulk of everyday interaction between peasant households is forever hidden from us. But there is no warrant for assuming that the 'functionally extended family' offered more than a temporary and partial remedy for economic misfortune. The medieval village was not the harmonious corporate community it was perhaps once thought to be.[47] Its members were indeed perhaps as calculating in their 'caring relationships' as the denizens of Victorian Preston. That much emerges with particular clarity from their treatment of the old.

In the maintenance agreements recorded by manorial courts, elderly peasants handed over the management of their land to children or other kin (or very occasionally non-kin) in return for an annuity of food, money, and clothing and, it seems, more direct assistance when they became sick or impoverished. This might be thought a surprising invasion of a contractualist ethos into the domain of family relations, whether it came at the behest of the court or of the parties to the contract. And the surviving written agreements could be only the visible tip of an iceberg of informal and unrecorded arrangements that were similar in effect – a tip generated by those families in which the two generations involved displayed little mutual trust.[48] When viewed in the context of later instances of family care subsidized by the Poor Law, or of the continental analogues mentioned in this volume by Cavallo and Dinges, the arrangements seem less remarkable, however.

Halesowen cannot stand for all pre-plague manors. In the Suffolk manor of Redgrave, with its different economic and demographic regime, family networks were, to judge by the court roll, considerably fewer, narrower, less durable. Neighbours instead performed many supportive functions, those of them with large holdings acting somewhat like patrons toward their poorer cohabitants.[49] Nor was the functionally extended family in Halesowen destined to last indefinitely. Indeed, its demise during the fifteenth century can be charted with some precision.[50] Yet such variation with place and period is entirely to be expected, and matches the variation which is probably responsible for the uncertainties of early modern historians adverted to above.

V

British historiography offers probably the longest and more or less continuous narrative of informal relief arrangements – from the thirteenth century onward. It also, probably, offers the best documented one. Which is not of course to say that no good examples could be derived from other parts of Europe, but that they would be narrower in scope and span a shorter period.[51] There seem, for instance, to be few companion studies to Segalen's evocation of the changes evident in inter-household kin interaction across two centuries of modern Breton history.[52] Elsewhere, we must be content with a keyhole view, the more vivid and tantalizing for being so narrow. A view of Paris, say, on the eve of Revolution:

> When a master turner living in the rue de la Cordonnerie suddenly felt ill his wife called the two men who lived opposite. An innkeeper, attacked by a man to whom he owed money, called for help and was rescued by about twenty neighbours! . . . A woman who sold coal in the rue de la Tannerie explained that as one of her sub-tenants, a printing-worker sick with venereal disease, had no one to look after him, 'she as well as several other neighbours took care of him and from time to time took him soup and other assistance.'[53]

If that seems to anticipate life in a Mexican shantytown, other vignettes are reminiscent of the child sharing typical of the Flats.

> In an interview, a remarkable [Sicilian] woman, a peasant and healer who has recently died aged 101, recounts how she was orphaned . . . when she was nine years old. The parish priest wanted to send her to an orphanage, but the neighbours insisted on a sort of collective adoption. The young girl should live in her own house; she would be cared for by all of them, and she would earn her keep by doing small tasks for the neighbours.[54]

Vignettes are no substitute for a coherent corpus of work, however limited it may be in local detail or chronological depth. Much the most useful for historians, and already 'applied' several times to the interpretation of antiquity,[55] is the social anthropology of Mediterranean Europe. This can be taken to include not only standard ethnography but in addition the 'ethno-ecological' study of (primarily) Greek peasants.[56] It is particularly useful in the present context, not just because, handled delicately, it is suggestive of the ancient past, but also because it adds a further rural clutch of examples to set beside the urban ones that have predominated so far.

Few arresting individual details emerge; but there is considerable *cumulative* evidence of all-pervasive reciprocity among kin, friends, and neighbours. It is a reciprocity which, like that portrayed in several previous examples, is born as much of calculation as of warmth, and would not have seemed sentimental in Preston. Resources are all perceived as scarce. Competition for access to them is a 'zero-sum game', one family's gain necessarily being another's deprivation. Alliances and exchanges between families are therefore undertaken instrumentally. In the longer term, their successful manipulation offers the prospect of 'getting ahead'.[57] In the short term, reciprocity – of finance, labour, technology, commodities – belongs under the same general heading as storage and crop diversification: all three are mechanisms of 'risk buffering', of insurance against agricultural hazard. Once more, it seems, informal support has its limitations. Simple demographic pressure combines with the effects of distance to limit the size of the available kin group. Poverty combines with competitiveness to limit what the kin group will provide. In critical years of food shortage, those living nearby, whether kin or friends, are after all likely to have been subject to the same disaster that prompts the appeal for help.

> Clearly Greek peasants [in the past as much as the present] could not rely solely on kinsmen, friends and neighbors for their subsistence insurance. Instead they had to expand their support networks outward in space and upward in the social hierarchy. Links had to be forged with men who controlled greater quantities of food supplies . . . One way to accomplish this was through the creation of interpersonal relationships with men of wealth and power, relationships best described by the term clientism.[58]

Patrons enter the picture once again, as they did in Lomnitz's account, or (as sympathetic landladies) in that of Ross, or (as lords of the manor) in Razi's.

Now to move around Europe in this way, invoking testimonies impartially from Britain and France, Italy and Greece, is to cross what some, following a pioneering analysis by John Hajnal, have supposed to be a boundary of sorts between two different regimes.[59] This boundary should be explored. It was originally drawn with respect to marriage practices and rules of household *formation* (as distinct from household *structure*). At least since the 'high' Middle Ages, the north-western European pattern has been one of delayed marriage for both sexes; couples establish new households after marriage, perhaps at some remove from their relatives, and young unmarried people circulate between households as servants. That, it may uncontroversially be said, is the regime forming the background to several contributions to this book – those dealing with England and the chapter by Dinges – as well as the British sociological and historical examples just rehearsed, reaching from modern Bethnal Green back to medieval Halesowen (and in the latter, retirement contracts entirely bear out Hajnal's generalizations about the lot of the elderly).

North-western families have been for the most part nuclear and households small – particularly the households of the poor.[60] Elsewhere – which in this context means southern and eastern Europe and indeed all of Eurasia apart from its north-western corner – joint household systems have prevailed. Marriage comes earlier in the life cycle and celibacy is highly unusual. Young married couples often start life together in another household of which an older person (typically the husband's father) remains in charge. Households with several married couples in them may split to form two or more new households, each containing one or more couples; and these latter households will be different in kind from those established neo-locally under the north-western regime. In other words, at any given time a significant proportion of all households will be extended, and most of that proportion will contain more than one conjugal family. This is the regime that – supposedly – provides the context to the contributions by Cavallo and Zhao below, and the Mediterranean evidence referred to earlier in the present chapter.

Does this distinction of regimes matter in the present context? Does it have any implications for the history of 'the locus of care'? Peter Laslett has argued influentially that it does.[61] He has proposed that, under the north-western regime of neo-localism and nuclearity, the death, physical incapacity, or loss of earning power of a member of a conjugal household would threaten its self-sufficiency. It would be liable to what he has called 'nuclear hardship'. The death of parents or spouse obviously brought a reduction in potential family support, though not necessarily a critical one. Widows could remarry and thus in effect rebuild their households. Beyond that, since those left on their own could not easily rejoin their families of origin, 'the only sources from which support might be forthcoming were the extended kin – that is, relatives beyond the household – and what is usually called the community or what I prefer to call the "collectivity" – friends and neighbours, along with the church and charitable institutions, as well as the village, town or state'.[62]

In logic, that is unimpeachable. If there was to be any support at all, and it could not be found within the household, it had to come from somewhere outside it. When Laslett turns from logic to life, however, he (like Hajnal[63]) projects a picture in which the extra-household collectivity is defined more narrowly. The north west is reduced to England, where most of the data comes from. And in the extreme English version of the north-western system, kinship interaction is presumed to be weak. This is not least because, according to computer projections of the kind made later in this volume by Zhao, the universe of available kin was likely to be very small.[64] Support from the collectivity is therefore, in Laslett's analysis, increasingly equated with the *non-kin* sector of the collectivity, and comes to mean the operation of the Poor Law.

With this bleak vision of tiny households saved from extinction only by Poor Law overseers, we are invited to contrast the joint household system. Under this regime the household's capacity as a source of support can supposedly be viewed with far more optimism. Children house and care for their needy parents without resorting to retirement contracts; domestic welfare provision indeed flows in every possible direction. At the extreme, instantiated in the occasionally vast *dvor* of imperial Russia, the typical household is almost coterminous with the effective kin group, and the family is self-sufficient, in need of little or no external welfare agency.

To report on the proposed contrast in this way is of course to caricature – for clarity's sake. In fairness it should be added immediately that both Hajnal and Laslett qualify their closely related interpretations in important ways. Hajnal allows, for instance, that differences in household formation and size between northern and southern Europe may be more than counter-balanced by similarities; he also shows that, in most household formation systems, the bulk of coresident groups will be nuclear families.[65] Laslett emphasizes that not even English society has fully implemented the north-western household formation rules, so that a number of households were extended for substantial parts of their developmental cycle. He is aware that there was significant extra-household kin interaction in some medieval English villages.[66] And he concedes that the capacity of the joint or extended family outside the north west cannot be taken for granted. Evidence from eighteenth-century China (provided elsewhere by Zhao) and from modern Kenya shows elderly people living alone, and 'warns us that the non-nuclear family systems may not be quite so different from the nuclear system in respect of their welfare functions as we are disposed to think'.[67] Even the large Russian *dvor* could, for demographic reasons, have a limited collective life and might need support from the village *mir* or the owner of the estate (the patron in yet another guise). For all these qualifications, ideal types have been established. They point to only selected aspects of a difficult area of investigation. And yet they maintain a seductive hold on the historiographical imagination and are always in danger of being confused with general reality – if not by Laslett and Hajnal, then certainly by the many scholars who have been profoundly influenced by their interpretations.

In the points that I derived from later chapters in this volume, some reasons have already been given why other ideal types might, for present purposes, be preferred to Laslett's. On the basis of the case studies reviewed subsequently, other reasons can now be added. In the process, a more coherent case can perhaps also be made for beginning to conceptualize major geographical differences in family care rather differently.

Firstly, a more complex picture of the distribution of household types – more nuanced than that available to Hajnal and Laslett – is slowly emerging (and where it has not emerged, it ought to be encouraged). This emergence is most obvious with respect to Mediterranean Europe.[68] Here a diversity too great to be captured in any simple formula is progressively being discovered – a diversity that includes a good proportion of small and simple households. Eastern Europe is however urgently in need of comparably wide-ranging scrutiny: the generalizations ventured by Laslett, Hajnal, and subsequent comparativists rest on a perilously small number of case studies. These seldom reach further back in time than 1800; the case for 'perennial complexity' may have been too ambitiously stated in them; and they leave unexplored a range of sources that might shed some light on welfare provision from both within and beyond the household.[69] Other scholarship has begun to restore the imbalance, giving due weight to mutual aid between poor villagers living in nuclear or small extended households, and challenging some of the received demographic distinctions between East and West.[70] But as yet there is no accepted synthesis. Synoptic studies covering substantial portions of 'the rest of the world' – such as would make accessible to students of Europe the relevant characteristics of the joint households of Asia, the 'tentholds' of parts of the Middle East, or the (supposedly) lineage-dominated structures of sub-Saharan Africa – are all, however, still urgently required.[71] Pending their appearance, we must be content with registering the implications of individual works such as John Iliffe's history of African poverty. He hastens to dispel the version of the 'myth of Merrie Africa' according to which the extended family ensured that *no* poverty existed in pre-colonial times. But he then on several occasions evinces surprise at just how little evidence he finds of effective domestic care, and how often he encounters very weak or severely circumscribed networks of kin or neighbourly support.[72]

Secondly, the similarities in average household size between East and West remarked on by Hajnal surely have some implications for the availability of support from within the household, even when allowance is made for regional differences in characteristic age structure.[73] Quite apart from any other considerations, these similarities begin to suggest that we should be chary of attributing greater caring capacity to the coresident group the further east (or south?) we go.

Thirdly, a minor but not entirely trivial matter: the terminology in vogue is surely either question-begging or misleading. The conjunction of nuclearity and hardship begs the question of whether or not a nuclear household can be effectively helped by outside agencies: it implies that all but the most capacious support systems, such as the Poor Law, will be inadequate to the task. But 'nuclear hardship' is also misleading in that it implies that the hardship is felt when the family is nuclear. Misfortune afflicts the nuclear family – according to Laslett's theory – when it is somehow functioning at *less* than full strength; the hardship really arises, if at all, when the household is 'sub-nuclear'.[74]

The fourth point relates to the previous one, but is of greater moment (and was anticipated earlier). It is that caring capacity cannot be assumed to increase in proportion to household size. 'Sub-nuclear' is associated with vulnerability – and doubtless rightly so. But is the nuclear household so solid and unitary as to be accounted an adequate welfare agency when functioning normally? And has the implied opposite of nuclear hardship – 'extended well-being' or something to that effect – really been so prevalent as Laslett and Hajnal appear to believe? Evidence from later chapters in this volume can be coupled with that of studies giving due weight to family dissensions or power struggles,[75] and also with those works (some of them mentioned above) which show extended households requiring outside help.[76] In combination they answer a resolute 'no': extended well-being cannot be taken for granted, whether in Europe or elsewhere in the world.

To take just one example which has been put forward as evidence of the supportive potential of the joint household: in the Bangladeshi and Indian villages studied by Cain, the elderly are indeed included within joint households. There is nowhere else for them to go. But sons living under separate roofs from the main household may also need to contribute to their maintenance; household and welfare networks are still not coterminous. Also, there are limitations to the obligation to care which would not be out of place in the world of nuclear household formation rules. For instance, a man is not under pressure to look after his wife's parents. Nor is it everywhere possible for elderly folk left without children to count on brothers.[77] Extended families in Asia are certainly not merciless; yet nor are they the infinitely soft cushions imagined by students of the north west. At the end of this volume Zhongwei Zhao argues that the large supportive coresident family of 'traditional' China, able to see the declining generation through a comfortable old age, is to a great extent a myth, an unattainable ideal. If the willingness was there, the personnel were not – at least within the household. In the 'margins' of other chapters we encounter the large kin and neighbourhood support network of an early modern Japanese village (Suzuki), and the extended and caring Xhosa family of pre-apartheid times (Burman and van der Spuy). It is tempting to speculate that these may not also be reassuring stereotypes that would crumble in the face of similarly painstaking demographic computer simulation and sociological research.[78]

Fifthly, a related matter of terminology: all the evidence we have mustered from earlier case studies and the chapters below suggests that the household may not be the best unit on which to base comparative analyses. Its shape is too mutable, its boundaries too flexible – a point that anthropologists and historians working outside the European mainstream have perhaps been the quickest to appreciate.[79] The important distinction is not that between household on one hand and wider collectivity on the other – for even if the household can be held in focus, 'collectivity' is shorthand for too wide a range of structures and institutions to be of much analytical use. (It also has overtones of collectivism – overtones which Laslett's emphasis on the Poor Law as the collectivity's principal incarnation is not calculated to dispel.) The appropriate distinctions to be drawn are rather between different types of inter-household network.

Such networks of extended family or of friends and neighbours have been found (and described in this chapter) linking both nuclear and extended households, in England, continental Europe and the Americas. Comparable networks are detectible further afield – in Taiwan for example, where large coresidential units coexist with a strangely neglectful attitude to kinship and the development of complex inter-household ties.[80] At this stage of the investigation (very much a preliminary stage, of course) the similarities will probably tend to obscure the regional and chronological differences. For the moment we have an overall picture of the history of mutual support networks in which some degree of continuity seems to be widespread. This is of course (I repeat) emphatically *not* to say that there have been no changes with respect to time and space – simply that we cannot yet state clearly what they are. Very likely, north-western networks *will* prove, on the whole, to have been less dense, or more fragile, than those further east, but we are still unsure how that contrast is to be captured – what geographical boundaries and local evolutions are really in question, and what conceptual tools will most suitably disinter them. When more evidence has been accumulated, however, and several convenient stereotypes banished, a more subtle conspectus should be possible. In that conspectus, household formation seems likely to be only one of a number of possible correlates of network size, purpose, and efficiency.

VI

How is this preliminary picture of the *relative* continuity and ubiquity of informal networks – even of their flourishing – to be reconciled with those generalizations that I earlier derived from subsequent chapters? Certainly the evidence offered of the ways in which networks of support and health care actually function clearly endorses some of the points made – about the sheer variety of care (1); the common irrelevance of 'national' ideology and religion and the importance of local economic and social conditions (3); the impossibility of specifying any simple secular evolution in informal care – for we have found evidence neither of golden ages nor of particularly decadent ones (6); and the occasional inadequacy or unavailability of neighbourly care (7). But what of the emphasis on the limitations of caring networks (9) and the interpenetration of domestic and other sectors (5 – and, to some extent, 2)?

I submit that there is no profound dissonance between the two bodies of information. The differences between them are superficial, the result of approaching informal networks from different directions – perhaps of the inevitable contrast of tone between an 'outsider' and an 'insider' view. Subsequent chapters mostly have to infer the character of networks from institutional evidence, which throws limitations into prominence. The ethnographic and historical accounts drawn on above are mostly attempting something less indirect and more evocative and sympathetic: limitations win less attention than successes. On closer inspection, however, the 'inside' views also lose their reassuring warmth. They yield numerous testimonies to the fragility and unpredictability of support networks among the poor; to the calculating, instrumental manner in which transactions are undertaken; to the narrowness of the sphere within which support may be hoped for (whether because of reluctance or unavailability); and finally, crucially, to the frequency with which the 'horizontal' world of informal networks is very seldom self-contained but continually intersects with the 'vertical' world of patronage and institutions. The network is no more an independent welfare republic than the household. *Some* degree of 'mixture' in the economy seems well-nigh inescapable.

VII

The final question that I want to raise takes us back to the opening of this chapter, with its vignette. It returns to the possible contribution that antiquity and the Middle Ages might make to the larger, and differently conceptualized, comparative history of informal relief which I have been urging. So far, the main task has been one of summary and comparison, and the main result – naturally at a level of considerable abstraction – has been one of continuity. But how far back can the comparisons be taken and the continuity projected? The first step toward an answer must be to challenge, yet again, the myth of the golden age. Demographers, sociologists, and social historians are now more or less unanimous in their opinion that the kinds of small household, precarious network, and mixed economy of welfare that we have been reviewing are evident in the Middle Ages, from around the thirteenth century – in England if less obviously elsewhere.[81] But the idea of some golden age of informal care, evident in a preceding period, is a tenacious one. Kinship, as historians see it, is nearly always in decline. Traditional structures, such as informal support mechanisms, are always found to have withered. In earlier times – so it is conventionally said – familial or neighbourly support was more readily available, more sustaining. I hope to have set out enough evidence in previous pages to dispel the notion that the English (or north-western) case is quite as special as has been supposed, and that vestiges of the golden age are more discernible elsewhere. I now, unsurprisingly, want to assert once more that, in the terms proposed, such an age has not existed – in gold or even in copper. It has not existed in Europe or the Mediterranean world since antiquity – and one might be forgiven for doubting that it has ever existed anywhere. In other words, domiciliary care and inter-household networks were no less limited in scope or fragile in quality in say the fourth century (BC or AD) than they were in the thirteenth century, or the eighteenth; and a range of other sources of support for the needy should be envisaged as an indispensable part of the picture. Such, at least, is the spirit in which I hope that we may approach the meagre deposits of antiquity – challenging them to disprove the null hypothesis rather than reading them through mythopoeic spectacles.[82]

VIII

'I am being wronged by Dionysius and my daughter,' wrote the woman to the king (in this chapter's epigraph). 'For though I had nurtured her . . . when I was stricken with bodily infirmity . . . she would not furnish me with the necessaries of life'. Such complaints to high authority were doubtless rare. But do they therefore present an acutely biased view of informal networks? Even from the relatively abundant papyrological evidence of pre-Roman and Roman Egypt, we cannot be certain that the solidarity of the kin group could usually be counted upon. It is impossible to tell whether those addressed in correspondence as, for instance, 'brother' were actual relatives. And, in any case, few of the everyday letters to survive come from the hands of obvious paupers in desperate need.[83] All we can say is that the occasional shafts of light do not illumine a happy scene. Some time around the end of the fourth century AD (to pursue morsels of evidence forward in time to the end of the Roman period) a city councillor fell in love with a public prostitute, but eventually, over dinner, he murdered her. The case came to trial before the governor. According to a transcript of the official record, the prostitute's mother,

> an old woman and a pauper, asks that [the councillor] be compelled for her support to provide some small consolation for her daughter's life. For she said, 'this is why I gave my daughter to the pimp, so that I might have a means of support. Now that my daughter is dead I am deprived of my support'.[84]

Seemingly no kin group to the rescue there. Nor do such groups figure prominently in that body of material that throws the broadest, if not always the most powerful, beam on social relations among the needy in late antiquity and the early Middle Ages – the biographies of saints.[85] Groups of friends and neighbours do occasionally appear as helpers, for example in the 'outdoor' care of the mentally ill or the possessed.[86] But they are not portrayed as large groups; nor (to my knowledge) is their charity ever extolled. The characteristic vignette of domestic care is more like that to be found in the fifth-century *Life* of Porphyrius of Gaza by Mark the Deacon. Escaping a pagan mob, the saint and his biographer finally take refuge above a rude house-top dwelling, to which only a skylight gives access. A poor orphan girl of 14 lives there. She is working to support her aged grandmother. The detail is incidental enough not to have been embroidered to make a hagiographical point. The scene is not a cosy one.[87]

'Thine own friend, and thy father's friend, forsake not; neither go into thy brother's house in the day of thy calamity; for better is a neighbour that is near than a brother who is far off.' The Book of Proverbs (27.10) anticipates – or is a source of – a piece of Palestinian folk wisdom recorded in the 1900s: 'he who is near is your neighbour but he who is far is not your brother'.[88] It also harmonizes with the advice tendered by Hesiod in *Works and Days* (lines 342–51):

> invite to dinner him who is friendly, and leave your enemy be; and invite above all him who lives near you. For if something untoward happens at your place, neighbours can come ungirt but kin take time to arm themselves. A bad neighbour is as big a bane as a good one is a boon: he has got good value who has got a good neighbour . . . get good measure from your neighbour, and give good measure back, with the measure itself and better if you can, so that when in need another time you may find something to rely on.[89]

Were even neighbours so dependable? A second-century AD poet imagines this appeal from one peasant farmer to another.

> A violent hailstorm has sheared off our standing grain, and there is nothing left to keep us from famine. Because we have no money we cannot buy imported wheat. But I hear that you have something left over from last year's good harvest. So please lend me twenty bushels, to give me the means to save my own life and that of my wife and children. And when a year of good harvest comes along, we will repay you . . . Please do not let good neighbours go to ruin in times such as these.[90]

The answer to the plea for help is not given. The ideal of reciprocity among the poor, with its ethos of calculation and instrumentality, could not be better evoked, however. Nor could the interdependence of storage and reciprocity as 'risk-buffering' mechanisms. But the resources in question are perceived as scarce; in ancient as in modern times, competition for them is a zero-sum game; neighbours are as likely to steal your animals or destroy your crops as to make good your losses;[91] networks of reciprocity once again seem delicate creations.

Which is not to argue that they functioned hardly at all. There is certainly evidence of the sorts of local interchange that we have been extracting from the record of much later centuries. Some of that evidence is again – inevitably – literary. In the early second century AD the orator Dio Chrysostom paints an elaborate and clever picture of rustic simplicity contrasted with urban decadence.[92] Unlike the farmer in the previous vignette, the family depicted here have diversified their means of subsistence. They have plenty of wheat, barley, and millet in store – though not beans, 'because they didn't grow this year'. Their other resources include a garden, two vines, the produce of hunting, and some livestock. But they also look to the benefits of having a functionally extended family. Their daughter has married a man of some substance in the local village. 'We don't want for anything,' the woman of the house says, 'but they [her daughter and his husband] take a bit of game when we have it or fruit or vegetables – they don't have a garden. And last year we had some of their wheat, threshed seed, and gave them it back as soon as harvest was in.' The detail is imagined, no equivalent of an ethnographic record. But Dio's presentation, though stylized, does need to be plausible.

Moreover, aspects of it can be matched from non-literary sources. Gallant provides what is in effect an extended commentary on it with respect to earlier Greek material.[93] For the Roman period, we have in rabbinic sources hints of a similar level of exchange, even across religious boundaries.[94] In the villages of Galilee during the second and third centuries, a Jewish woman might lend her blouse to a gentile friend or a Jewish man his ass or some farm equipment. Between as within religious communities, there could be mutual aid in the work place or in the sharing of a storehouse to deposit goods. Men living in the same alleyway or courtyard might pool their resources so as to be able to buy in bulk; women living close together lent each other sieves or ovens.[95]

What we do not find men or women doing, in this or indeed in any equivalent sources, is cooperating with, or benefiting from, members of a large supportive *household*. The coresident groups encountered in the preceding *aperçus* have been nuclear or sub-nuclear. Neighbours sharing courtyards and rooftops emerge from such evidence with more credit than do kin. So it is in rabbinic texts generally. The rabbis assume that farmers have only nuclear families to assist them – apart from occasional hired help. 'There is little evidence of any kind of the extended family sticking together in this period. One text alone suggests that a young couple might dwell in the same courtyard or house as the husband's parents, whereas there is a striking absence of halakha dealing with relations between a woman and her mother-in-law or with property relations between a man and his father.'[96] There are no early versions of the retirement contract, then. And, more generally, there are, it appears, few extended households.

Of course extension both vertically and laterally was a phase that numerous households would go through at some point in their developmental cycle. But any demographic 'snapshot' that we can envisage seems likely to reveal as great a preponderance of *poor* nuclear households as would later be characteristic of many parts of early modern Europe, even its famed north-western sector. 'All the instruments we have agree', as Auden wrote in his elegy for Yeats. The very narrow circle of those family members commemorated on the tombstones that survive in their thousands from the ancient and late antique worlds, and have been submitted to computerized analysis; the oblique references to household membership in hagiography and other literary genres; the registers of dependent peasants on the great estates of the early medieval West; the more limited evidence from that period of property transmission among peasants – by any measure, and with respect to any period, from the late Roman Republic to the tenth century AD and further into the Middle Ages, most poor households were small and many of these were simply conjugal.[97]

This does not mean that they were isolated. We may guess – though can never prove – that the household was no more the fundamental unit and source of welfare provision in this early period than it would be later on. The informal systems of mutual support that we have found would, typically, be operating *between*, at least as much as *within*, dwellings. To say more about these systems than has already been said, and to show how they relate to patterns of residence, is extremely difficult. It may eventually be possible to glean some relevant evidence from the archaeology of towns and villages, by looking carefully at the topography of neighbourhoods and the subdivision of houses. But studies of that kind, likely to be inspired by Andrew Wallace-Hadrill's discussion of Pompeii, are in their infancy.[98] Even when pursued more vigorously and maturely, moreover, they will yield at best proxy evidence, from which only bold inferences will be possible. All that can be asserted for the moment – upon the basis of a not inconsiderable volume of source material – is that there is no sign, either around the ancient Mediterranean or in early medieval Europe, of the widespread existence among the poor of households large enough to be self-sufficient in welfare terms. (Households or 'tentholds' in early Islam are rather more elusive; but it is certainly not obvious, from what little can be known, that they would present a substantially different picture, even in tribal nomadic society.[99]) In sum, there is no sign of the sort of coresident family or household upon which the myth of the golden age is largely predicated.

The networks of this early period are, I am proposing, comparable in several important respects to those of modern times. They are recognizable to students of other cultures – to readers of Lomnitz, Stack, Finch, Anderson, and Razi, and indeed to readers of papers in this volume. It would be reasonable to expect that they should also be comparable in one more respect: that they should intersect at every turn with the world of 'vertical' relations of patronage, or with the still larger world of institutions. These worlds – of 'euergetism' (civic benefaction), rural lordship, confraternities, hospitals – have been abundantly studied. To recall even their summary conclusions here would be to rehearse a substantial part of the social history of the period; and it would not necessarily be conclusive because the points, or the occasions, of intersection would remain mostly hidden from us.[100] Instead, keeping resolutely to the theme of informal 'horizontal' ties, I shall close with one more example. It concerns Iceland.

Like all other Scandinavian countries apart from Finland, Iceland is conventionally included within the sphere of the north-western European household formation system.[101] It is also the country for which the greatest degree of continuity in welfare arrangements, particularly those respecting the elderly, has been hazarded by historical demographers – from the early Middle Ages to the nineteenth century[102] – a continuity far outstripping that posited for England. In the national law book of Iceland, a vernacular compilation dating, in its surviving version, from the later twelfth century but embodying material from before the Christianization of the country over two centuries previously,[103] we read:

A man must first maintain his mother. If he can manage more, then he must also maintain his father. If he can do better still, then he must maintain his children. If still better, then he must maintain his brothers and sisters. If better again, then he must maintain those people whose heir he is and those he has taken in against the promise of inheritance. If yet better, he must maintain the freed man to whom he gave liberty.[104]

Anyone unable to support his parents as the law prescribed should approach the nearest kinsman who had any resources to spare and offer to work as his slave in order to pay off the loan of whatever was necessary to keep his parents alive. If some such family support proved impossible, then responsibility passed to the *hreppr*, a commune of twenty or so farms. It is all highly reminiscent of the Elizabethan Poor Law – 'the father and grandfather, mother and grandmother, and children of every poor . . . person . . . shall at their own charges relieve and maintain every such poor person'. But the Icelandic law-makers seemingly take an even less optimistic view than would the Tudors[105] of the potential of family support and of the range of kin from whom it might be expected. They do not expect much spontaneous generosity. A nice illustration of the interplay of household, extended family, and institutional care, it is uniquely specific in early medieval legislation on incapacity.

Does it report an extreme situation? It is tempting to hypothesize that the need for such a law arose in the absence of traditional means of supporting the needy that had broken down in the trauma of migration to Iceland from Norway in the ninth century.[106] But to rely on that hypothesis is to ignore partial analogues in other Scandinavian codes, where it is insisted that kin rather than non-kin take in the poor and elderly – in return for a right to the inheritance.[107] It is also to give further credence to the myth of the declining kin group. I hope to have shown that there are at least grounds for supposing that Icelandic law articulates something not far removed from an ancient and medieval norm.

NOTES

1 Trans. A. K. Bowman, *Egypt after the Pharoahs 332 B.C.–A.D. 642*, 2nd edn (London, 1996), p. 58; cf. P. Garnsey and G. Woolf, 'Patronage of the Rural Poor in the Roman World', in A. Wallace-Hadrill (ed.), *Patronage in Ancient Society* (London, 1989), pp. 155–6.
2 Cf. J. Lewis, 'Family Provision of Health and Welfare in the Mixed Economy of Care in the Late Nineteenth and Twentieth Centuries',

Social History of Medicine 8 (1995), p. 1: 'it is more accurate to see Britain as always having had a mixed economy of welfare'.

3 Two very different studies suggest ways forward: E. K. Abel, 'A "Terrible and Exhausting" Struggle: Family Caregiving during the Transformation of Medicine', *Journal of the History of Medicine and Allied Sciences* 50 (1995), pp. 478–506; A. Kleinman, *Patients and Healers in the Context of Culture: An Exploration of the Borderland between Anthropology, Medicine, and Psychiatry* (Berkeley, Los Angeles, and London, 1980), ch. 6: 'Family-based Popular Health Care'.

4 Cf. J. K. Walton, 'Casting Out and Bringing Back in Victorian England: Pauper Lunatics, 1840–1870', in W. F. Bynum, R. Porter, and M. Shepherd (eds), *The Anatomy of Madness: Essays in the History of Psychiatry*, vol. 2 (London, 1985), pp. 132–46. A. Scull, '*Museums of Madness* Revisited', *Social History of Medicine* 6 (1993), pp. 3–23, for household care among wealthy families and the occasions of their resort to institutionalization.

5 Contrast H. Bolkestein, *Wohltätigkeit und Armenpflege im vorchristlichen Altertum* (Utrecht, 1939), with the greater caution of P. Brown, *Power and Persuasion in Late Antiquity: Towards a Christian Empire* (Madison, WI, 1992), pp. 92–3.

6 Cf. J. Henderson and R. Wall, 'Introduction', in J. Henderson and R. Wall (eds), *Poor Women and Children in the European Past* (London, 1994), pp. 18–21, with references.

7 Several contributors to Henderson and Wall, *Poor Women and Children*, provide parallel instances of foundling hospitals' functioning as a temporary resource: see pp. 10, 44, 71, etc. cf. also pp. 172, n. 41, and 244 below.

8 Cf. S. Cavallo, *Charity and Power in Early Modern Italy: Benefactors and their Motives in Turin* (Cambridge, 1995), for some extreme instances of self-regard. Cf. for antiquity, P. Veyne, *Bread and Circuses: Historical Sociology and Political Pluralism* (London, 1990).

9 Cf. D. Thomson, 'The Welfare of the Elderly in the Past: a Family or a Community Responsibility?', in M. Pelling and R. M. Smith (eds), *Life, Death, and the Elderly: Historical Perspectives* (London, 1991), pp. 194–221; Lewis, 'Family Provision of Health and Welfare'.

10 E.g. F. Newall, 'Wet Nursing and Child Care in Aldenham, Hertfordshire, 1595–1726: Some Evidence on the Circumstances and Effects of Seventeenth-Century Child Rearing Practices', in V. Fildes (ed.), *Women as Mothers in Pre-industrial England* (London, 1990), pp. 122–38.

11 Cf. M. Pelling, 'Apprenticeship, Health and Social Cohesion in Early Modern London', *History Workshop Journal* 37 (1994), pp. 33–56.

12 R. Lesthaeghe, 'On the Social Control of Human Reproduction', *Population and Development Review* 6 (1980), pp. 527–48.

13 R. M. Smith, 'Charity, Self-Interest and Welfare: Reflections from Demographic and Family History', in M. Daunton (ed.), *Charity, Self-Interest and Welfare in the English Past: The Neale Colloquium in British History* (London, 1996), pp. 23–49, at pp. 35–6.

14 Henderson and Wall, *Poor Women and Children*, esp. chs 3 and 5, again offer parallels.
15 Cf. Cavallo, Wright, below. J. Finch and D. Groves (eds), *A Labour of Love: Women, Work and Caring* (London, 1983).
16 E.g. R. M. Smith, *Land, Kinship and Life-Cycle* (Cambridge, 1984); S. Cavallo, *Charity and Power in Early Modern Italy*; M. W. Dupree, 'Family Care and Hospital Care: The "Sick Poor" in Nineteenth-Century Glasgow', *Social History of Medicine* 6 (1993), pp. 195–211; T. Hitchcock, P. King and P. Sharp (eds), *Chronicling Poverty: The Voices and Strategies of the English Poor, 1640–1840* (London, 1997); Henderson and Wall, *Poor Women and Children*, Part I, with the caveat that the contributors mostly accept a broad distinction between northern and southern Europe, with respect to the relationship between family size and need for institutional relief – a distinction which we are here inclined to question.
17 Compare J. Finch, *Family Obligations and Social Change* (Oxford, 1989), ch. 1.
18 L. A. Lomnitz, *Networks and Marginality: Life in a Mexican Shantytown* (New York, 1977), pp. 64, 211.
19 Lomnitz, *Networks*, p. 89.
20 Quotations from Lomnitz, *Networks*, pp. 3, 101.
21 Lomnitz, *Networks*, p. 202.
22 C. B. Stack, *All Our Kin: Strategies for Survival in a Black Community* (New York, 1974), the quotations in what follows from pp. 35, 62–3.
23 Stack, *All Our Kin*, p. 85.
24 E.g. B. Valentine, *Hustling and Other Hard Work: Life Styles in the Ghetto* (New York, 1978).
25 M. Nolan, G. Grant, and J. Keady, *Understanding Family Care: A Multidimensional Model of Caring and Coping* (Buckingham and Philadelphia, 1996), is a handy synthesis and literature survey.
26 M. Bulmer, *The Social Basis of Community Care* (London, 1987), p. 23, ch. 3.
27 Bulmer, *Social Basis*, chs 2, 4.
28 Cf. Nolan, Grant, and Keady, *Understanding Family Care*, ch. 2, for various possible classifications.
29 Bulmer, *Social Basis*, pp. 20–1.
30 Finch, *Family Obligations*.
31 M. Young and P. Willmott, *Family and Kinship in East London*, (London, 1957). Quotation from Pelican edn (London, 1962), p. 47; cf. pp. 55, 86. Contrast J. Cornwell, *Hard Earned Lives: Accounts of Health and Illness from East London* (London, 1984).
32 Young and Willmott, *Family and Kinship*, ch. 8.
33 G. Allan, *Kinship and Friendship in Modern Britain* (Oxford, 1996), is a useful conspectus.
34 Bulmer, *Social Basis*, chs 6–7.
35 Finch, *Family Obligations*, p. 129.
36 J. Finch and J. Mason, *Negotiating Family Responsibilities* (London, 1993).
37 Finch, *Family Obligations*, ch. 2.

38 E. Ross, 'Survival Networks: Women's Neighbourhood Sharing in London before World War I', *History Workshop Journal* 15 (1983), pp. 4–27; quotations in what follows from pp. 5, 6, 11.

39 For what follows, M. Anderson, *Family Structure in Nineteenth-Century Lancashire* (Cambridge, 1971), pp. 48, 51, 53, 65, 137–9, 143, 146, 148, 152; quotations from pp. 56–7, 147, 165.

40 Finch, *Family Obligations*, pp. 75–7, Bulmer, *Social Basis*, pp. 161–71.

41 S. Rappaport, *Worlds within Worlds: Structures of Life in Sixteenth-Century London* (Cambridge, 1989); J. Boulton, *Neighbourhood and Society: A London Suburb in the Seventeenth Century* (Cambridge, 1987).

42 The flavour and supporting literature of recent debates can be sampled in Smith, 'Charity, Self-Interest and Welfare'; B. Reay, 'Kinship and the Neighbourhood in Nineteenth-Century Rural England: The Myth of the Autonomous Nuclear Family', *Journal of Family History* 21 (1996), pp. 87–104; K. Wrightson and D. Levine, *Poverty and Piety in an English Village: Terling, 1525–1700*, 2nd edn (Oxford, 1995), esp. the Postscript, reviewing reactions to the discussion of kinship structures in the first edn of 1979.

43 Finch, *Family Obligations*, p. 58; A. Macfarlane, *The Origins of English Individualism* (Oxford, 1978); cf. A. Macfarlane, *Marriage and Love in England, 1300–1840* (Oxford, 1986).

44 Z. Razi, 'The Myth of the Immutable English Family', *Past and Present* 140 (1993), p. 5; cf. pp. 14–15.

45 See also E. Clark, 'Social Welfare and Mutual Aid in the Medieval Countryside', *Journal of British Studies* 33 (1994), pp. 381–406.

46 See now Z. Razi and R. M. Smith (eds), *Medieval Society and the Manor Court* (Oxford, 1996), chs 9, 10.

47 R. M. Smith, '"Modernization" and the Corporate Medieval Village Community in England: Some Sceptical Reflections', in A. R. H. Baker and D. Gregory (eds), *Explorations in Historical Geography: Interpretative Essays* (Cambridge, 1984), pp. 140–79; A. Macfarlane, 'History, Anthropology and the Study of Communities', *Social History* 5 (1977), pp. 631–52; C. Dyer, 'The English Medieval Community and its Decline', *Journal of British Studies* 33 (1994), pp. 407–29, with bibliography.

48 R. M. Smith, 'The Manorial Court and the Elderly Tenant in Late Medieval England', in M. Pelling and R. M. Smith, *Life, Death, and the Elderly*, pp. 49–50, 42.

49 R. M. Smith, 'Kin and Neighbors in a Thirteenth-Century Suffolk Community', *Journal of Family History* 4 (1979), p. 245.

50 Razi, 'Myth of the Immutable English Family', p. 33.

51 R. Jütte, *Poverty and Deviance in Early Modern Europe* (Cambridge, 1994), pp. 88–9, for Germany.

52 M. Segalen, 'Nuclear is Not Independent: Organization of the Household in the Pays Bigouden Sud in the Nineteenth and Twentieth centuries', in R. McC. Netting, R. R. Wilk, and E. J. Arnould (eds), *Households: Comparative and Historical Studies of the Domestic Group* (Berkeley, Los Angeles, and London, 1984), pp. 163–86; cf. M. Segalen, *Fifteen Generations of Bretons: Kinship and Society in Lower Brittany, 1720–1980* (Cambridge and Paris, 1991), ch. 9.

53 D. Garrioch, *Neighbourhood and Community in Paris, 1740–1790* (Cambridge, 1986), p. 19, but cf. p. 65 for limitations on such assistance.

54 G. Fiume, 'Cursing, Poisoning and Feminine Morality: The Case of the "Vinegar Hag" in Late Eighteenth-Century Palermo', *Social Anthropology* 4 (1996), p. 126.

55 P. Walcot, *Greek Peasants Ancient and Modern: A Comparison of Social and Moral Values* (Manchester, 1970); T. W. Gallant, *Risk and Survival in Ancient Greece: Reconstructing the Rural Domestic Economy* (Oxford, 1991).

56 P. Halstead, 'Waste Not, Want Not: Traditional Responses to Crop Failure in Greece', *Rural History* 1 (1990), pp. 147–64, with full bibliography.

57 Gallant, *Risk and Survival*, pp. 144–5, with references.

58 Gallant, *Risk and Survival*, p. 158, cf. p. 155. Halstead, 'Waste Not, Want Not', pp. 157–8.

59 J. Hajnal, 'Two Kinds of Pre-industrial Household Formation System', *Population and Development Review* 8 (1982), pp. 449–94. R. Wall, J. Robin, and P. Laslett (eds), *Family Forms in Historic Europe* (Cambridge, 1983).

60 Though cf. T. Sokoll, *Household and Family among the Poor: The Case of Two Essex Communities in the Late Eighteenth and Early Nineteenth Centuries* (Bochum, 1993), for some possible exceptions to the generalization.

61 P. Laslett, 'Family, Kinship and Collectivity as Systems of Support in Pre-industrial Europe: a Consideration of the "Nuclear-Hardship" Hypothesis', *Continuity and Change* 3 (1988), pp. 153–75.

62 Laslett, 'Family, Kinship and Collectivity', p. 154.

63 Hajnal, 'Two Kinds', p. 477.

64 Laslett, 'Family, Kinship and Collectivity', pp. 161–4; cf. D. Cressy, 'Kinship and Kin Interaction in Early Modern England', *Past and Present* 113 (1986), pp. 56–9.

65 Hajnal, 'Two Kinds', pp. 460–1, 476; cf. Laslett, 'Family, Kinship and Collectivity', p. 159.

66 Laslett, 'Family, Kinship and Collectivity', p. 161.

67 Laslett, 'Family, Kinship and Collectivity', p. 154.

68 Cf. Cavallo below; D. I. Kertzer and C. Brettell, 'Advances in Italian and Iberian Family History', *Journal of Family History* 12 (1987), pp. 87–120; J. de Pina-Cabral, 'The Primary Social Unit in Mediterranean and Atlantic Europe', *Journal of Mediterranean Studies* 2 (1992), pp. 25–41; S. R. Epstein, *An Island for Itself: Economic and Social Change in Late Medieval Sicily* (Cambridge, 1992), pp. 349–50.

69 A. Plakans, 'Interaction between the Household and the Kin Group in the Eastern European Past: Posing the Problem', *Journal of Family History* 12 (1987), pp. 163–75, with references, and esp. p. 172.

70 Some chronological depth was already available from E. A. Hammel, 'Household Structure in Fourteenth-Century Macedonia', *Journal of Family History* 5 (1980), pp. 242–73; A. E. Laiou-Thomadakis, *Peasant Society in the Late Byzantine Empire* (Princeton, 1977). J. Klassen,

'Household Composition in Medieval Bohemia', *Journal of Medieval History* 16 (1990), pp. 55–75, brings out forcefully the similarities between at least one area of 'the East' and 'the north west' in the Middle Ages. C. Wetherell, A. Plakans, and B. Wellmann, 'Social Networks, Kinship, and Community in Eastern Europe', *Journal of Interdisciplinary History* 24 (1994), pp. 639–63, suggestively discover networks of *non*-kin neighbours in a farming community of a Russian Baltic province in the late eighteenth to nineteenth centuries. The major monographs are C. D. Worobec, *Peasant Russia: Family and Community in The Post-Emancipation Period* (Princeton, NJ, 1991) – see esp. pp. 20–4, 84–6; S. L. Hoch, *Serfdom and Social Control in Nineteenth Century Russia: Petrovskoe, a Village in Tambov* (Chicago, 1986). See also R. D. Bohac, 'Widows and the Russian Serf Community', in B. E. Clements, B. A. Engel, and C. D. Worobec (eds), *Russia's Women: Accommodation, Resistance, Transformation* (Berkeley, Los Angeles, and Oxford, 1991), pp. 95–112. I am grateful to Judith Pallot for advice.

71 Although a series of monographs by J. Goody is some interim compensation: cf. his *Production and Reproduction: A Comparative Study of the Domestic Domain* (Cambridge, 1976) and, most recently, *The Oriental, the Ancient and the Primitive* (Cambridge, 1990), pp. 114, 211, 307 *et passim*; *The East in the West* (Cambridge, 1996), esp. pp. 169–71. An older local study well worth consulting is P. H. Gulliver, *Neighbours and Networks: The Idiom of Kinship in Social Action among the Ndendeuli of Tanzania* (Berkeley, Los Angeles, and London, 1971).

72 J. Iliffe, *The African Poor: A History* (Cambridge, 1987), pp. 7, 16, 29, 58, 180, 245, etc.

73 Hajnal, 'Two Kinds', p. 449; Goody, *The East in the West*, p. 169.

74 Wetherell *et al.*, 'Social Networks', propose 'kinship crisis' as a substitute for nuclear hardship.

75 E.g. A. Collomp, 'Tensions, Dissensions, and Ruptures inside the Family in Seventeenth and Eighteenth-Century Haute-Provence', in H. Medick and D. W. Sabean (eds), *Interest and Emotion: Essays on the Study of Family and Kinship* (Cambridge, 1983), pp. 145–70.

76 Cf. D. I. Kertzer, D. P. Hogan, and N. Karweit, 'Kinship Beyond the Household in a Nineteenth-Century Italian Town', *Continuity and Change* 7 (1992), p. 119. More optimistic is L. Valverde, 'Illegitimacy and the Abandonment of Children in the Basque Country, 1550–1800', in Henderson and Wall, *Poor Women and Children*, pp. 51–64.

77 M. Cain, 'Welfare Institutions in Comparative Perspective: The Fate of the Elderly in Contemporary South Asia and Pre-industrial Western Europe', in Pelling and Smith, *Life, Death, and the Elderly*, pp. 227–8. Cf. J. Briscoe, 'Energy Use and Social Structure in a Bangladesh Village', *Population and Development Review* 5 (1979), pp. 615–41, on the need for patronage to underwrite the needs of poor clients. For the wider context of village-wide social security arrangements, E. Ahmad, J. Drèze, J. Hills, and A. Sen (eds), *Social Security in Developing Countries* (Oxford, 1991).

78 Cf. the still salutary paper by T. Yamane, 'The Nuclear Family within the Three-Generational Household in Modern Japan', in L. Lenero-Otero (ed.), *Beyond the Nuclear Family: Cross-Cultural Perspectives* (London and Beverly Hills, CA, 1977), pp. 79–95. On poverty among the Xhosa in the nineteenth century see Iliffe, *African Poor*, pp. 72–4.

79 S. J. Yanagisako, 'Family and Household: The Analysis of Domestic Groups', *Annual Review of Anthropology* 8 (1979), pp. 161–205; J. Guyer and P. E. Peters, 'Introduction', *Development and Change* 18, special issue: 'Conceptualizing the Household: Issues of Theory and Policy in Africa' (1987), pp. 197–214; J. I. Guyer, 'Household and Community in African Studies', *African Studies Review* 24, nos 2–3 (1981), pp. 87–137. I am grateful to David Parkin for references.

80 B. L. Foster, 'Family Structure and the Generation of Thai Social Networks', in Netting *et al.*, *Households*, pp. 84–105.

81 P. Laslett and R. Wall (eds), *Household and Family in Past Time* (Cambridge, 1972); Smith, *Land, Kinship and Life-Cycle*; Laslett, 'Family, Kinship and Collectivity'; Razi, 'Myth of the Immutable English Family', pp. 3–5, with full bibliography.

82 Only essential references are given in what follows. I shall attempt to justify conclusions at greater length in a forthcoming monograph. On the invocation of the null hypothesis see the cautionary remarks of P. Laslett, 'The Character of Familial History, its Limitations and the Conditions for its Proper Pursuit', *Journal of Family History* 12 (1987), pp. 278–9.

83 *Pace* Garnsey and Woolf, 'Patronage of the Rural Poor', p. 155; although cf. R. S. Bagnall, *Egypt in Late Antiquity* (Princeton, 1993), p. 203, for some interaction among members of nuclear households.

84 *Aegyptische Urkunden aus den Koeniglichen Museen zu Berlin: Griechische Urkunden*, vol. 4.1 (Berlin, 1904), no. 1024.7 (pp. 19–20); trans. M. R. Lefkowitz and M. B. Fant, *Women's Life in Greece and Rome*, 2nd edn (London, 1992), p. 125; Bagnall, *Egypt in Late Antiquity*, p. 197.

85 L. Theis, 'Saints sans famille? Quelques remarques sur la famille dans le monde franc à travers les sources hagiographiques', *Revue historique* 225 (1976), pp. 3–21; P. Horden, 'The Sick Family in the Early Middle Ages', forthcoming.

86 P. Horden, 'Responses to Possession and Insanity in the Earlier Byzantine world', *Social History of Medicine* 6 (1993), pp. 177–94.

87 H. Grégoire and M.-A. Kugener (eds), *Marc le Diacre: Vie de Porphyre évêque de Gaza* (Paris, 1930), ch. 97 (p. 74).

88 G. Hamel, *Poverty and Charity in Roman Palestine, First Three Centuries C.E.* (Berkeley, Los Angeles, and Oxford, 1990), p. 213.

89 Hesiod, *Theogony and Works and Days*, trans. M. L. West (Oxford and New York, 1988), p. 47 (adapted).

90 Alciphron, *Letters 2* (*Letters to Farmers*), 3, trans. B. Shaw, 'Our Daily Bread', *Social History of Medicine* 2 (1989), p. 205; the penultimate sentence alludes to Hesiod, *Works and Days*, for the context of which see P. Millett, 'Hesiod and His World', *Proceedings of the Cambridge Philological Society*, n.s. 30 (1984), pp. 84–115.

91 Gallant, *Risk and Survival*, 144–5, 148, 158.

92 *Euboicus* (= *Oratio* 7) 69, in D. A. Russell (ed.), *Dio Chrysostom: Orations VII, XII and XXXVI* (Cambridge, 1992). Cf. P. Garnsey, *Famine and Food Supply in the Graeco-Roman World* (Cambridge, 1988), pp. 56–7.

93 Gallant, *Risk and Survival*, ch. 6.

94 M. Goodman, *State and Society in Roman Galilee, A.D. 132–212* (Totowa, NJ, 1983), p. 44.

95 M. Peskowitz, 'Family/ies in Antiquity: Evidence from Tannaitic Literature and Roman Galilean Architecture', in S. J. D. Cohen (ed.), *The Jewish Family in Antiquity* (Atlanta, GA, 1993), p. 33.

96 Goodman, *State and Society*, p. 36.

97 For supporting references, ranging from late antiquity to well into the Middle Ages, see B. Shaw, 'Latin Funerary Epigraphy and Family Life in the Later Roman Empire', *Historia* 33 (1984), pp. 457–97. Shaw's seminal article was written with R. P. Saller: 'Tombstones and Roman Family Relations in the Principate: Civilians, Soldiers and Slaves', *Journal of Roman Studies* 74 (1984), pp. 124–56; see also, for an even heavier emphasis on nuclear family relationships in the later epigraphy of the Christian population of Rome, B. Shaw, 'Seasons of Death: Aspects of Mortality in Imperial Rome', *Journal of Roman Studies* 86 (1996), pp. 109–10. See further R. S. Bagnall and B. W. Frier, *The Demography of Roman Egypt* (Cambridge, 1994), ch. 3; R. P. Saller, *Patriarchy, Property and Death in the Roman Family* (Cambridge, 1994). The criticism of Shaw's method – that it promotes confusion of family *relations* with family *structures* – advanced by D. B. Martin, 'The Construction of the Ancient Family: Methodological Considerations', *Journal of Roman Studies* 86 (1996), pp. 40–60, need not affect the present argument, since Martin also stresses (pp. 46–7, 52) that even extended households attested were small.

98 A. Wallace-Hadrill, *Houses and Society in Pompeii and Herculaneum* (Princeton, NJ, 1994). See also D. Fiensy, *The Social History of Palestine in the Roman Period* (Lewiston, 1991), p. 145; G. Tate, *Les campagnes de la Syrie du Nord du IIe au VIIe siècle* (Paris, 1992).

99 W. B. Kubiak, *Al-Fustat: Its Foundation and Early Urban Development* (Cairo, 1987), pp. 71–2; S. D. Goitein, *A Mediterranean Society*, vol. 3: *The Family* (Berkeley, Los Angeles, and London, 1978), pp. 37–40. For modern analogies cf. J. Gulick, *The Middle East: An Anthropological Perspective* (Lanham, MD, 1983), pp. 130–1, and D. F. Eickelman, *The Middle East: An Anthropological Approach* (Englewood Cliffs, NJ, 1981), pp. 122–3. Near-residence seems to have outweighed coresidence.

100 From a vast literature that could be cited I shall, e.g., mention only P. Veyne, *Bread and Circuses*, for euergetism; Wallace-Hadrill, *Patronage in Ancient Society*; E. Patlagean, *Pauvreté économique et pauvreté sociale à Byzance* (Paris, 1977); P. Horden, 'The Confraternities of Byzantium', *Studies in Church History* 23 (1986), pp. 25–45, for references to 'horizontal' associations of all types, pagan and Christian, in antiquity and the early Middle Ages.

101 Hajnal, 'Two Kinds', p. 449; although on Finland see now B. Moring, 'Marriage and Social Change in South-Western Finland, 1700–1870', *Continuity and Change* 11 (1996), pp. 91–113.

102 G. A. Gunnlaugsson and L. Guttormsson, 'Transitions into Old Age: Poverty and Retirement Possibilities in Late Eighteenth- and Nineteenth-Century Iceland', in Henderson and Wall, *Poor Women and Children*, pp. 251–68; G. Gunnlaugsson, 'Living Arrangements of the Elderly in a Changing Society: the Case of Iceland, 1880–1930', *Continuity and Change* 8 (1993), pp. 103–25. P. Laslett, *A Fresh Map of Life: The Emergence of the Third Age* (2nd edn, London, 1993), pp. 158–9.

103 M. Stein-Wilkeshuis, 'The Right to Social Welfare in Early Medieval Iceland', *Journal of Medieval History* 8 (1982), pp. 343–52.

104 *Grágás*, cap. 128, trans. P. Foote and D. M. Wilson, *The Viking Achievement* (London, 1970), p. 120. Cf. Stein-Wilkeshuis, 'Right to Social Welfare', pp. 345–6.

105 39–40 Elizabeth I, caps 3–5. Thomson, 'Welfare of the Elderly in the Past', pp. 197–8

106 Stein-Wilkeshuis, 'Right to Social Welfare', p. 351. Cf. J. L. Bycock, *Medieval Iceland: Society, Sagas, and Power* (Berkeley and Los Angeles, 1988), pp. 52–4, 57. On medieval Icelandic kinship structures, not redolent of breakdown to the non-specialist, see K. Hastrup, *Culture and History in Medieval Iceland* (Oxford, 1985), ch. 3.

107 Stein-Wilkeshuis, 'Right to Social Welfare', p. 346. Note her evolutionary kin→non-kin outline of the general history of poor relief in northern Europe generally.

Part II

NETWORKS AND INSTITUTIONS IN WESTERN EUROPE
c. 1500–*c.* 1800

2

NETWORKS OF CARE IN ELIZABETHAN ENGLISH TOWNS

The example of Hadleigh, Suffolk[1]

Marjorie K. McIntosh

I

Providing appropriate assistance to those unable to take care of themselves has for many centuries been a responsibility shared among various individuals and groups within English communities. During the later medieval and Tudor periods, relatives, neighbours, and wealthier households continued to offer most of the informal or person-to-person aid as they had in previous centuries, while organizations such as religious bodies, parish fraternities, and town governments increasingly offered more structured or formal relief.[2] Support might be provided in the needy person's own home, through boarding and care in someone else's home, or in residential institutions – hospitals for the infirm and almshouses for the elderly. From the middle of the sixteenth century, some communities began to experiment with the use of compulsory rates, local taxes levied upon more prosperous citizens for the benefit of the poor. This process culminated in Parliament's passage of the Poor Laws of 1598 and 1601, which required that all parishes provide minimal help for the needy, supported by rates. The kinds of people who qualified for help were defined throughout the later medieval and Tudor years in terms of their inability to perform the labour necessary to support themselves: those who were ill or injured, were physically or emotionally disabled, or were unable to work because of age or domestic situation – especially the elderly, orphans, and widows with young children.

The networks of care that developed during the Elizabethan period were flexible and diverse, marked by complementarity and a lack of rigid definition. No one was thinking in terms of the categories that have characterized most historical study of such care: whether it was family- or community-based, formal or informal, public or private. Instead, it included all these things. Of course many families took care of their own relatives, but there was no requirement that wealthier people had to assume the burden of looking after their kin. If needy people had no family members living nearby who were able or willing to help them, neighbours, friends, or local officials were prepared to step in. A contrast between formal and informal or between public and private care would likewise have puzzled Elizabethans: when an official body provided care, it expected that many recipients would be living in their own or other people's houses, not in residential institutions, and it worked through employees who were themselves local people, often neighbours of much the same social standing as those being assisted. The help paid for by the town was an extension of the informal care that was already being provided, and as much as possible it shared the features of informal assistance. Nor was care for disabled, infirm, and elderly persons living in their own homes or boarded with other families sharply distinguished from that offered by the almshouses, which were normally located in the midst of communities and integrated as much as possible into the life of the village or town. At times of particular hardship, extra assistance was provided by both private people and community bodies, and needy individuals could move between the various types of assistance in any sequence, depending upon their own circumstances.

The patterns found in the later sixteenth century emphasize the need for alternative modes of conceptualization that promote inclusive and relative analysis of the various components within a network of care. The kinds of questions that recur in this volume (such as the character of care, the source of its provision, and the points of delivery) seem more likely to bear fruit than do rigid dichotomies. The only contrast which appears useful in examining the Elizabethan situation concerns the issue of choice in providing assistance: did people give assistance purely on a voluntary basis, as was true until the 1550s and 1560s, or were at least the wealthier members of the community compelled to give aid through officially imposed rates? As long as a local system of relief rested upon voluntary payments, it would remain to some extent haphazard. Only when the force of local or national government backed compulsory rates could communities include a predictable, regular element within their system of relief. Yet even when rates were employed, they generally accounted for a smaller share of the total aid provided than did voluntary contributions or landed endowments.

In this paper we shall explore the forms of assistance provided in Elizabethan England through an examination of the situation in the woollen-cloth town of Hadleigh, Suffolk. Here the survival of exceptionally detailed records permits us to analyse the ways in which this community of 2,000–2,400 people provided assistance to about 10 per cent of its members.[3] We shall see how Hadleigh experimented with methods of looking after the disabled, infirm, elderly, and orphans as well as a group found less often in pre-modern systems of relief: poor children whose parents were unable to provide adequately for them. The forms of assistance that grew up in Hadleigh are impressive in their scope and flexibility, providing a fine illustration of the blending of categories so characteristic of this period. After a summary of the situation in Elizabethan England more generally, we will turn to the context and scope of Hadleigh's system of relief, describing the kinds of people who received assistance and the settings in which aid was provided. In closing we will consider how Hadleigh dealt with poor children and adolescents.

II

The community's role in supporting those in need increased during the later fifteenth and sixteenth centuries in England.[4] Private, voluntary assistance from one person to another could not keep up with the rising demand that resulted from a cluster of economic and demographic changes felt in some areas during the later fifteenth century and conspicuous throughout the country by the later sixteenth: larger scale production in agriculture and crafts, a greater reliance on wage labour, a rising birth rate that contributed to a high rate of inflation and a decline in real wages, and increased geographic mobility, particularly among the poor. The great medieval hospitals, scattered irregularly throughout the country, provided beds for a few of the infirm and elderly, but these were insufficient even before many of the hospitals were closed as a result of the religious changes of the 1530s and 1550s; almshouses for the elderly, a popular type of foundation between 1460 and 1600, likewise failed to meet the need.

Because Parliament and the crown offered little direction in developing methods of assisting the poor, local communities were left to experiment on their own. The most innovative and extensive programmes were established in certain Elizabethan towns that met three conditions: they had undergone pronounced economic development, such as clothmaking, which produced a group of wealthy citizens while at the same time increasing the fraction of poor people reliant upon their wages; they had a strong sense of community identity and strong communal institutions accustomed to dealing aggressively with local problems; and most if not all of them contained a vigorous reformed Protestant presence, with ministers and/or members of the leading families eager to establish a truly Christian community on earth. London was the prime example, with its reforms of the 1550s which created a series of residential institutions for the ill and elderly, orphans, and the insane, all supported by obligatory rates.[5] A number of communities in East Anglia and the western clothmaking areas followed suit in the 1570s, 1580s, and 1590s. In cities like Norwich, Ipswich, and Salisbury, we can observe the efforts made to provide care for the elderly, the ill and handicapped, and the poor. Paying for ambitious systems of relief such as these, even with the use of rates, was difficult and weakened their long-term viability. The period of local experimentation was curtailed by the legislation of 1598 and 1601, and as the Poor Laws were enforced in the seventeenth century, the scope of relief became narrower, limited now to widows, some of the elderly, and occasionally orphans.[6]

Although Elizabethan attempts to devise new forms of relief were influenced by ethical and religious goals as well as practical ones, they were not merely Utopian visions. The towns that were trying out new kinds of assistance for the deserving poor were at the same time experimenting with how to handle idlers and the shiftless.[7] Local leaders tried to keep undesirable people from settling in their areas, to remove beggars from the streets, and to force lazy people to work, often requiring them to live and labour in some sort of a Bridewell or workhouse, modelled on the institution established in London. We therefore need to see Elizabethan efforts at providing care as growing up hand-in-hand with coercive measures designed to control those people whom local leaders saw as unworthy of assistance and disruptive to the good order and harmony of their communities.

One of the most broadly conceived and energetic efforts at structuring a network of relief was made in Hadleigh, located fourteen miles west of Ipswich.[8] Hadleigh's concern with the needy was influenced by its economic, administrative, and religious situation. As the result of the growth of its woollen cloth manufacturing industry during the fifteenth century, Hadleigh was by 1524 the twenty-fourth wealthiest town in England, equal in taxable land, goods, and wages to Southampton.[9] By the later Elizabethan years, the town's relative economic position was beginning to decline, as only a few of its clothiers shifted to production of the lighter 'new draperies'.[10] In addition to the demographic and economic problems that confronted all Elizabethan communities, Hadleigh faced severe outbreaks of plague in 1582 and 1592 and was subject to widespread if temporary unemployment during periods when the cloth trade to Europe was disrupted. Helping their workers' families to get by during periods of reduced production may have been one motive behind the activity of the master clothiers who played so important a role in Hadleigh's experiments with relief.

Although Hadleigh was not formally chartered as a borough until 1619, it demonstrated a strong sense of identity in the sixteenth century. Its 'principal inhabitants' supervised the activity of the local market and managed an array of urban and rural properties acquired over previous centuries. In 1573 the town bought back its late medieval Guildhall, which had served as the home of Hadleigh's vigorous lay fraternities or guilds prior to its confiscation by the crown in the 1550s. During the Elizabethan period community decisions were made by a group of about twenty men, most of them clothiers or gentlemen who lived in or near Hadleigh, drawn from the same families that had previously dominated the fraternities.

The sense of civic community in Elizabethan Hadleigh was not, however, supported by shared religious beliefs. Although the town had been a centre of early Protestantism and produced several Marian martyrs, some of its citizens opposed the new Church under Edward and continued to support a traditional position under Elizabeth. By the 1570s and 1580s, many of the principal inhabitants were sympathetic to Puritan beliefs while the minister and other lay leaders remained far more conservative. Since, however, the social teachings of both a tradition-based Anglicanism and Calvinism emphasized the Christian duty of caring for the needy, religious divisions did not weaken the ability of the town heads to cooperate in charitable activities.[11] To the contrary, it is possible that an aggressive and highly visible social policy promoted and expressed a sense of community within Hadleigh which no longer held true in religious terms.

A close examination of Hadleigh's system of relief is made possible by the fortunate preservation of the detailed accounts of the Collectors between 1579 and 1596.[12] These men, two of whom were chosen each year by the principal inhabitants, were responsible for the collection and distribution of all money and goods to the needy and the provision of personal care. The long span of their records is of great importance, for it allows us to trace assistance given over time, rather than providing data for merely a single year or two as is true for the other Elizabethan towns studied to date. The weekly or monthly accounts of Hadleigh's Collectors record a total of 6,535 payments of cash or goods to nearly 600 different people, all of which have now been entered into a computer. In addition, lists survive of the residents of Hadleigh's almshouses in 1594 and 1602, giving their full names, ages, and marital status.[13] We also have demographic information from the earliest parish register, which includes the full Elizabethan period.[14] From this array of sources a family cluster has been constructed for each person receiving relief. This material can be set into context through a range of other economic and religious records, including the fine town book and local wills.[15] We are thus able to offer an unusually full case study of Hadleigh's network of relief.[16]

An overview of the town's role in providing relief suggests the scope of its system. Between 1579 and the early 1590s, an average of ninety-two people received help from the town each year, with an average payment of 18s. 11d. annually; up to thirty poor children and idle adults were housed temporarily and perhaps trained in a workhouse, which cost the town £20 per year. By the later 1590s, Hadleigh was spending as much as £180 annually on 120 to 130 needy people.[17] Some of the assistance went to people living in their own homes who were essentially self-sufficient: they received aid merely in the form of occasional grants of goods or cash. Others were supported when sick or if their families could not provide a decent burial. A smaller group of poor or handicapped people received regular, weekly payments at a level dependent upon their other earnings. For those adults temporarily unable to look after themselves due to illness or injury, the town paid for boarding with another family; boarding was also used for orphans and poor children. In addition Hadleigh operated two types of residential institution for the needy: a workhouse, and two almshouses in which thirty-two elderly people lived rent-free while receiving a weekly cash allowance plus firewood and occasional gifts of bedding or cloth. In total, those living in their own homes received about 35 per cent of the amount expended annually, boarding consumed 5 per cent, the stipends of the almshouse residents came to 41 per cent, and the workhouse received 19 per cent.

This system was supported through a combination of rental income from properties owned by the town, endowments for the poor, current gifts and bequests distributed by the Collectors, and compulsory local rates. The rates, which provided about a quarter of the annual total for the poor, were imposed on the wealthiest 25–30 per cent of Hadleigh's household heads. The most prosperous citizens paid by the week, others by the quarter, with annual individual totals ranging from 4d. to 26s. It is striking that more than a third of the recipients of relief had relatives or people of the same surname living in the town who were required to pay rates. Hadleigh was thus willing to provide public support for poor people even if they had wealthier relatives in the community: there was clearly no sense that extended families were solely responsible for their own poorer members.

Who were the recipients of relief in Hadleigh? A total of 583 people were given some sort of help from the town between 1579 and 1596. Forty-nine per cent of these were male, 46 per cent female, and 5 per cent of unknown sex. Of those aided in 1579 whose status is known, 5 per cent were children or adolescents, 24 per cent were parents of children under age c. 15 years (of whom 9–11 per cent were widows), 67 per cent were older people above age c. 50 years (of whom 9–30 per cent were widows), and 2 per cent were physically handicapped. This distribution contrasts with the pattern observed during the seventeenth century, which includes a much higher preponderance of elderly widows; the distribution common during the eighteenth century, with more male recipients, is closer to that seen in Elizabethan Hadleigh.

Hadleigh's recipients fell within 260 surname groups, with an average of 2.2 people per family. Three-quarters of those assisted thus had relatives who also received help during these years. Slightly under half were given help in just a single year, while on average people were assisted in two years. This was true even though 13 per cent received relief over a period of ten or more years.

Hadleigh's needy fell into several main categories, each assisted in different ways. Most people needed help only temporarily, due to a problem with health or employment. Illness, for example, might force people to ask for care who had otherwise been self-sufficient. Sixty-three people (11 per cent of the total) were given sickbed assistance, in the form of payments either to them or to others for nursing them. Most of the care was provided by other local people, who came to the patient's house or boarded them in their own homes; in more serious cases, the town hired one James, a surgeon, to heal people.[18] Should such efforts fail, the town was willing to pay for the important social ritual of a decent burial. Money was granted for the burial of eighty-three people (14 per cent of the total), with peaks in the plague years. Of this group, two-thirds had received some form of assistance from the town in the past, but a third had been self-reliant until their death.

Others needed help over longer periods. The elderly poor, those no longer able to work to support themselves, received money payments and in-kind contributions in their own homes for as long as possible. Once they became too frail to live entirely independently, they might be given a place in an almshouse, where some kind of informal care was probably available for those who needed physical assistance.[19] Twenty-four people with physical or mental handicaps likewise received financial relief or personal care; six of these were children.[20] Boarding was also provided for a man who was 'out of his wits,' and several of the leading citizens took in girls who were physically handicapped or retarded as long-time, protected servants.

While most people in Hadleigh were helped by the town only as the result of abnormal circumstances or during a particular stage in their life, nine families had six or more members spread over several generations who required assistance. For these families, need and dependence were ongoing conditions. Thus, eight members of the Gedge family were assisted, many of them at high levels of support: in the oldest generation, blind father John Gedge and a widow Gedge who had probably been married to John's brother; in the middling generation, Ann Gedge, whose husband Edmund was unable to provide for his large family; and in the youngest generation, two sons and two daughters of Ann and Edmund, aged between 3 and 15 years at the time they received help, together with the youngest of three illegitimate sons of Elizabeth Gedge, Edmund's unmarried sister. Moral objection on the part of the town's heads to extra-marital sexual activity did not preclude aid to the children that might result from fornication or adultery.

Hadleigh's relief was provided in one of three settings: in people's own homes, as boarders in other households, or in a residential institution. Most of the needy received help while living at home. Some of these were virtually self-reliant, needing only a boost now and then to be able to remain independent. Thus, a number of widows received an occasional cash payment or some goods (bedding, clothing, or fuel) but never needed regular relief. Other people required ongoing assistance. At the most modest end of the spectrum were those given payments for a few months in times of special need, for a total of less than 8s. annually. Many of these were parents of small children who were hampered by sickness or the birth of a new baby, while others were tended while ill or after an injury. A middling group received regular payments but at a low level of 2–5d. per week. In this case assistance from the town must have supplemented a limited income from other sources. Between a third and a half of these recipients were elderly, while another 40 per cent were parents of young children. At the highest level of those assisted at home were people who received ongoing payments of 6–12d. each week. Six pence per week could sustain a very modest standard of living for an individual, and in many instances the town's contribution was augmented by some earnings and private charity as well. The majority of the recipients of heavy relief were described as 'father', 'mother', or 'old' – people who were normally over 50 years of age and in most cases over 60 years. Physically handicapped adults and needy parents of young children comprised the rest of the high-support group.

Boarding constituted a second method of care. In this arrangement, the town paid to have someone live with another household for a given period of time while receiving care there. Adults constituted a third of the sixty-three people boarded between 1579 and 1596. A third of them were boarded for less than one month and only three were in another home for more than four months. This was obviously care during a period of special need, not a long-term provision for the elderly or bedridden. More than a third of the boarded adults were old people, who probably needed care due to an injury or illness. Of the younger women, most were either ill or giving birth. Once they were back on their feet, such adults would return to their own homes or an almshouse. Here we see clearly the integration of the town's aid with other sorts of care: the Collectors supported those people who were not included in the informal and reciprocal networks of relatives or neighbours that must commonly have provided care to their own members, but the town complemented such networks rather than attempting to replace them.

Boarding raises the question of who provided care. Whereas studies of other Elizabethan communities emphasize the importance of older women, often widows and often themselves poor, in tending the sick and elderly, Hadleigh offers a more varied pattern.[21] Of the people paid by the town to board others, somewhat more than half were men. Since many were married at the time, their wives presumably did the actual work of tending the needy visitor. Of the women paid directly for boarding, only a quarter were said to be widows, while nearly half are known to have been married. Male household heads commonly provided boarding for a period of just over a year, whereas women's boarding fell into two separate patterns: some boarded other adults for no more than a few months at a time, while others kept children for several years. Nearly a third of the men and nearly half of the women who provided boarding were themselves aged 60 years or more. These elderly households were used especially for care of young children, leading to longer periods of boarding and higher amounts paid by the town for their care. In economic terms the households which provided boarding spanned a considerable range. About half of the men and four-fifths of the women were themselves poor people who received relief at some point in their lives. In these cases the town heads filled two social needs at once by sending to them people needing care and then providing substantial payments to the household. Other boarders, however, were comfortably off, some of them found among the top quarter or third of Hadleigh's inhabitants who were required to pay poor rates. The rate payers, several of whom were important clothiers in the town, commonly boarded poor children between the ages of 5 and 10.

Hadleigh also had two kinds of residential institution. For elderly people, the almshouses operated by the town provided considerable security: close neighbours and the financial benefits of free housing and fuel, a weekly payment of at least 6*d.*, and occasional gifts of clothing and bedding. Twenty-four people lived in the house established in Mawdelyn Street in 1497 by William Pykenham, Rector of Hadleigh and an important lawyer/ administrator within the late medieval Church; another eight people lived in the almshouse on Benton Street founded by John Raven and his son, both wealthy clothiers, between 1500 and 1555.[22] Each of the houses was less than half a mile from the market and church, and their inhabitants seem to have remained involved in local society as long as they were mobile.

Although neither Pykenham nor the Ravens stipulated an age qualification for people in their almshouses, these institutions were used exclusively for the elderly during the Elizabethan period. Only three of the thirty-two inhabitants in 1594 were younger than 60 years, and they were married to older residents. (The presence of a few younger people may have been intentional, to provide some degree of physical assistance for the infirm.) Fourteen people were in their 60s, ten in their 70s, four in their 80s, and one in his 90s.[23] Twenty-two of the full group were women (69 per cent), and there were six married couples; of the remaining sixteen women and four men, three had apparently never married while the majority were widows or widowers.

Whereas some almshouses elsewhere required that their residents be unmarried, Hadleigh's leaders seem to have looked with favour upon remarriage among the elderly – presumably for the care which a spouse could provide as well as for the companionship and financial effectiveness of shared households. Hadleigh's elderly obviously shared this view. Many of the married inhabitants of the almshouses, both men and women, had wed their current or most recent spouse after the age of 40, suggesting a second or later marriage: of the seventeen whose date of latest marriage is known, four had married in their 40s, three in their 60s, two in their 70s, one in his 90s, and one had been described as 'old' prior to his last marriage.[24] Surely we must include marriage on our list of caring institutions for the elderly.

Some of the almshouse dwellers were people who had been

81

entirely self-sufficient until they reached old age, while others had received relief for a much longer period. Among the first type was John Mychell, who moved into the almshouse in 1594, when he was 74 years old and his wife Joan was 64. When John was in his 50s and 60s, he had paid rates for the poor, suggesting that he was among the upper group of Hadleigh's household heads. In 1565, aged 45, he married Marian Trascan, a second or third wife, and after her death he wed Joan Pryor, an older widow with children of her own. Neither John nor Joan had needed any assistance from the town prior to the time they took a place in the almshouse when John was in his mid-70s. Both Mychells were still living there eight years later. Robert and Margaret Colbrone, aged 60 and 40 in 1594, illustrate a different pattern. Robert had married Katherine Grene when he was aged 25, and they had a large family of children. After Katherine's death twenty years later, Robert married Margaret Rywett, aged 25 years, who came from a family with seven other members who received poor relief in this period. During the first decade after Robert's and Margaret's marriage, they were given occasional money, fuel, and cloth by the Collectors, and a son and daughter from Robert's first marriage were assisted in their early teens, when they were taking positions as servants. In 1590, when Robert was aged 56, the Colbrones began to receive a weekly stipend of 4*d.* while still living in their own home. The following year they moved into the almshouse, where they both remained for at least eleven years.

The other residential institution in Hadleigh which played a role in the lives of some of the poor was initially called a hospital but later gained the more accurate title of a taskhouse or workhouse. The house was set up in 1577 in one wing of the Guildhall as a place in which poor children as well as 'idle rogues and masterless persons' were to live while learning to prepare woollen yarn.[25] From the mid-1580s the town provided £20 annually to a keeper of the house, who was to use the money to maintain up to thirty people between the ages of 8 and 50 years as sent to him by local officials. The keeper agreed to provide food and clothing (the town furnished bedding) together with instruction in simple spinning techniques (for which the town furnished cards, spindles, spinning wheels, and raw materials).[26] This rather idealistic attempt to teach the poor a skill they could use to support themselves was paralleled in other communities in south-east England in the later Elizabethan years.[27] As time passed, however, the educational focus of Hadleigh's house weakened in favour of a more punitive approach. In 1598 the keeper of what was now termed the House of Correction was ordered to take up any people found begging in the town and bring them forcibly into the institution.[28] Nevertheless, the workhouse continued to be used for short-term training of poor children and adolescents.

The assistance provided by the town was supplemented by several forms of private aid, though these are less visible in the records. There was certainly a good deal of undocumented help provided by economically comfortable families to less prosperous relatives and perhaps more distant kin. Many wealthier households were surely assisting their needy neighbours, friends, and servants. The poor must likewise have been helping their fellows, in part through informal tending of the sick, elderly, or young. Much of this personal assistance was presumably delivered by women, in their roles as providers of food, clothing, and care. In addition, a number of people left bequests for the poor in their wills, some given to the town to be administered by the Collectors in the fashion we have observed, others to be supervised by the church-wardens or the executors of that will. In 1587, for example, two wealthy clothiers, Robert Rolff and Julian Beamonde, left bequests to the poor. Rolff ordered that two great white broadcloths and forty ells of canvas were to be distributed among the poor annually for five years, while Beamonde left £10 to be used in buying wood during the summer when it was inexpensive so that it might be sold to the poor at the same price during the winter.[29] Five years later, Thomas Alabaster, another clothier, bequeathed an annuity of just over £5 in perpetuity. This sum was to be distributed by the churchwardens as grants of 2d. each week to twelve 'honest, aged, impotent poor men and women', to be given to them every Sunday 'immediately after evening prayer within the south chapel of the church of Hadleigh'.[30] Although we do not know the names of the recipients of these kinds of private assistance, they were probably chosen from among the same people who received help from the town.

The categories of people whose assistance we have described thus far were commonly included among those relieved in many pre-modern communities, regardless of the precise forms of assistance or payment. In addition, however, Hadleigh's principal inhabitants were concerned with a group not normally assisted: children and adolescents from poor families. Although the town seems never to have provided relief to unemployed adults, it was aware of the plight of the children of needy families and apparently took steps to minimize the negative consequences of ongoing poverty.[31] Some young children were supported through payments while they were still living at home with their own parents: these grants might be made to the children directly or to their parents. In other circumstances, the town decided to board poor children with another family. A total of forty-two children were boarded between 1579 and 1596, half boys and half girls, and they remained in other households from anywhere between a few weeks and seven years. Boys were boarded for an average of fifteen months, girls for an average of nineteen months; five children who were physically handicapped or chronically ill were boarded for longer periods. Some children were placed into a different household at an early age, between 2 and 4 years old. When we are able to identify the cause, we find that nearly all had recently lost their mothers, usually at the birth of another baby, or were full orphans. These children, whose parents might not have received assistance, usually remained in care as supported by the town for at least a year, sometimes until they reached the age of 10 to 15 and were old enough to go into service.[32]

In a more interesting pattern, accounting for the majority of the boarded children, the youngsters were put into another household at a somewhat older age, between 5 and 9 years. Nearly all these came from poor families already receiving substantial relief in other forms, and they had younger siblings at home. Here we cannot be sure whether town officials were simply attempting to relieve the burden on the home family by removing one mouth to feed, whether they felt that the child was at risk at home or might thrive better in a situation where there were fewer children, or whether they thought the child needed closer supervision and a stricter upbringing. Although children in this age range generally remained in their boarding household until they reached their teens, the town paid for their care for only a short period of time because families would keep them free as they became older – children of 8 to 12 years could be of some use in the household, craft work, or agriculture.

Once poor children approached their teens, they might be placed into service by the town. They henceforth worked for and lived within the household of a master or mistress, bound by a series of one-year contracts, until they were old enough and financially able to marry, usually around their middle 20s. The institution of adolescent service, widely practised in England among all but the wealthiest families, provided an opportunity for a young person to acquire occupational or domestic skills together with a small annual salary which together made it possible to set up an independent household at the time of marriage.[33] Hadleigh's town leaders were thus adapting a pattern used throughout society to the special needs of the poor in a way that promoted the maintenance of both short-term and long-term order: keeping poor adolescents under the watchful eye of a master and offering them the training needed to become self-supporting adults. While many of the children put into service were within the normal age range of 13 to 18 years, Hadleigh sometimes sent out children as young as 10 years. The town made arrangements for the placement and provided a set of new clothing and shoes for the child at the start of service. If a boy showed particular aptitude, the town might pay the fee to a craftsman to take the lad as a formal apprentice for a longer period of years. Hadleigh also utilized its workhouse in dealing with poor children and adolescents. Seven young people were placed into the workhouse, generally for just a few weeks or months at a time, immediately before being boarded in another household or being placed into adolescent service. Probably they were sent to learn basic spinning skills.

This account of Hadleigh's Elizabethan experiment with relief of the needy makes it clear that such a network of care cannot be readily categorized or discussed according to the conventional terms of historical analysis. To some extent this results from the fact that we are looking at a period of transition in how care was provided: formal assistance as offered by the town and supported in part by rates was a relative newcomer as compared with a strong and ongoing tradition of informal and voluntary help given by individual people or households. Yet one feels that Hadleigh's leaders were conscious of the merits of the complex and flexible system that had grown up in their community and were deliberately cultivating its strengths. Their pattern of support enabled people to remain in their own homes as long as possible and to be part of familiar community patterns even when they were being boarded or lived in an almshouse. For those who needed temporary care, the town filled in the gaps within the older network of informal assistance generated throughout the community; at the same time it ensured that the elderly, handicapped people, orphans, and parents of young children who needed ongoing support would receive it. Hadleigh's approach lessened the contrast between those who required help and those able to live independently, as well as that between recipients and providers of care. Encouragement of voluntary assistance among the poor and by wealthier families served to lessen the burden of obligatory rates. These may be regarded as positive features of a network of care in any historical period or place.

NOTES

1 The research for this paper was supported by a Fellowship from the National Endowment for the Humanities in 1983–4, by a Visiting Research Fellowship in the Arts from Newnham College, Cambridge, in the same year, and by a Faculty Fellowship from the University of Colorado in 1990–1. Computer assistance was kindly provided by Caren Corbitt and Elspeth McIntosh. I am grateful for the comments received at a presentation of similar material at the Seminar on the History of Poverty at Oxford University in May 1991 and at the conference out of which this volume arose.

2 For a fuller description of changing patterns and attitudes between *c.* 1350 and 1600, see M. K. McIntosh, 'Local Responses to the Poor in Late Medieval and Tudor England', *Continuity and Change* 3 (1988), pp. 209–45, which also provides references to studies of poverty in later medieval and early modern England and on the continent.

3 Total population figures have been estimated from the number of marriages per quinquennium, using the conversion figures given in E. A. Wrigley and R. S. Schofield, *The Population History of England, 1547–1871* (London, 1981), Table A3.1. The number of births provides less reliable figures for the adult population of Elizabethan Hadleigh, because of a net emigration of young people before the age of marriage. For the parish registers, see note 14 below; for the percentages receiving assistance, see note 17 below.

4 These changes are discussed more fully in McIntosh, 'Local Responses to the Poor'.

5 See, e.g., P. Slack, 'Social Policy and the Constraints of Government, 1547–1558', in J. Loach and R. Tittler (eds), *The Mid-Tudor Polity, c. 1540–1560* (London, 1980), pp. 94–115; and P. Slack's *Poverty and Policy in Tudor and Stuart England* (London, 1988). For the towns mentioned below, see J. F. Pound (ed.), *The Norwich Census of the Poor,* Norfolk Record Society 40 (Norwich, 1971); J. Webb (ed.), *Poor Relief in Elizabethan Ipswich*, Suffolk Records Society 9 (Ipswich, 1966); and P. Slack, 'Poverty and Politics in Salisbury, 1597–1666', in P. Clark and P. Slack (eds), *Crisis and Order in English Towns, 1500–1700* (London, 1972), pp. 164–203.

6 See, e.g., T. Wales, 'Poverty, Poor Relief and the Life-Cycle: Some Evidence from Seventeenth-Century Norfolk', in R. M. Smith (ed.),

Land, Kinship and Life-Cycle (Cambridge, 1984), pp. 351–404; and W. Newman Brown, 'The Receipt of Poor Relief and Family Situation: Aldenham, Hertfordshire, 1630–1690', in Smith, *Land, Kinship and Life-Cycle*, pp. 405–22.

7   See, more fully, McIntosh, 'Local Responses to the Poor'.

8   For a general account, see W. A. B. Jones, *Hadleigh through the Ages* (Ipswich, 1977), esp. chs 3–4.

9   Jones, *Hadleigh through the Ages*, ch. 3, based on the 1524 Lay Subsidy returns.

10 Most important were the bays and says that the Dutch and Walloon immigrants were introducing into Norwich and Colchester. Jones, *Hadleigh through the Ages*, ch. 3.

11 There were, of course, differences between the denominations in terms of how this responsibility was to be carried out and in the intensity with which proponents of each position implemented their goals. I intend merely to stress that a concern with the poor could serve as a common and shared focus for members of both groups.

12 Hadleigh MSS 21/7–26. I am grateful to the late W. A. B. Jones, then Town Archivist of Hadleigh, and to the Town Council for permission to use and cite these records and to Mr Jones for his assistance in using the documents and for many valuable and happy conversations about Hadleigh.

13 Hadleigh MSS 11/A/3 and 22/4.

14 Suffolk Record Office, Ipswich branch, MS FB 81/D1/1, copied by kind permission of the Rector of Hadleigh. The fact that Hadleigh was a single parish facilitated the collection of demographic data.

15 The town book is Hadleigh MS Box 4/1; local wills are preserved at the Essex Record Office in Chelmsford (because Hadleigh was a peculiar of the Rector of Bocking) and the Public Record Office in London.

16 A complete account of this project will be included in M. K. McIntosh, *Local Responses to the Poor in England, 1350–1598*, forthcoming.

17 Hadleigh MSS Box 4/1, p. 261, and 21/7–26, plus the £20 given to the keeper of the taskhouse. Paul Slack suggests that one should double the number of actual recipients to obtain an approximate figure for all those being assisted within household units (*Poverty and Policy*, Table 8, p. 177). That yields a figure of around 250 for the later 1590s, constituting 10–11 per cent of the total estimated population.

18 Cf. M. Pelling, 'Healing the Sick Poor: Social Policy and Disability in Norwich, 1550–1640', *Medical History* 29 (1985), pp. 115–37.

19 Some almshouse charters from the fifteenth and sixteenth centuries specify that younger and more vigorous women shall attend to their neighbours who are bedridden. The presence of a few women younger than age 60 among the residents of Hadleigh's almshouses points to that pattern here too. In the later twentieth century, the trustees of Pykenham's almshouse have tried to assign one place to a somewhat younger retired nurse who is then 'on call' for the older residents (personal communication from the late W. A. B. Jones).

20 Of the handicapped, fourteen were blind, six lame, one deaf, and three had defective limbs.

21 See, e.g., M. Pelling, 'Old Age, Poverty, and Disability in Early Modern Norwich: Work, Remarriage and Other Expedients', in M. Pelling and R. M. Smith (eds), *Life, Death, and the Elderly: Historical Perspectives* (London, 1991), pp. 74–101, and D. Willen, 'Women in the Public Sphere in Early Modern England: The Case of the Urban Working Poor', *Sixteenth Century Journal* 19 (1988), pp. 559–75.

22 Pykenham, like many founders of almshouses in this period, imposed fairly rigorous conditions upon the inhabitants of his institution. To be admitted to a place candidates had to be 'known of good and honest conversation and living'; they had to have 'fallen to extreme poverty' through misfortune, not through any negligence or misdeeds of their own (Hadleigh MS 25/30). Once accepted into the house, they were commanded to eschew 'variance and strife' among themselves. Moreover, one of the inmates was to toll the bell of the almshouse's chapel every morning at 8 o'clock and every afternoon at 4, whereupon all the able-bodied inhabitants were to come into the chapel to pray. Pykenham dictated that those of the poor who were literate should recite a long list of daily prayers, with a shorter list for those 'as be not lettered'. For the Ravens' foundations, see Hadleigh MSS 25/36 and 25/38.

23 The oldest inhabitant in 1594 was Father John Cromer, aged 90, who lived with Katherine, his 63-year-old wife. This was probably not the first marriage at least for John, as they had wed in 1565 when he was 61 and she was 34. The Cromers moved into the almshouse in 1592 or 1593, where their next-door neighbour was Mother Anne Berdwell, aged 68, then unmarried. Mother Berdwell was evidently more fit than the Cromers, for she received an average weekly payment in 1594 of only 7*d.* as compared with Father Cromer's 9*d.* and Mother Cromer's 8*d.* Katherine Cromer died in 1595, and the following year, John married Anne Berdwell, when he was 92 and she was 70. He lived on for another two years, while she survived at least to the age of 78.

24 This group includes five men (aged 45, 45, 73, 92, and 'old' at their last marriage) and six women (aged 41, 42, 62, 65, 68, and 70 when last married). For the four pairs in which the age of both partners at the time of last marriage is known, the ages of husband/wife were as follows: 39/68, 45/25, 73/62, and 92/70. For a discussion of remarriage among the elderly in Norwich, including large gaps between ages, see Pelling, 'Old Age, Poverty, and Disability'.

25 Hadleigh MSS 4/1, folio 122ff., and 21/27.

26 For a sample contract, that of 1595 with John Allen, see Hadleigh MS 4/1, p. 248. By this stage, the clothiers of the town were furnishing more of the materials in return for receiving the completed yarn.

27 E.g. the taskhouse established in the village of Linton, Cambridgeshire, and the decision by the Collectors of the poor in the rural parish of Eaton Socon, Bedfordshire, to pay 2*d.* per week in 1596 to a woman 'that teacheth the poor children to work bone lace'.

E. M. Hampson, *Treatment of Poverty in Cambridgeshire 1597–1834* (Cambridge, 1934), p. 10, and Bedfordshire Record Office P 5/12/1.

28 Hadleigh MS 4/1, p. 264.

29 Public Record Office, PROB 11/72/20 and PROB 11/70/1.

30 Public Record Office, PROB 11/80/51.

31 Relief aimed at children was not always identified as such, but there is not a single instance of support given to able-bodied adults between the ages of 25 and 50 unless they had children beneath the age of around 15 years living with them.

32 An example of the ways in which Hadleigh assisted children is provided by the experience of the appropriately named Sadde children. Their family received clothing from the town in 1579, and the following year the Collectors provided winding sheets for the burial of the father and mother. These deaths left three orphaned children: William, then aged 8; Alice, aged 7; and Oliver, aged 2. All three children were placed into boarding care with the family of Richard Smith, a woadsetter or dyer. In 1581 Smith gave bond to the town for £6, acknowledging that he had received £3 from the leading inhabitants in return for his agreement 'to educate and to bring up of his own proper costs and charges' Oliver and Alice Sadde. He promised to raise them 'with godly, virtuous education and information of the Lord especially, as also with sufficient meat, drink, and clothes meet for them, until the said children and either of them do accomplish their several ages of 14 years'. Alice died the following year, but Oliver remained with the Smiths until he was 13 or 14, when the town paid for him to spend a short period in the workhouse before he went into formal service with another family. The older Sadde boy, William, was not included in Smith's contract with the town. Instead, Hadleigh paid Smith for William's care on a short-term basis until the boy was 10, after which he remained with the family until he was 17, presumably earning his own keep as an informal servant. At age 19 he too was sent to the workhouse, apparently before he entered service elsewhere.

33 For a fuller discussion, see M. K. McIntosh, 'Servants and the Household Unit in an Elizabethan English Community', *Journal of Family History* 9 (1984) pp. 3–23.

3

FAMILY OBLIGATIONS AND INEQUALITIES IN ACCESS TO CARE IN NORTHERN ITALY, SEVENTEENTH TO EIGHTEENTH CENTURIES

Sandra Cavallo

I

In the context of early modern Europe, the English relief system is often seen as unique in its ability to mobilize substantial resources for the provision of care and financial aid to the poor.[1] Through the collection and redistribution of poor rates, it is argued, the old Poor Law succeeded in freeing the majority of the labouring classes from their obligation to assist family members, especially the elderly.[2] In England, therefore, it was the community rather than the family which assumed responsibility for supporting the indigent, old, and disabled. The amount of relief which public agencies on the Continent were able to provide is held to have been far more limited. The poor laws introduced during the 1500s were never consolidated so that, by the turn of the century, there was a considerable divergence between the English system of relief and the continental ones. The latter, it is claimed, increasingly tended to assist the poor in institutions located exclusively in the towns, and was therefore much less widespread and effective than the parish-based system available in England. Futhermore, the kind of care which these institutions offered to the poverty-stricken is seen as radically different from that provided across the Channel. For in England assistance was given in the home – or at least within a domestic environment – through the practice of entrusting the care of the needy to poor widows and other kinds of sick-keeper.[3] The impotent poor therefore were not isolated from the community. On the Continent, in contrast, when the poor gained access to public relief, it was usually within the context of structures likely to produce a sense of social stigma and alienation. The received image of institutions for the poor remains in fact substantially unchanged from that put forward by Foucault in his early works (namely his *Histoire de la Folie*).[4] Continental institutions are thus seen as compulsory and segregated from the outside world, and characterized by day-to-day procedures inherently dehumanizing. A number of studies have subsequently emphasized the non-coercive nature of these institutions and stressed their role as centres for the provision of outdoor relief as well as shelter;[5] however, the tendency to describe them primarily as places of confinement persists.[6]

A range of arguments has been put forward, from different perspectives, to explain the different courses that the organization of relief took in England and on the Continent. In the context of the present discussion, however, I would like to concentrate on the approach which traces the origins of such divergent patterns back to differences in the nature of social organization, especially of family and kinship ties. This influential view has been authoritatively expounded by Peter Laslett. He argues that an inversely proportional relationship exists between the size and structure of the coresidential family (or family-household) and the importance of the wider kinship group on the one hand and the development of an extensive public welfare system on the other.[7] This interpretation is a corollary of the thesis, originally proposed by Hajnal and developed by Laslett, according to which a specifically north-western European pattern of marriage emerged in the early modern period. It is argued that, given the peculiarly nuclear tradition of the English family, its members tended to be more individualistic in outlook and the idea of taking responsibility for the needs of relatives was alien to their mentality.[8] This in turn encouraged the development of collective responses to the problem of dependence brought about by economic hardship, age, and ill-health. In regions where the family was, on the contrary, extended – in eastern and southern Europe, according to Laslett – and where family considerations tended to dictate individual choices far more, there was a greater sense of obligation towards members of the kinship group, family solidarity saw to it that the need for care was met, and public welfare structures were consequently much less sophisticated and less widespread.

This interpretation seems to me to be important, not because of its somewhat rigid distinction between northern and southern European family types (an approach which has been widely criticized and shown to be unconvincing) but because Laslett makes explicit an assumption, still broadly shared in the literature on welfare, that a close correlation exists between the size and form of the family-household and the extent of care this could offer.[9] Indeed in studies of both northern and southern Europe, recourse to public relief is explained in relation to the reduced size and vulnerability of the family unit which made a significant transfer of resources within the group of blood-relations unlikely. The paupers' household is described as small and often incomplete, broken, headed by women, or composed of single persons; much is made, moreover, of the fact that individuals were often unaware of their kinship group and that the number of their living relatives could be very small.[10] Economic and demographic constraints, in other words, prevented the family from fulfilling its obligations to members in terms of financial support and care, thus prompting them to resort to public welfare structures. The underlying assumption is that when the family was present, then it rather than an outside agency would attend to its members' needs. It should be pointed out that from this perspective, the family is seen as an entity almost biologically programmed to protect its members; as a structure that only when prevented by its fragile state would not fulfil its 'natural' role as provider of care and relief. In proposing this view, writers on welfare clearly reflect the idea that the family functioned according to loyalties which were not contractual but ascriptive. This assumption rests on an image of the family which has characterized a substantial part of literature on the subject over the last few decades: as an archaic form of social organization.[11] The persistence of strong family and kinship ties has been interpreted as a form of backwardness precluding the development of more advanced kinds of social, political, economic, and even personal relations.[12] And indeed, it is argued, it was precisely in English society, where the family was much less pervasive from relatively early on, that we witness a rapid transition to the market economy, to democratic forms of participation in public life, and, to return to our main theme, to a public welfare system.

In the discussion which follows, based on an Italian case, I seek to get away from the tendency to see the family as the primary provider of protection for its members. I suggest that it is mistaken to view it as a locus of 'disinterested' relationships untouched by contractual mechanisms and to assume solidarity between blood-relations. This would be to ignore the often conflictual relationships and power inequalities which cut across the family group, and the differing aspirations of its members which cause them to be in constant negotiation with one another.[13] A family's agreement to provide care was a negotiated one and this was the case not only among the poor. Using evidence from my research on Piedmont I shall attempt to shift the focus away from the biological family and the kinship group to the variety of non-familial arrangements which individuals in the early modern period could turn to in order to ensure care and assistance, and I shall suggest that, in continental Europe, institutions offering relief and medical care constituted one of these alternative arrangements.

The Italian case seems particularly appropriate for a discussion of these issues, as it has been seen as proof of the validity of the north-western European family model[14] and indeed, in recent works, it is still taken to exemplify a society in which family ties are particularly strong.[15] Italy is, finally, the place where the continental model of welfare, based on institutions rather than on outdoor relief, is said to have first developed.[16]

II

Contrary to what the stereotype of the Italian family might suggest, my findings indicate that, at least in an urban context, many domestic and kinship groups were unable to shoulder the burden of providing for their aged and infirm relations. My study of the requests for admission to the hospital for the poor in Turin (the Ospedale di Carità) has demonstrated that in fact it was not only the isolated person who turned to this institution for help.[17] The elderly or disabled men and, in far greater numbers, women who sought admission were often not without living offspring and kin who might even be resident in the same town. Furthermore, the institution often stood in for the family when it came to the maintenance of offspring; children of at least 7 years old could be left 'in deposit' at the hospital as could new-born babies who would be placed in the care of wet-nurses living in the countryside. Once they were 2 years old these infants would normally be returned to their families. Older children would sometimes be reclaimed once the period of difficulty at home was over, but more often than not they remained in the care of the hospital until the boys could be placed as apprentices with an artisan and the girls in domestic service in a family.

Families were thus prepared to delegate to an institution the task of raising their children – a task which might seem to us even more 'natural' than that of caring for ageing parents. This practice was far from exceptional among the labouring classes and appears to have been especially an option for large families, burdened with many mouths to feed, and for widowed mothers who wished to remarry. It should be pointed out, however, that in spite of the tendency to associate admission to a hospital with confinement, the inmates did not sever the relationships with the outside world. Up until the late eighteenth century the hospital does not appear to have been synonymous with segregation but was rather an open structure characterized by the continual comings and goings of the residents themselves, friends and relations paying visits, artisans and others who worked in the institution, fruit and sweet sellers who peddled their wares, or members of the elite who came to fulfil their devotional and charitable activities. Moreover, the inmates continued to play an active part in both the economic and the domestic life of their families. About one-quarter of the inmates (out of a total population of 800 to 2,000) would leave the hospital for periods of up to two to three months in the summer when living expenses were lower and when there was more demand for temporary seasonal labour on the land (especially for the grape harvest) and for peddlers. When their destination is mentioned, it appears that they were reclaimed by their families to look after grandchildren and little brothers and sisters or to care for a sick relation while the able-bodied members worked; the younger ones were expected to assist their parents in their seasonal tasks or to learn their trade, thus reproducing the family's occupational identity. In sum the poor inmates of the hospital were not considered 'lost' to their families but continued to represent an important resource for them.

III

Although the institution did not entirely replace a pauper's family it constituted nevertheless an important extension of it, taking on the responsibility of providing a basic upbringing and education for the children, a training for the young and dowries to enable the girls to marry. In a sense the institution came to represent a second family, and this was reflected in the language employed, describing the community of residents within it as 'la famiglia dell'ospedale' (the hospital's family). This familial language served not only to legitimize the hierarchical paternalism which characterized the governance of these institutions – the power, that is, of the governors ('fathers') and the housekeeper ('mother') over the residents ('sons and daughters'). It also invoked ties which did not cease to exist once an inmate had left the hospital, ties which implied obligations of help and protection on the part of the governors. The fact of having at one time belonged to the community of the hospital gave ex-inmates privileged access to its resources. The hospital also continued to serve as a place to which ex-residents could refer in times of need, and where they could return and find employment and shelter in their old age.

It should however be emphasized that these ties were characterized by a certain reciprocity. There was no one-way transfer between the institutions and the inmates but rather a relationship based on exchange; care and relief were not offered without the expectation of a return. The majority of poor given assistance by the hospital contributed their labour to the institution; not only the young and able-bodied but all those who were capable of participating in its activities were employed in the various manufactories and workshops housed in the hospital and in the various services needed to sustain this large-scale self-sufficient enterprise. They worked as laundresses, cooks, nurses, herdsmen, millers, and agricultural labourers, and even the aged and impotents who were not recorded as officially 'at work' were nevertheless employed in various useful activities such as collecting alms in the city, carrying dispatches, and attending to the children in the hospital.

The strong emphasis on work which characterizes the seventeenth-century hospitals for the poor has usually been seen as part of an attempt to instruct, discipline, and morally educate the disorderly labouring classes.[18] This is not an entirely convincing explanation, however, if one considers that for a long time the relationship between medical hospitals and patients was governed by a similar principle of exchange. In Turin's main hospital for the sick, where there were no productive processes, the transfer from patient to hospital took the form not of labour but of money or goods (although it should be noted that in this hospital, too, service jobs were given to ex-residents, that is to say, to foundlings who had been raised at the institution's expense).

In 1610 Gio Batta Marconi was accepted as an in-patient 'on condition that he should donate to the hospital his credit of 66 florins together with all his chattels'.[19] This kind of contract, according to which the hospital took responsibility for providing treatment and care for an indefinite period in exchange for some form of payment, was not exceptional. It appears to have constituted a common mechanism for gaining entry into a hospital, at least until the mid-seventeenth century when, with the growing use of these institutions for medical education and training, control over admissions gradually passed from governors to surgeons.[20] The system is documented by the wills of some female patients and by occasional entries in the hospital's minute books referring to donations made by male patients (it should be pointed out that while men could dispose of their estate during their lifetime by means, precisely, of making donations, women's dispositions had to be reserved for their wills as they had no real control over their property while they were alive).[21] These contracts involve patients considered to be incurable (the fact that the patient would die 'while within its [the hospital's] walls' was usually taken for granted) and presumably in quite serious condition (those for whom the date of death is known actually survived in the hospital for a period ranging from two months to over ten). The advanced stage of the illness would seem therefore to provide the explanation as to why these patients entered into an agreement with the hospital whereby they would hand over part (or all) of their property in return for the institution's commitment to look after them indefinitely. Their physical dependence and need for constant care probably diminished the likelihood of their finding any spontaneous help within the family or even of ensuring the assistance of the traditional figures (often innkeepers or solitary women) who provided care for the sick on payment in the community. Before they came to be monopolized by the medical profession, therefore, hospitals seem to have been one of the agencies which offered care for payment, and one disposed in particular to take on the most serious cases.

Seeking admission to hospital did not necessarily imply the absence of family ties. The existence of relatives is documented in all nine of the women's wills examined (unfortunately, the family circumstances of the male patients remain obscure given the much more concise nature of acts of donation). Four of the wills mention the existence of only distant kin, almost all male (two grandsons 'for many years in Flanders'; two 'female relatives' not otherwise identified; one brother-in-law and a *nipote*, i.e. a nephew or grand-son).[22] The wills of the remaining five women record the existence of closer relations, that is to say a brother, a daughter, and, in three cases, a husband.[23] However, in at least two of the wills reference is also made to the unreliability of the persons concerned. Both Mattia Ruspa and Maddalena Barbero accused their husbands of having denied them help during their long illness, having mistreated them on several occasions and even having been openly unfaithful to them while they were ill. It was not only solitude, therefore, but also the inability or refusal of the family to provide assistance which drove such women to seek admission to hospital. The institution would agree to take over a family's obligations but at the same time also appropriated some of its inheritance rights. All nine of the women for whom we have wills transferred the bulk of their property to the hospital and made only small bequests to relatives and others; even the closest heirs such as husbands and daughters saw their inheritance rights reduced to the minimum allowed by law.

As I have already mentioned, more agreements between women and the hospital survive than do those with men. This may point to the fact that there was more demand for care on the part of women (one should not forget, however, that male patients may partly be under-represented simply because acts of donation are documents far less likely to survive than wills). And yet examples of bequests to the hospital – sometimes quite substantial ones – by female (but not male) long-stay patients persisted well into the last decades of the eighteenth century, in spite of a new procedure that now regulated the admission of incurables. Following the creation, in the late 1660s, of a separate ward for incurables, access to the hospital was no longer gained through an agreement between the incurable patient and the governors but through the good offices of one of the benefactors (or one of their heirs), who had left funds for the maintenance of one or more patients in exchange for the perpetual right to nominate the beneficiaries of their charity. It seems even more significant, therefore, that although these patients' immediate obligation was to the patron and not to the hospital, women nevertheless felt it necessary to try to secure the good will of the agency responsible for actually providing the care.

Other features endorse the impression that the attitudes of female patients were affected by a severe sense of insecurity, among them the frequency, common to both earlier and later wills, with which these included legacies to fellow patients, nurses, and other female staff in the hospital. One telling example is the will of Susanna Beltramo, an incurable patient who, in 1773, divided her belongings between five women: Gioanna Caterina, another incurable to whom she gave the choice of getting either a legacy of 10 *lire* or the trunk in which she kept her personal possessions; Susanna, daughter of the late Giuseppina Caraglio, once a patient in the ward for incurables, to whom she left her purple bodice and skirt, her striped skirt and two bonnets; the two nurses, Elisabetta and Gioanna Battista (once foundlings brought up by the hospital) and Cecilia, 'Maestra' (guardian) of the younger children in the hospital, who each received 15 *lire* and one of her shawls. The remainder of her estate, consisting of credit bonds for 1,500 *lire*, was left to the hospital.[24] Dispositions of this kind document on the one hand a more marked effort on the part of women patients to establish solid and lasting relationships in the hospital. On the other hand, legacies to individuals directly involved in their care should perhaps be seen as a promise of reward for help received; as in the agreements entered into by the patient and the hospital, they contain a contractual element, an element of exchange. Wills left by female patients seem to reveal a special need to ensure that they would be given the necessary care and attention and so counteract the considerable apprehension that women seemed to feel about their dependent situation.

IV

The practices of placing children, the old and the sick in institutions, which we have examined so far, were not the only examples of familial obligations being fulfilled by external agencies: domestic service, husbandry, and apprenticeship might all serve a similar purpose. These forms of employment involved not only the assimilation of the individual within a domestic group different from that constituted by his or her family of origin but also the transfer to this group of a series of responsibilities otherwise undertaken by kin.[25] In the case of domestic servants, these responsibilities could even extend to supplying dowries for female servants and providing for the old age of servants who had been in a household for some time.

A detailed description of these provisions, which followed a consistent pattern, can be found in the instructions to heirs contained in employers' wills. They consisted of three main elements: an annuity to be paid either in money (generally a much higher sum than the salary received up until that time) or in the regular provision of grain and wine, firewood, and clothing; sometimes the guarantee of a place to live (for example one or two rooms in the employer's house or in one of his other properties); and, almost invariably, a legacy of furniture, chattels, and linen. In the case of female servants who chose on retirement to enter a convent, the annuity would be replaced by a one-off payment of the necessary dowry. Some domestic staff might also benefit from the influence of an employer and be able, for example, to secure a bed on the ward for incurables in the main city hospital. At least on paper therefore (since we do not know to what extent heirs respected the dispositions of testators) it was the relationship established through work and not, or not only, the biological family which was crucial in providing some servants with a substantial insurance against the disabilities of old age.

For the vast majority of servants, however, employment generally brought with it only a modest wage. To that board might be added, at least in the case of male servants (who were considered more representative of the public image of their masters), some items of clothing (almost always one or two pairs of new shoes, one for winter, one for summer, often a new suit – whether of livery or not – and sometimes a hat and stockings) supplied even when, as was often the case, the term of employment lasted only for a few months. Information concerning these and other matters relating to the treatment of servants can sometimes be gleaned from employers' account books. For example, the book kept from 1665 to 1680 by Count Carlo Benso, head of an aristocratic family from the town of Chieri, records in minute details for over fourteen years all transactions relating to his staff: the dates on which servants were engaged or left, agreements relating to their clothing and wages, and notes of all other payments (in money or otherwise) made on their behalf.[26]

Obligations towards servants in times of illness were not mentioned on the occasion of their being hired but subsequent entries would suggest that employers did accept responsibility for their staff's ill-health. In the three cases of sickness recorded by Count Benso, wages continued to be paid as usual during the servant's infirmity, even though this lasted for two out of a total of seven months' employment in the case of the footman Bartolomeo Mulassano and for fifteen days in the case of Mattia Ganotto. No wages were deducted even in the case of Anna Maria, the 'lady's maid' (employed for one and a half years), who required expensive medical treatment (blood-letting by the barber on two separate occasions, one month apart, and at a cost of 15 *lire* a time which, when set against wages of 3½ *lire* per month, was clearly a considerable sum).[27] It may at first seem strange that, of the seventy-one servants who passed through the Benso household at one time or another during the fourteen years covered by the book, only three suffered from health problems. If one takes into account, however, the brief – often very brief – duration of service (almost one-third of the seventy-one stayed for less than one year and only exceptionally did periods of service last for a number of years) the rare incidence of illness seems less anomalous.[28] It is possible furthermore that the master of the house made entries only in those cases of infirmity which were most serious and expensive – perhaps as a warning against hiring the same servant again in the future (a practice documented in some cases in the account book).

The high turnover of servants in the Benso household does not appear exceptional and in fact conforms to a practice which has been shown to be typical of other Italian states and other countries in this period.[29] But this pattern existed in parallel with another, according to which some domestic staff stayed for much more extended periods of employment, bonds of affection and obligation were established, and generous provisions, of the sort discussed above, were made as a result. I would like to argue that these two different patterns were linked to the changing personal circumstances and life-cycle phases not just of servants – as has often been suggested – but also of employers. In a relatively 'young' family, like that of the Benso, made up of the married couple, the widowed mother of the Count, and the children produced almost annually by the Countess, it is possible that the stability of the domestic staff was not seen as a priority. Between master and servant no particular bonds of loyalty developed nor were there debts of gratitude to be paid. Only one of the five staff who were in the service of the family at the time of the Count's premature death (the coachman who had been in the household for sixteen months) was mentioned in his will, with a legacy of 20 *lire* (equal to one-third of the servant's annual salary). No reference was made to the footman, Nicolao, who had been in the household for six years nor for the three female servants. The needs of the Benso family fitted well in fact with a situation in which a ready supply of temporary domestic labour could be found in a population which saw it not only, as has often been claimed, as a source of income in the pre-matrimonial phase of the life cycle, but as an intermittent form of occupation which could fill the seasonal gaps characteristic of the majority of rural but also industrial and commercial activities in the early modern period, and could respond to particular needs as they arose. (It seems clear from the Count's book, for example, that resort to domestic service was typical in critical periods when the peasant family was in urgent need of currency to pay off debts to tax-collectors or other creditors.) This temporary labour force made few demands and asked for nothing more than to receive its wages at regular intervals. As soon as the period of service extended over the year, however, we can see that the relationship between servant and employer became more binding; not only does a wage-rise seem to have been automatic but the purely monetary component of the salary assumed less importance while more complex forms of payment became common. Remuneration increasingly took the form of provision (wine and grain) for the family of the servant, deriving from the Count's properties and evaluated at a concessionary price ('prezzo agraziato'), that is, below the current market value; servants also successfully negotiated the rent of portions of the master's land to their families and benefited from the intervention of the Count in negotiations regarding their families' debts.[30] The employer, in a word, had to invest more in his servant and even if this meant that he gained more in the way of service and a greater loyalty in return, one wonders whether the increased commitment was always desired.

In other cases, however, employers' needs and those of their staff probably did converge, with both parties welcoming the possibility of longer-term relationships which also brought with them more substantial obligations. There certainly seems to have been a link between the age and marital status of testators and the rewards to which servants might aspire.[31] The latter's future needs seem to have been mainly taken into consideration by employers aged over 50 years, particularly unmarried men and, in even higher numbers, widows. These two categories are conspicuous not only for the frequency with which they made bequests to their servants but also for the fact that they were most likely to establish life annuities on their behalf (more than one out of three widows provided for the old age of their servants and only slightly fewer unmarried men made similar arrangements). Might we be justified in seeing these legacies as a form of exchange and in assuming that older servants and employers advanced in age had a common interest in ensuring some form of mutual assistance? Anxiety about old age and ill-health possibly affected the attitude of both servants and employers who felt unable to rely on their families for help and led them to put an otherwise somewhat tenuous relationship onto a firmer footing. The element of reciprocity was often made explicit in conditions attached to legacies which stated that a servant should still be in the testator's employment at the time of the latter's death. But wills could sometimes include an even more obviously contractual clause. In 1694, for example, that of Anna Camilla Barile Albanese, twice widowed and without issue, stipulated that at her death Cristina Singano was to receive an annual income of 270 *lire* 'on condition however that the said Cristina should live with her, being however permitted to go to Racconigi [her place of origin] in case of the sickness of her parents or brothers and sisters and for 15–20 days in each year, if she wished to see them'.[32]

Younger women, on the other hand, together with married men *of all ages*, only very exceptionally made bequests to their servants (and these almost never included pensions). Similarly, widowers, although they did leave servants legacies more often, never bequeathed annuities. This seems to suggest that the gender of employers as well as their ages and marital status played an important part in differentiating attitudes towards domestic staff. This becomes particularly clear if we compare the wills of married women who were already getting on in years with those of their male counterparts. As many as 60 per cent of the wives as against 20 per cent of husbands over 50 years old left legacies (although not many annuities) to their servants. Moreover, if we look at who exactly the beneficiaries of these provisions were we discover that significant variations exist depending on the identity of the testator. Whereas married men and widowers show a marked preference for their lower-ranking male staff (man-servants, footmen, and bearers) and do not mention the female staff, married women and widows, together with unmarried men tend to favour precisely this group (house-keepers, maids, and other female servants). Older women and widows further stand out for the fact that they made bequests to higher-ranking male servants, i.e. to agents, overseers, and secretaries who were involved in the administration of the estates of both husband and wife.

The fact that debts of gratitude towards female domestic staff seem to have been most keenly felt among unmarried men and older women – whether married or widowed – appears to be linked to the important role, which included the provision of care and assistance, that such servants were called upon to play in order to compensate for the isolation and vulnerability that employers experienced within their families. These employers certainly included unmarried men who usually had to contend with an old age spent in solitude; but there were also widowed women who, as the seventeenth century progressed, we find living less and less frequently with their married children – unlike their male counterparts. The relatively high incidence of legacies being left to servants by older women, even when they were still married, can, I believe, be explained precisely by the latter's awareness of their likely future predicament. As they grew older, the thought that as widows they might well find themselves living alone, except for a maid, in separate apartments, encouraged them to strengthen their ties with female servants who might one day become their principal source of support in case of illness or disability. It also became crucially important for a woman to ensure the loyalty of the clerks whose task it was to assist her in the difficult phase of succession to her husband's estate and who were also responsible for defending her rights against the attempts of heirs to usurp them.

The generosity of these women towards their servants would seem therefore to be linked, as in the case of female hospital patients previously discussed, to a perception of their vulnerability.

In their wills there is evidence of a strong sense of obligation for services rendered, often expressed in explicit declarations of gratitude – 'for the assistance during my widowhood'; 'for unfailing care during my illness'.[33] By contrast, a similar sense of indebtedness is largely absent from the testaments of unmarried men, despite the generosity they frequently show towards those in their service. This silence becomes absolute in the case of old married men and widowers, who make no mention at all of the care they certainly received not only from their wives, daughters, and daughters-in-law but also from the female staff supervised by them. The help that other members of the family had to secure for themselves through promises of material reward was obviously taken for granted as an indisputable right by men in this position.

V

Analysis of the provisions made for servants in their old age also sheds light therefore on the inequalities of status which cut across the families of employers and led to notable differences in the degree to which even the socially privileged could claim a 'right' to care. Although the need to guarantee care and assistance has until now been seen as a problem facing primarily the poor, and among them those without family in particular, the study of wills reveals that even within the more affluent classes those members who were most disadvantaged by demographic circumstances, inheritance practices, and models of household formation were often forced to negotiate solutions to the problems posed by their dependent state in times of sickness or in old age. We have observed in particular the insecurity which seems to surround old women, undoubtedly to be linked with the assault on their economic independence which intensified in the second half of the seventeenth century.[34] The vulnerability of their position seems to explain also other distinctive characteristics of their wills. It is certainly no accident that women, especially those whose husbands had died, are conspicuous for the frequency with which they left legacies to individuals who did not belong to their immediate familial and domestic environment and were often of lower social status. Men, especially those who had enjoyed upward social mobility and were therefore more anxious to protect the family's good name, showed frequent concern for the welfare of their less fortunate kin but their legacies to individuals outside the kin group are remarkably less numerous.[35] Moreover, when they did leave bequests to non-relatives, the recipients tended to be 'friends' and colleagues, i.e. peers in status.

These non-familial and non-domestic legacies by women once again frequently take the form of explicit statements of obligation for care bestowed upon them in times of sickness. Those mentioned as providers of care are often other women, presumably not of very low status but rather of the middling sort, as the use of the term 'madama' or 'signora' suggests – 'to *madama* Prelasca, wife of Cesare, for the care given to me over many months'. Medical practitioners (surgeons, physicians, and apothecaries) or their wives, who possibly assisted their husbands or acted as mediators between them and their patients, also frequently feature as beneficiaries 'for the long period of service during illness'. The third group often mentioned were members of the legal profession, merchants and bankers who, similarly to the clerks employed by the family, were rewarded for the help they had given in managing their financial affairs and dealing with law-suits.

I believe that the inter-class relations which these women's testaments evoke cannot simply be subsumed, as they usually have been, under the general umbrella of ties of patronage; they cannot, that is, be seen simply as examples of the ways in which family or individual influence was established and maintained. Women's legacies often document the benefactresses' need to call attention to themselves, rather than being an expression of their paternalism, piety, or compassion. The weakening of their position that women of the propertied classes experienced in the late seventeenth and eighteenth centuries might explain the considerable investment in social relations in the community they seem to have made. This was true especially in the case of those who had no children, but even those who did were anxious about their old age. The promise of remuneration in exchange for care which, it has been argued, lay at the heart of women's bequests to hospital nurses, servants, and acquaintances was sometimes extended to family members as well. There is no lack of examples of women negotiating with expected heirs the bequest of the property of which they could dispose in exchange for a guarantee of care. In her will, drawn up in 1761, the widow Vittoria Verna left a dowry worth 1,000 *lire* (and all her underwear) to her granddaughter, the child of one of her own daughters, Rosa Reyneri. Rosa was to be permitted to make use of the interest on this sum until such time as the young woman got married 'but on condition that the death of the testator should occur in the Reyneri house where she currently resides'.[36]

The family, even in cases where it existed and was financially solvent, did not automatically represent a solution to the need and dependence of its members. In this chapter I have suggested that in the early modern period family relations were only one of the several agencies to which an individual could turn for protection and that they should not be expected to have functioned according to principles radically different from those which governed the relationships between the providers and recipients of care in other settings. The scenario described here, however, should not be seen as unchanging. There is evidence for example of an expansion of the role played by the family as an agent of welfare in the second half of the eighteenth century when we see a growing number of provisions being made on behalf of less fortunate members of the kinship group.[37] Previous to such developments, however, expectations concerning sources of care were distributed much more equally than is often supposed between family, community, and institutions.

NOTES

1 See for example P. Slack, 'Comment: Some Comparative Problems in the English Case', in T. Riis (ed.), *Aspects of Poverty in Early Modern Europe* (Stuttgart, 1981), pp. 281–5; and P. Slack, *Poverty and Policy in Tudor and Stuart England* (London, 1988), p. 11.
2 For a sample of this positive view, D. Thomson, 'The Welfare of the Elderly in the Past: a Family or Community Responsibility?', in M. Pelling and R. M. Smith (eds), *Life, Death, and the Elderly: Historical Perspectives* (London, 1991), pp. 194–217.
3 M. Pelling, 'Healing the Sick Poor: Social Policy and Disability in Norwich, 1550–1640', *Medical History* 29 (1985), pp. 115–37; A. Wear, 'Caring for the Sick Poor in St. Bartholomew Exchange: 1580–1676', in W. F. Bynum and R. Porter (eds), *Living and Dying in London, Medical History* Supplement no. 11 (London, 1991), pp. 41–60.
4 M. Foucault, *Histoire de la Folie à l'Age Classique* (2nd edn, Paris, 1972). For a perceptive analysis of the evolution of Foucault's thought on this subject, S. Loriga, *Soldati. L'Istituzione Militare nel Piemonte del Seicento* (Rome, 1992), Introduction.
5 For instance S. J. Woolf, *The Poor in Western Europe in the Eighteenth and Nineteenth Centuries* (London and New York, 1986).
6 R. Jütte's recent overview, *Poverty and Deviance in Early Modern Europe* (Cambridge, 1994), for example, in spite of the attention it pays to

the poor's informal networks of support, ignores the part played by welfare institutions themselves in such self-help strategies. Relief institutions are dealt with in a separate chapter and only in terms of their role in the 'marginalization' of the poor, a framework which just reconfirms the negative, reductive view of institutional intervention.

7 P. Laslett, 'Family, Kinship and Collectivity as Systems of Support in Pre-industrial Europe: a Consideration of the "Nuclear-Hardship" Hypothesis', *Continuity and Change* 3 (1988), pp. 153–75.

8 J. Hajnal, 'European Marriage Patterns in Perspective', in D. V. Glass and D. E. C. Eversley (eds), *Population and History: Essays in Historical Demography* (London, 1965), pp. 101–43; and 'Two Kinds of Pre-industrial Household Formation System', in R. Wall, J. Robin, and P. Laslett (eds), *Family Forms in Historic Europe* (Cambridge, 1983), pp. 65–104; P. Laslett, 'Family and Household as Work Group and Kin Group: Areas of Traditional Europe Compared', in Wall and Laslett (eds), *Family Forms*, pp. 513–63.

9 The validity of this model in the Italian case has been questioned by F. Benigno, 'The Southern Italian Family in the Early Modern Period: A Discussion of Co-Residential Patterns', *Continuity and Change* 4 (1989), pp. 165–94; and M. Barbagli, 'Three Household Formation Systems in Eighteenth- and Nineteenth-Century Italy', in D. I. Kertzer and R. P. Saller (eds), *The Family in Italy from Antiquity to the Present* (New Haven, CT, and London, 1991), pp. 250–70. For the complexity of the Iberian and more generally Mediterranean situation, R. Rowland, 'Sistemas matrimoniales en la peninsula iberica: una perspectiva regional', in V. Pérez Moreda and D. Sven Reher (eds), *La Demografia historica en España* (Madrid, 1988), pp. 72–137.

10 Slack, *Poverty and Policy*, pp. 76, 85; Jütte, *Poverty and Deviance*, p. 40; Woolf, *The Poor*, pp. 15–16; Laslett, 'Family, Kinship and Collectivity', pp. 161–3.

11 In David Sabean's words, kinship 'has often been seen as something ascriptive and so the map of social history has looked something like "from kin to contract"'. D. W. Sabean, *Property, Production and Family in Neckerhausen, 1700–1870* (Cambridge, 1990), p. 24.

12 On the family as an obstacle to the development of civic life and to the emergence of democratic political structures, see the classic study by E. C. Banfield, *The Moral Basis of a Backward Society* (Glencoe, IL, 1958), and the works of anthropologists of Mediterranean societies, for example J. K. Campbell, *Honour, Family and Patronage: a Study of Institutions and Moral Values in a Greek Mountain Community* (Oxford, 1964). On the importance of the family as an impediment to the development of a land and labour market and therefore of a capitalist economy, A. Macfarlane, *The Origins of English Individualism: the Family, Property and Social Transition* (Oxford, 1978). On kinship ties as an obstacle to individual freedom of choice see, as well as Macfarlane, L. Stone, *The Family, Sex and Marriage in England 1500–1800* (London, 1977).

13 For a critique of this approach see B. Thorne and M. Yalom (eds),

Rethinking the Family: Some Feminist Questions (rev. edn, Boston, MA, 1992), especially pp. 14, 20.

14 This followed in particular the publication of a study of the Florentine Catasto, on which see the discussion in R. M. Smith, 'The People of Tuscany and their Families: Medieval or Mediterranean?', *Journal of Family History* 6 (1981), pp. 107–28.

15 D. I. Kertzer, *Sacrificed for Honor: Italian Infant Abandonment and the Politics of Reproductive Control* (Boston, 1993), pp. 3, 170; Laslett, 'Family, Kinship and Collectivity'.

16 B. Geremek, 'Renfermement des pauvres en Italie (XIV–XVIIe siècle): remarques préliminaires', in *Mélanges en l'honneur de Fernand Braudel: histoire économique et sociale du monde méditerranéen 1450–1650* (Toulouse, 1973), vol. 1, pp. 205–17; K. Park and J. Henderson, '"The First Hospital among Christians": The Ospedale di Santa Maria Nuova in Early Sixteenth-Century Florence', *Medical History* 35 (1991), pp. 164–88.

17 S. Cavallo, 'Conceptions of Poverty and Poor Relief in Turin in the Second Half of the Eighteenth Century', in S. J. Woolf (ed.), *Domestic Strategies: Work and Family in France and Italy, 1600–1800* (Cambridge, 1991), pp. 148–99; and 'Bambini abbandonati e bambini "in deposito" a Torino nel Settecento', in *Enfance abandonnée et société en Europe XIVe–XXe Siècle*, Collection de l'Ecole Française de Rome 140 (Rome, 1991), pp. 341–76.

18 For instance K. Norberg, *Rich and Poor in Grenoble 1600–1814* (Berkeley, CA, 1985).

19 Archivio Ospedale S. Giovanni (hereafter AOSG), Ordinati, 29 June 1610.

20 S. Cavallo, *Charity and Power in Early Modern Italy: Benefactors and their Motives in Turin, 1541–1789* (Cambridge, 1995), pp. 209–11.

21 Although the number of fully documented cases is small (fourteen agreements have so far been traced, nine with women and five with men for the fifty-five years between 1585 and 1640, and three for the second half of the seventeenth century), it is not insignificant if one considers that the hospital did not house more than two dozen patients until the mid-1660s. These were mostly made up of syphilis sufferers, who remained there only for the period needed to undergo special sweating treatments. A second, small group of patients was represented by casualties (people in need of urgent treatment who were admitted for very short periods). The remaining patients were the long-stay cases I am concerned with here, and represented therefore only a small proportion of the total.

22 Archivio Comunale di Torino (hereafter ACT), 'Volume Congreghe tenute dalla direzione dell'ospedale'; AOSG, Categoria (Cat.) 4, classe (cl.) 1, vol. 44, fascicolo (fasc.) 2, 7 June 1597, and vol. 38, fasc. 5, 12 September 1622.

23 'Volume Congreghe', 2 March 1587; AOSG, Cat. 4, cl. 2, vol. 2, fasc. 2, 14 October 1590; vol. 38, fasc. 4, 8 July 1621; vol. 7, fasc. 1, 23 August 1635; vol. 34, fasc. 1, 21 February 1640.

24 AOSG, Cat. 4, cl. 2, vol. 3, fasc. 33, 26 April 1773.

25 For the negotiations between the apprentice's family and the master concerning matters of health, M. Pelling, 'Apprenticeship, Health and Social Cohesion in Early Modern London', *History Workshop* 37 (1994), pp. 33–56.

26 Archivio di Stato di Torino (AST), sezioni riunite (s.r.), Doria di Cirié 113, 'Libro di memorie di diversi affari domestici del S. Conte Carlo Benso di Chieri di pochissima entità'.

27 A similar degree of tolerance was shown towards servants who were absent from work for family reasons: for example, no deductions were made from the salary of a certain Laura who went to Turin for fifteen days 'to attend her sick husband'.

28 As many as seventeen stayed from between only a few days to three months, eleven up to six months, eighteen up to one year, twelve from between one and two years, four for two to three years and only two for more than three years (with eight years as the maximum). The number of servants in the Benso household was modest and usually extended to no more than four, two men (one coachman and one footman) and two women (one 'lady's maid' and one servant 'to cook'). Only towards the end of the period covered by the book, when the older offspring of the family reached adolescence, was a 'serva dei figlioli' (a servant for the boys and girls) employed. The highest turnover was amongst the female ordinary servants, followed by the footmen.

29 A. Arru, 'The Distinguishing Features of Domestic Service in Italy', *Journal of Family History* 15 (1990), pp. 547–66; D. Romano, 'The Regulation of Domestic Service in Renaissance Venice', *Sixteenth Century Journal* 22 (1991), pp. 661–77; D. A. Kent, 'Ubiquitous but Invisible: Female Domestic Servants in Mid-Eighteenth Century London', *History Workshop Journal* 28 (1989), pp. 111–28.

30 This highlights the danger of assessing the treatment received by different categories of servant in purely monetary terms, as in the case of Kent, 'Female Domestic Servants', p. 121.

31 The following remarks are based on an ongoing study of wills left by members of the aristocracy and the merchant and professional classes of Turin and its province between the late sixteenth and the middle of the eighteenth century. All calculations in the following pages have been carried out on a random sample of 200 wills, referring to the 1690–1761 period, which has been isolated for the purpose of this article.

32 AOSG, Cat. 4, cl. 2, vol. 2, fasc. 17, 23 July 1694.

33 These acknowledgements should perhaps be interpreted also as an attempt to justify their wishes to their heirs and make sure that they would be respected.

34 Cavallo, *Charity and Power*, ch. 4, and 'What did Women Transmit? Ownership and Control of Household Goods and Personal Effects in Early Modern Italy', in M. Donald (ed.), *Gender and Material Culture: Historical Perspectives*, forthcoming. A similar trend is outlined for the English case by A. Erickson in her *Women and Property in Early Modern England* (London, 1993).

35 For example, more than two-thirds of the widows compared with less than half of the unmarried men benefit non-family members.

36 Vittoria's remaining possessions, consisting of her personal clothing and the furniture from her widow's apartments, were to be divided between the three daughters (an equal share of the former) and her unmarried son (the latter). Vittoria was in a relatively strong position compared with other women of the propertied classes because, heiress to the property of both her parents and of an uncle without issue, she had a modest capital with which to bargain. AST, s.r., Insinuazione di Torino, bk. 9, vol. 2, 2 September 1761.

37 Cavallo, *Charity and Power*, pp. 221–3.

4

SELF-HELP AND RECIPROCITY IN PARISH ASSISTANCE

Bordeaux in the sixteenth and seventeenth centuries

Martin Dinges

I

It is a striking fact that, despite the centralization of poor relief and medical care in the hospitals of the early modern period, and the emergence of the hospital as the dominant medical institution in the nineteenth century, the system of parish relief has not only continued to exist but has also experienced repeated revivals. It does indeed have an important role again nowadays. This is essentially due to its success in fulfilling certain tasks in the care of the sick and poor.

In this paper I shall be concentrating on the social practices and moral values which form the basis of the parish relief system. It is my theory that they are largely responsible for its relative success and longevity. The town of Bordeaux in early modern times serves as an example which is sufficiently distant from us to allow the clarification of certain facts and concepts. To do this, the position of the parish relief system between self-help and outside help will first be discussed systematically. Then I will examine the effect of two fundamental values on the way the relief system worked and what it achieved. These two values are self-help and reciprocity. Both must be considered as essentially social practices which are, however, closely connected to certain moral values. Finally, I will discuss the problem of where the organizers of the parish relief system and its recipients agree and where they differ in their view of moral values.

First of all, however, I would like to outline the relative importance of parish relief within the total system of urban poor relief. In the sixteenth and seventeenth centuries the town of Bordeaux, with a predominantly Catholic population of 35,000, offered a wide range of different ways of helping the poor and sick. After its extension in the sixteenth century, the central hospital of St André could accommodate 200 or at the most 300 people and there were special smaller hospitals for the care of orphans and pilgrims (St James) and for the seriously ill or crippled (St Charles). A workhouse existed after the middle of the seventeenth century (La Manufacture) which basically assumed the functions of poor relief, especially for former prostitutes and elderly women.[1] Additionally parish relief had been in existence in many Catholic parishes since the beginning of the seventeenth century as a result of counter-reformatory initiatives. Here it concentrated on the care of the sick. The Calvinist minority comprising approximately 2,000 people was particularly efficient in its organization of parish relief.[2] Alms were also given to the poor by convents and monasteries.

The relative importance of all these sources of help on the relief market can be determined for the years 1660–70 from the income and expenditure of the individual institutions (see Table 4.1).

This indicates that parish relief still had an important function even after the considerable expansion of the hospitals and the

Table 4.1 Annual expenditure on poor relief in Bordeaux
(1660–70)*

		Total	Percentage
Hospitals		44,170	73.2
Parish relief			
Protestants	8,890		
Catholics	2,500		
Jews	1,000	12,390	20.5
Donations		1,000	1.7
Alms distribution			
at funerals	540		
direct	1,920		
at monasteries	300	2,760	4.6
Total		60,320	100

* Figures in Tournois pounds.

founding of a workhouse: parish relief accounted for a good fifth of the total expenditure on relief, the hospitals for just under three-quarters. The study of parish relief is, therefore, concerned with an area which was essential in the fight against poverty and disease.

II

When considering ways of fighting poverty and disease in the early modern period systematically, we can differentiate between two forms, self-help and outside help. Self-help was the strategy employed to solve the majority of problems, which is the reason for its being placed at the top of the diagram (see Figure 4.1).

I define self-help in this context as 'the ability of individuals to endure a period of poverty or distress beyond the short-term logic of the market economy without asking for assistance'.[3] Self-help operates best in a certain social structure characterized by social relations with a low specificity.[4] This means for example that working relations are as effective as personal relations in coping

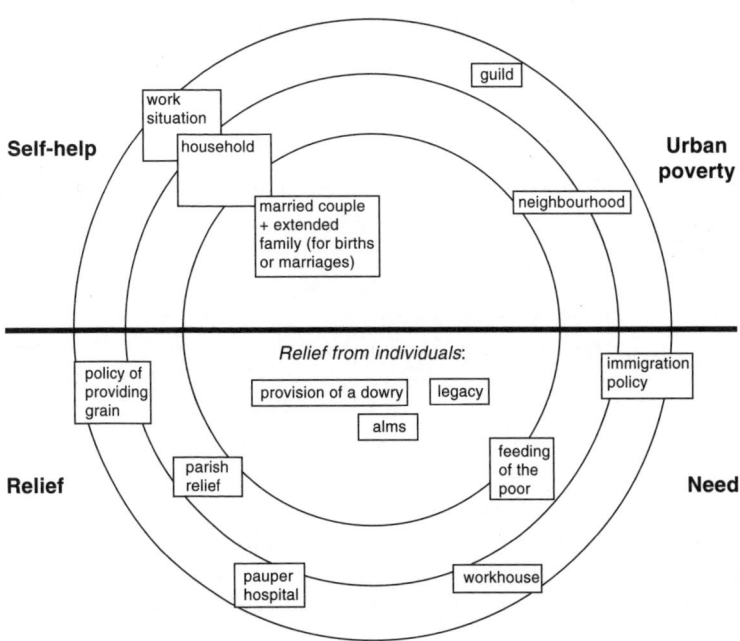

Figure 4.1 The position of need between reciprocal help and help from outside

with poverty, and that neighbourhood relations may have the same useful effects as family relations during a period of distress. Social relations of this type have a twofold effect: they can substitute for one another and they can be combined. This leads to a profusion of solid social ties.

They become even stronger when used as a network.[5] Normally people have a family, as well as neighbourhood acquaintances, colleagues at work and friends, or at least one or two of these. The famous 'friends of friends' represent other possibilities and a more substantial 'social capital'.[6] I use this term to suggest the ability of a person to mobilize others to help him.[7] An individual with many relationships has a substantial social capital, which may prove useful in times of distress.

These networks consist of different types of relation: those between equal partners (brothers, friends, etc.), between unequal ones (parents and children, employers and employees, etc.), or relations between persons who are not defined by rank and power (housekeeper and tenant, etc.). Asymmetric relations have to be considered as extremely common. This does not however destroy the possibility of exchange as long as every participant in a network has something to give.[8]

Here we encounter the principal motivation of networks: the idea of reciprocity. Every participant in such a network gives because he supposes that the other will reciprocate at another point in time. I do not exclude altruistic motives, but I maintain that social institutions work best if there is a real balance of interests. The donor's interest in the actual gift is by and large underlined by the fear that he too may find himself in a similar situation, i.e. in need of a reciprocal gift. Thus every gift is an investment for the future, for himself and his friends.

In the short space available I can only list here the conditions essential to the success of self-help networks. Long-term social relationships in one place favour self-help. Reciprocity assumes a code of 'honest' behaviour which makes it possible for the likelihood of a reciprocal gift to be calculated.[9] Self-help therefore encourages expectations of conforming behaviour within the network. The code of behaviour within such networks can, however, be changed autonomously by its members. Outside help, which is shown in the lower half of Figure 4.1, becomes necessary when people are no longer able to help themselves and so sink from poverty to destitution.

There are structural differences between assistance and self-help. First of all assistance is not based on reciprocity but is a sort of one-way enterprise. Third persons render services to other persons. Their motives may be very different: charitable, religious, social, ostentatious. They usually do not give because they may become needy themselves.[10] Secondly, assistance tends to a more institutionalized form than self-help. Since assistance cannot rely on the mutuality of social interaction it needs stronger forms to stabilize its practice. Private foundations have a low degree of institutionalization. They are followed by parish assistance and by hospitals, which themselves become larger and more centralized. 'Bureaux des pauvres', poor taxes, and workhouses are in early modern times at the highest degree of institutionalization. Large institutions foster administrative and bureaucratic tendencies and develop their own logic. Thirdly, institutionalization tends to be expensive. The basic principle of assistance is that a third party raises the funds for others. With institutionalization the costs mount up and call for funds from the whole of society. In this way assistance naturally becomes a political issue. My fourth point: since assistance is expensive and financed by a third party but gratuitous for the assisted, it attracts social parasitism. To counter-act this tendency the administrators of assistance develop rules regulating access. These rules represent one-sided expectations of behaviour. Programmes with behaviour expectations have the tendency to become quite universal. The famous project of the early modern elites to spread social discipline by work and prayer has one manifestation in the treatment of the poor in hospitals or of their children in special schools.[11] From this point of view assistance can be defined as a means of coping with poverty not based on reciprocity but, rather, one-sided, financed by a third party, tending to institutionalization and developing its own programmes of one-sided expectations of behaviour.

Parish relief is to be classified indisputably as outside help. On this basis, it is interesting to examine more closely what social practices and moral values it relates to and depends on.

III

The following is based on the consistorial registers of the Calvinist community in Bordeaux from 1660 to 1670. Their parochial relief system was entirely dependent for its income on donations from the wealthy Bordeaux merchant community. Of the twenty-one 'elders', four were always noblemen, ten merchants, two lawyers, two civil servants, two craftsmen, and one a doctor. They met once a week. The consistorial registers provide detailed records of the total expenditure of this charitable institution together with the name of the recipient and the purpose of the payment, so that not only can the distribution of the various areas of help be reconstructed but also the history of individual cases over several years. This is a relatively unusual situation for records on the Continent. This register is unique in having been preserved, although it is the fifth of its kind. Sources of similar detail do not exist in Bordeaux for the Catholic community.

Between 66 per cent and 80 per cent of the expenses recorded in the consistorial registers were spent on relief in the town, 5 per cent to 10 per cent each on travellers and prisoners. The consistory allowed itself between 1 per cent and 10 per cent for legal assistance in the tense period before the revocation of the Edict of Nantes. Just under 10 per cent of the total sum was spent on the training of future priests. In what follows we will be concerned only with the largest item, local charity.

Two-thirds of the requests for relief were made by the poor directly to the consistory. The other third appealed to a neighbour or a member of the consistorial council living nearby. A representative of the council then determined whether the applicant was a practising Calvinist and checked the information given about family situation, housing costs, etc. If the applicant was deemed to be truly in need he usually received assistance immediately. A formal decision to provide this support, which had usually been pre-paid by the consistorial representative, was not then made by the consistory until its next meeting.

The reasons given in the records for providing relief show not only why it was required but also the elders' aims in providing it (see Table 4.2). Sickness and unemployment make up the main reasons for giving relief, accounting for just over and just under a third of the cases respectively. Illness is seldom diagnosed – accidents at work and gynaecological problems were involved to a certain extent. I will come back to the question of relief in the case of sickness in due course.

A striking point is that a high proportion of payments, i.e. just under a third of the cases of relief, were connected with work. Forty-five of the total of 160 entries were allowances for clothing to

Table 4.2 Reasons for supporting recipients of alms in Bordeaux*

Reasons	Cases	%
Illness, accident, etc.	195	37.2
Unemployment, wage supplement	160	30.5
Destitution	156	29.8
Damage (theft, hail)	13	2.5
Total	524	100

* Protestants, 1660–70.
Source: M. Dinges, Stadtarmut in Bordeaux (1525–1675): Alltag, Politik, Mentalitäten (Bonn, 1988), p. 147.

enable a pauper to start an apprenticeship or a job. Apprenticeship fees were paid for by the consistory for forty-four boys. Sometimes different masters were consulted so as to select the most reasonable offer. Any preferences the young men may have expressed for a particular craft were seldom taken into account. The consistory helped craftsmen in difficulty twenty-five times. They were bought raw materials or coal or granted a credit. Assistance was also given in starting a business. Unemployment benefit was paid thirteen times 'until a new job is found'. Finally relief was paid to those unfit for work, wage supplements paid when wages were too low, or temporary allowances paid when wages were in arrears.

These examples demonstrate clearly what the consistory's aims were in providing relief. Its main aim was to make it possible for the poor to help themselves. So paying for a servant's clothes could enable him to work just as raw materials could a craftsman.

The quantitative analysis of payments in cases of 'acute need', the second most important cause of poverty, also supports the theory that the consistory's main aim was to encourage self-help. Apart from one-off payments towards, say, redeeming a pledge or rebuilding a house after a fire, there were long-term payments as shown in Table 4.3.

The first point to note is that the level of poor relief paid to households of the same size varied considerably. This meant that each individual was given assistance according to specific need, which is not unexpected in a class-based society. Larger households did not automatically receive higher contributions, although a greater number of people must have had more requirements. Thus a woman with three children was paid less than a single woman, a

Table 4.3 Examples of long-term payments to the poor*

Household	Annual sum		
Woman, single	30	80	100
Widow	39	60	78
Woman and daughter	48	104	
Woman with 2 small girls	104		
Woman with 3 children	75	100	
Married couple with at least 1 child	75		
Married couple with 2 children	80		
Married couple with 4 or 5 children	150		
Man, single	72	104	
Young girl	60	73	
Child	50		

* Protestants, 1660–70; figures in Tournois pounds.
Source: M. Dinges, *Stadtarmut in Bordeaux (1525–1675): Alltag, Politik, Mentalitäten* (Bonn, 1988), p. 450

widow, or a single man. This alone leads us to the conclusion that the long-term payments by the consistory were to be understood merely as a supplement to the pauper's own income.

We can test this by looking at the cost of living. For a single person in Bordeaux around 1660 to 1670 this was at least 75 *livres* per year, for a larger household at least 60 *livres* per person. The contributions paid by the consistory therefore seldom reached subsistence level and the larger the family the less adequate they became. Thus the payments of parish relief served merely as a supplement and were subsidiary to the self-help of the person concerned. The paupers were expected to look for one of the many temporary jobs which the economy of the Ancien Régime in this port offered. The idea that payments were made in relation to the opportunities for self-help available is supported by the increases agreed to by the consistory when the head of the household fell ill (see Table 4.4). It is an interesting fact that the examples of this are mostly single mothers who received assistance which did in fact cover the cost of living when they were ill.

The following reconstructed history of a pauper can be taken in the place of many others from the day-to-day routine of the elders to illustrate the way in which the consistory relied on, encouraged, and made demands on the individual's own potential for self-help. The example concerns the family of the master goldsmith, Thevenin,[12] where the father lived apart from his wife and three

Table 4.4 Examples of changes in payments to the poor when head of household ill*

	Weekly payment		Annual total	
Household	*Healthy*	*Ill*	*Healthy*	*Ill*
Woman, single	15 *sous*	30 *sous*	39 *sous*	78 *sous*
Woman, single	15 *sous*	45 *sous*	39 *sous*	117 *sous*
Mother and daughter	2£	3£	104£	156£

* Protestants, 1660–70; figures in Tournois pounds (1 pound = 20 *sous*)
Source: M. Dinges, *Stadtarmut in Bordeaux (1525–1675): Alltag, Politik, Mentalitäten* (Bonn, 1988), p. 450

children. At the beginning of 1662 they received financial aid individually, the mother with her three children 100 *livres* a year and the father Thevenin 'in an emergency' 40 *sous* a week. The husband must have already been very poor since he was bought clothes so that he could be lodged with his brother-in-law, Tostee. At the end of 1663 he was 'extremely poor', was visited by a member of the consistory and placed on the list of paupers with a payment of 20 *sous*. At this time he was again living alone. Three months' rent were paid for him in the hope that he would then be able to find work. In March he received another 12 *livres* to enable him to find work to support himself. This must have failed since in July he had to be assisted with a further 12 *livres* as a result of his 'poverty'. This situation began to cause the consistory concern. They decided to continue to pay him 20 *sous* a week but at the same time to look for a job for him. The 'elders' also tried to obtain some support from his family and asked Tostee to take his brother-in-law in again. After his negative experiences in 1662–3, however, Tostee preferred to contribute towards his relief (36 *livres*) and so to avoid having to live with Thevenin again.

Here the close connection between relief payments and appeals to the individual's potential for self-help is evident more than once. Paying Thevenin's rent was supposed to help him to get work. Later the consistory still paid him relief but looked for a job for him at the same time. They relied on his own potential for self-help by involving his brother-in-law's family and by buying him clothes to make it possible for the family to lodge him in the first place. Although the family's experiences were not positive the first time, the consistory still expected further help from them, which they later provided by taking on part of the relief payments.

We can summarize the results of this section as follows. The consistory

(a) takes it for granted that the pauper will be prepared to mobilize all existing ways of helping himself;
(b) relies throughout for the form of its payments on the pauper's own capacity for self-help by providing only supplementary relief;
(c) develops the individual's self-help potential by providing temporary relief;
(d) extends the potential for self-help by involving third parties such as the extended family;
(e) teaches self-help by making low payments and encouraging work and thrift.

IV

I now come to the second fundamental value in parish relief, and that is reciprocity. By this I mean the conviction held by both sides in an interaction resulting in help, that anything done by one party will at some time be repaid by help, possibly in a completely different form, from the other party. This is the basis of the practice of 'do ut des'. In the case of reciprocity, social practice and moral values are again closely connected.

There is a tight link between self-help and reciprocity. In a self-help network only somebody who helps himself is an acceptable partner for help based on reciprocity. Thus self-help is a basic requirement for reciprocity. As I have already mentioned, reciprocity strengthens the functioning capacity of self-help networks.

In the practical workings of the parish relief system, relations based on reciprocity can be observed on various levels. Firstly, the consistory and the community help each other. Here we can point to the many cases where consistory councillors use their contacts to find a job or an apprenticeship. Frequently they approach a colleague in business, administration or trade and so are able to find a temporary post for a pauper in a business, with a family, or as an apprentice. The sense of community created by belonging to a threatened religious minority certainly contributed to a particularly marked willingness to help.

Secondly, relations based on reciprocity existed between the consistory and its councillors. If any of their servants fell ill they nursed them initially in their own homes, but if servants were ill for a longer time they were in some cases transferred to the parish sick-room for further care. The point at which the councillors turn to outside help from the consistory marks the limitations of their self-help. Here reciprocity is based on the rule that those members of the community who are particularly involved in its running may also be unburdened of it at the cost of the community.

Thirdly, relations based on reciprocity also develop between the consistory and its 'business partners'. Examples of these are certain doctors and chemists whom the consistory has more or less under contract. Sick people were sent only to them for treatment or medicine. The consistory then paid their fees, which were not always particularly low, directly. Thus the doctors and chemists had a secure source of income. For that they were obviously sometimes prepared to treat the poor free of charge. Naturally the commercial nature of this relationship is predominant here, but rules of reciprocity also counted. To this must be attributed the fact that doctors informed the consistory about the health of the paupers so that relief was paid only to the deserving.

Fourthly, relations based on reciprocity existed between those financing the consistory and the consistory itself. I have already portrayed the case of Thevenin, whose brother-in-law Tostee took him in for a while. Later Tostee contributed towards Thevenin's upkeep, which eased the consistory's poor fund. So Tostee had helped the consistory. Accordingly the consistory paid for one of Tostee's dismissed servants to be cared for in the parish sick-room some years later. Anyone who helped the community received help himself.

The councillors acted according to this principle in the case of Mr and Mrs Coutin who were in charge of the community sick-room. They are mentioned occasionally in the registers in connection with new bedlinen and towels. It was a room in the parish of Sainte Croix which was always filled with two or three sick people, mostly from elsewhere. It was possible, therefore, to find accommodation as lodgers for most of the sick people in the parish. The Protestants presumably intended the sick-room to prevent their fellow Protestant travellers from having to stay in the large Catholic infirmary in the town, where a mass was celebrated daily in each sick-room. The consistory found a flat for the Coutins which was nearer since the husband had grown old and could no longer manage the long distances. When he died and his wife was no longer able to manage the sick-room, she was put on the parish poor list and so received a small pension. Again the principle was valid; whoever helped the community received help themselves.

My fifth point is that the consistorial councillors and the needy helped each other. So people in need who could no longer look after themselves alone were often put by the consistory as lodgers in other households because they were ill or needed temporary nursing. The parish assumed responsibility for the costs, the guest family for their care. Households which were not very affluent were mentioned remarkably frequently in this connection. The households who took in the sick can be found repeatedly elsewhere in the registers as recipients of relief themselves. The consistory obviously felt that a family that had already received alms from the parish or wanted to at a later date should be prepared to make their contribution by taking in lodgers. Additionally, every sick person was visited twice a week by the consistorial councillor responsible for him, who brought him his sick money, and by another elder. The priest also cared particularly for his spiritual welfare.

My sixth point is that one can at least wonder whether by placing paying guests in other families new relations based on reciprocity were not generated between the paupers involved. The fact that someone was placed in a strange family indicates that he was not able to mobilize any more help within the self-help network. Life in another family integrated the sick person, which meant that his social capital could be strengthened and reciprocal relations established for the future.

It is clear therefore that relations based on reciprocity were important on various levels in the practical workings of the parochial relief system. Just as in the case of self-help, the consistory put help based on reciprocity into practice itself, it relied on reciprocity from the poor, and encouraged them in it.

V

We have shown that self-help and reciprocity are basic social practices and values within the parish relief system. On the other hand self-help and reciprocity also form the basic means of overcoming the problems of poverty and disease in the early modern period. It would therefore appear at first sight that the parish relief system is based on the same value orientation as are the everyday strategies of the poor themselves. So a certain correspondence can be perceived between the values of the poor and those of the consistory councillors.

One can, however, observe different attitudes towards these values in the two groups. Self-help means something different to the pauper and to the consistory. For the poorer members of the community it was a strategy for survival especially in emergencies. The members of the consistory are certain to have experienced self-help in the same way in their everyday lives. But for them self-help was important for two further reasons. Firstly, it reduced the costs of the poor fund, since every sick person who helped themselves meant less relief money spent. Secondly, developing the capacity for self-help can be justifiably interpreted as an attempt, not surprising for Calvinists, to confront the lower classes with demands for a certain moral attitude towards work and everyday conduct. In this respect referring to self-help is also a way of spreading the values of the successful members of the community. This means that on one hand there are common values but on the other an imbalance of power, which can lead to the same values' being applied differently by different social groups.

The emphasis on reciprocity is also connected with the everyday practices of the poor. But again this value has different meanings for the consistorial councillors and the poor. While the readiness of the poor to take in lodgers is certainly based on reciprocity with the consistory, they presumably have no other choice than to agree to its demands if they want to be supported themselves again later. Since their relationship to the consistory is determined by a weaker position they are more or less forced into reciprocity. For the consistorial councillors on the other hand, asking the poor for reciprocal help is a further chance of teaching a certain work ethic which in these cases is of advantage to the community. At the same time, when reciprocity has emerged it is naturally intended to strengthen ties within the denominational group.

When it comes to the consistorial councillors themselves, their relations to the consistory based on reciprocity are characterized by their voluntariness and by a balance of power. This reciprocity may cost them some free time but also proves a financial benefit. The relationships of the financiers of the consistory and its business partners are similar. Since in the context of parish relief self-help and reciprocity do not mean the same to all those involved, the social differences must be carefully examined before these values are uncritically ascribed to socio-political change or blurred by nostalgia. Nevertheless the fact that there was agreement on a certain level of moral values between the paupers and the consistorial councillors certainly contributed substantially to the success of the parochial relief system. It remains to further research to ascertain whether these results suitably characterize the parish relief system in general or whether more emphasis should be put on the peculiarities of different denominations or European regions.[13] The social practices and moral attitudes I have described serve at any rate to explain the aversion displayed in the early modern period to the most important institution of outside help, the hospital.[14] Unless the latter was totally unavoidable, self-help was always preferred.

We can assume that social conditions will continue to exist in the future in which self-help and reciprocity are esteemed. So it is likely that even in the changed conditions of an industrial society parish relief will retain a certain importance.

NOTES

1 For further details, see M. Dinges, *Stadtarmut in Bordeaux (1525–1675): Alltag, Politik, Mentalitäten* (Bonn, 1988), and more particularly, 'L'assistance paroissiale à Bordeaux à la fin du XVIIe siècle – l'exemple du consistoire protestant', *Histoire, Économie et Société* 5 (1986), pp. 475–507; and 'L'hôpital Saint-André de Bordeaux: objectifs et réalisations de l'assistance municipale au XVIIe siècle', *Annales du Midi* 99 (1987), pp. 303–30.

2 The written records of the Jewish community do not begin until the eighteenth century. We can, however, justifiably assume that similar relief existed in earlier centuries; cf. J. Cavignac, 'L'assistance chez les juifs portugais de Bordeaux au XVIIIe siècle', *Actes du 108 Congrès National des Sociétés Savantes*, Colloque sur l'histoire de la Sécurité Sociale, Grenoble 1983 (Paris, 1983), pp. 27–35.

3 This definition excludes self-help such as begging and criminal activities as well as more formal types of mutual aid offered by corporations and unions, which have been carefully studied. On criminality of the poor in France, see A. Farge, *Déliquence et criminalité: le vol d'aliments à Paris au XVIIIe siècle* (Paris, 1974); Dinges, *Stadtarmut in Bordeaux (1525–1675)*, pp. 154ff. On begging see N. Schindler, 'Die Entstehung der Unbarmherzigkeit', *Bayerisches Jahrbuch für Volkskunde* (1988), pp. 61–97. Quite traditional is E. Sableyrolles, 'Le vagabondage en Haut-Alsace sous l'Ancien Régime', *Révue d'Alsace* 113 (1987), pp. 151–62. See also C. Küther, *Menschen auf der Straße: vagierende Unterschichten in Bayern, Franken und Schwaben in der 2. Hälfte des 18. Jahrhunderts* (Göttingen, 1983).

4 For more details and empirical evidence see Dinges, *Stadtarmut in Bordeaux (1525–1675)*.

5 On networks and the poor cf. now R. Jütte, *Poverty and Deviance in Early Modern Europe* (Cambridge, 1994), pp. 83–99; on networks and health, see K. Hurrelmann, *Sozialisation und Gesundheit: somatische, psychische und soziale Risikofaktoren im Lebenslauf* (Weinheim, 1988), p. 112; and H. Keupp and B. Röhrle (eds), *Soziale Netzwerke* (Frankfurt, 1987). On networks in history, see A. E. Imhof, *Die verlorenen Welten* (Munich, 1984), pp. 43ff.; W. Reinhard, *Freunde und Kreaturen: 'Verflechtung' als Konzept zur Erforschung historischer Führungsgruppen. Römische Oligarchie um 1600* (Munich, 1979); A. Maczak (ed.), *Klientelsysteme im Europa der Frühen Neuzeit* (Munich, 1988), esp. pp. 9, 13, and the discussion on pp. 344ff. Methodologically inspiring is R. M. Smith, 'Kin and Neighbors in a Thirteenth-Century Suffolk Community', *Journal of Family History* 4 (1979), pp. 219–57.

6 J. Boissevain, *Friends of Friends: Networks, Manipulators, and Coalitions* (Oxford, 1974); J. C. Mitchell, *Social Networks in Urban Situations: Analyses of Personal Relationships in Central African Towns* (Manchester, 1969).

7 I developed this concept empirically from the Bordeaux sources. The notion of social capital used by Pierre Bourdieu is wider, cf. his 'Ökonomisches Kapital, kulturelles Kapital', in R. Kreckel (ed.), *Soziale Ungleichheit* (Göttingen, 1983), pp. 183–98.

8 Asymmetry is a normal feature in the bargaining concept, see T. Scheff, 'Negotiating Reality', *Social Problems* 16 (1968), pp. 3–17.

9 On honour as a code of behaviour see M. Dinges, 'Die Ehre als Thema der Stadtgeschichte: eine Semantik im Übergang vom Ancien Régime zur Moderne', *Zeitschrift für historische Forschung* 16 (1989), pp. 409–40, and *Der Maurermeister und der Finanzrichter: Ehre, Geld und soziale Kontrolle im Paris des 18. Jahrhunderts* (Göttingen, 1994).

10 N. Luhmann, 'Formen des Helfens im Wandel gesellschaftlicher Bedingungen', in N. Luhmann, *Soziologische Aufklärung*, vol. 2 (2nd edn, Opladen, 1982), pp. 134–49.

11 Y. Poutet, 'L'enseignement des pauvres dans la France du XVIIe siècle', *Dix-Septième Siècle* 90–1 (1971), pp. 87–110, and *Le XVIIe siècle et les origines lassaliennes* (Rennes, 1970). B. Garnot, *Le Peuple au siècle des lumières: échec d'un dressage culturel* (Paris, 1990), pp. 123ff. U. Herrmann (ed.), *Das pädagogische Jahrhundert: Volksaufklärung und Erziehung zur Armut im 18. Jahrhundert in Deutschland* (Weinheim and Basel, 1981).

12 Dinges, *Stadtarmut in Bordeaux*, p. 453.

13 Cf. R. Jütte, 'Parochialverbände als Träger städtischer Armenfürsorge: Die "Armenbretter" der Stadt Köln in der Frühen Neuzeit', *Geschichte in Köln* 12 (1982), pp. 27–50.

14 Cf. P. Loupès, 'L'hôpital Saint-André de Bordeaux au dix-huitième siècle', *Revue d'Histoire de Bordeaux* n.s. 21 (1972), pp. 79–111; M. Dinges, 'Attitudes à l'égard de la pauvreté aux XVIe et XVIIe siècles à Bordeaux', *Histoire, Économie et Société* 10 (1991), pp. 359–74.

5

COMMUNITY SPONSORSHIP AND THE HOSPITAL PATIENT IN LATE EIGHTEENTH-CENTURY ENGLAND

Amanda Berry

I

Voluntary hospitals provided an important new locus of care for the treatment of the sick poor in eighteenth-century England. Established in both London and the provinces, their numbers grew from one in 1720 to thirty-three in 1800. Financed by charity and sustained by 'that most characteristic eighteenth-century device, the subscription', voluntary hospitals were joint enterprises, in whose support the moderately wealthy could join forces with the rich and famous.[1] Subscribers were central to these institutions. They governed and administered the charities through courts and committees, they elected the physicians and surgeons, and (of particular significance to the present discussion) in proportion to the value of their subscriptions, they had the right to nominate patients for admission.

Conventional interpretations of the characteristics of subscribers have focused principally on the underlying ideology of the founders and supporters of these charitable institutions. Charity sermons preached on behalf of hospitals and the hospitals' own appeals have been used to assess the religious and humanitarian motives of subscribers.[2] Lists of names published in hospital annual subscription lists have been cited in support of the argument that noble patronage was vital to hospitals and to demonstrate how the power of aristocratic example served to attract the support of the middle classes.[3] Historians have emphasized that the participation of the

126

urban middle classes in voluntary hospitals was widespread. It has further been maintained that hospitals served to narrow the social space between the middle classes and the gentry; that, by providing a local focus for charitable activity, hospitals served to unify and integrate the propertied of all ranks and religious persuasions.[4] Connection with hospitals not only provided an opportunity for ordinary citizens to become involved in civic affairs, it also 'reinforced the power of the elite by enabling them to dispense selectively a new form of largesse'.[5]

A hospital subscription carried the right to nominate patients for treatment. Subscribers' letters or tickets were issued on a graduated scale to match their generosity. Although rules varied slightly between hospitals, usually a subscription of 2 guineas a year accorded the right to recommend one in-patient and one or two out-patients at a time.[6] Voluntary hospitals were strictly for the treatment of the 'deserving poor', for those whom the hospitals referred to as 'real objects of charity'. Prospective patients had to obtain the written recommendation of a hospital subscriber who was obliged to confirm that the sick person was a 'suitable object' and was not able to afford private advice or medicines. Only accident or emergency cases were normally able to by-pass these procedures. Even so, only those suffering from maladies believed to be curable were to be admitted for treatment.

Hospital subscribers were themselves members of their local communities; but in addition there is evidence that a significant and changing share of subscribers were also 'communities' – in the form of parishes, commercial firms, and friendly societies. This growing 'community' support of voluntary hospitals in the late eighteenth-century has largely been overlooked. Although it has been noted that 'in due course it became common for parishes to subscribe [to voluntary hospitals] on their own behalf' and that business firms and friendly societies began to appear on some hospital subscription lists, such 'community' support was not characteristic of all voluntary hospitals.[7] There were regional variations in hospital patronage. It is argued in this paper that these variations were closely associated with the economic problems of the late eighteenth century, problems which also influenced the voluntary hospitals' policies relating to the admission and treatment of pauper patients.

The rapid increase in population, falling real wages, the prevalence of wage labour and the growing seasonality of agricultural employment, particularly in the rural south, predated the French Revolutionary Wars.[8] The consequent increasing underemployment and poverty meant that parishes were faced with increasing levels of poor rates and expenditure on poor relief. Recent work has shown that the annual expenditure on poor relief in England and Wales between 1783 and 1785 averaged £2 million, an increase of 33 per cent on expenditure in 1776 and an increase of 190 per cent on expenditure in 1748–50.[9] Conditions worsened after 1795, and the effect of sustained high prices and periodic shortages experienced during the Revolutionary and Napoleonic Wars were felt most especially by the labouring poor. Labourers' wages lagged well behind price inflation; structural unemployment and widespread underemployment became typical, especially in the arable farming counties of southern England.[10]

As expenditure on the able-bodied poor rose and a larger share of Poor Law expenditure was given as outdoor relief, parishes attempted to cut costs. They strove to halt the rise in the cost of relief not only by initiating or reviving schemes for farming out the maintenance of the poor but also by adjusting their systems of relief for medical purposes. Both rural and urban parishes increasingly drew up annual contracts with local surgeons and surgeon-apothecaries in an attempt to provide more cost-effective treatment than fee-based medical care.[11] A hospital subscription taken out by parishes and friendly societies was an additional means these 'communities' used to limit their expenditure on the treatment of the sick poor. Business firms, on the other hand, had an economic interest in securing hospital-based care for their workers. Employers subscribed to hospitals to gain the right to nominate their employees for treatment.[12]

Certainly the voluntary general hospitals attempted to meet a major medical and social need in treating the non-pauperized working class.[13] Cherry has argued that 'sick paupers were rarely admitted to voluntary hospitals, partly because they were mistakenly believed to have access to suitable medical facilities under the Poor Law, unlike the sick but non-pauperized poor, and also to avoid the off-loading of chronic sick patients from poor relief into the hospitals'.[14] Although it is widely believed that voluntary hospitals stated in their rules that pauper patients were prohibited, and that, according to one account, 'obvious paupers were redirected to the workhouse',[15] hospital statutes seldom mention pauper patients. Marland has pointed out that some hospitals excluded paupers altogether.[16] Yet others encouraged parish sub-scriptions. Overall, whatever the rules stipulated, there was a degree of latitude in policy and practice.

Through an exploration of the extent of community support and of these communities' recommendations of patients to volun-tary hospitals, this chapter attempts to place the emergence of community sponsorship in the context of late eighteenth-century society, particularly in terms of contemporary concerns about increasing pressures on the poor rate. I argue that community use of hospitals was not so much detached from the stereotypical system of hospital patronage by individuals, but that it became part of the system because it was an economic means of treating the sick poor, one means of minimizing the risk of incurring additional costs of parish relief.

The obvious sources for documenting the mechanism of the patronage system of voluntary hospitals, the social groups involved, and the degree of community sponsorship are the hospitals' pub-lished accounts and subscription lists, minute books and patient records. Evidence has been drawn from such surviving records of three provincial voluntary hospitals, the Bristol Infirmary, the Devon and Exeter Hospital, and Northampton General Hospital for the period from 1765 to 1815.[17] This case study approach facili-tates detailed analysis of patrons, patients, and their sponsors.[18] Research has demonstrated that there was incipient 'community' patronage of these charitable institutions. Groups of people were taking collective decisions to subscribe to voluntary hospitals, an aspect of patronage which was of increasing importance as the period progressed.

Figure 5.1 lends support to the view that 'corporate' support of both the Bristol Infirmary and the hospital at Northampton was of growing importance in the late eighteenth and early nineteenth centuries. The number of parishes, friendly societies, business partnerships and commercial firms on the hospitals' annual subscription lists increased over the period, relative to the number of individual patrons; their relative financial contribution also increased, though to a lesser degree. In contrast, 'community' patronage of the Devon and Exeter Hospital throughout the period under review was negligible when compared to the patronage of individuals and so does not feature in Figure 5.1.[19]

Community support of Northampton's hospital stemmed primarily from parishes, clustered in the south of the county

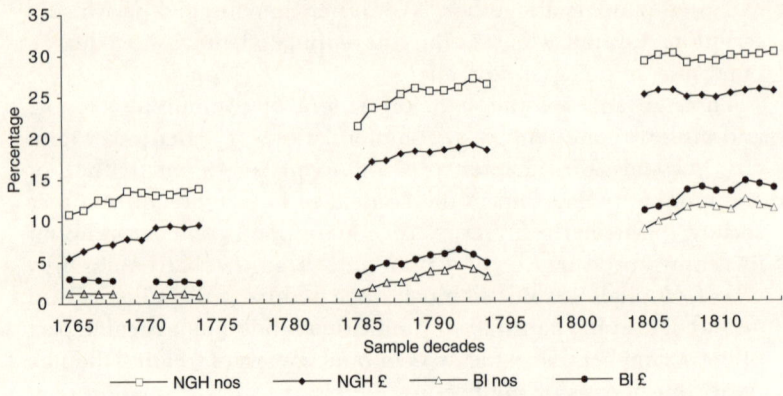

Figure 5.1 Corporate patrons as percentage of all patrons, Northampton General Hospital and Bristol Infirmary

around Northampton itself. There were twenty-eight parishes on the hospital's subscription lists in 1765 (8 per cent of Northamptonshire's parishes). By 1814, 177 parishes were listed as subscribers. Of these, 151 were Northamptonshire parishes (45 per cent of the county's parishes), and nineteen were Buckinghamshire parishes, the remainder being in the neighbouring counties of Bedfordshire, Huntingdonshire, Leicestershire, and Warwickshire. Some of these parishes subscribed for only a few years. Subscriptions ranged between 1 and 10 guineas, the larger sums being paid by the most populous parishes, and there was a tendency for parishes to increase their subscription levels early in the nineteenth century. Kingsthorpe parish (population 909 in 1800),[20] for instance, subscribed 1 guinea a year until the 1790s, 2 guineas in 1805 and 1806, and raised its subscription to 4 guineas in 1808.

Local friendly societies or benefit clubs were also listed as subscribers to the hospital at Northampton. Members of these societies generally paid a monthly subscription into their society's box, held by the landlord of the public house at which the society met, and when they were sick and unable to work their members' benefit was taken from the box. Since such arrangements should have served to reduce the poor rate, they were in general much approved of by late eighteenth-century social commentators.[21] While only one such society subscribed to the hospital at Northampton in 1765, eight were listed as subscribers in 1814 as 1 or

2 guinea subscribers; seven of these friendly societies were based in parishes where the parish also concurrently subscribed to the hospital.

Business firms were of minor importance as community patrons of Northampton's hospital, only two firms being listed in 1765 and five in 1814. In contrast, community support of the Bristol Infirmary stemmed primarily from business partnerships and commercial firms. In 1765 there were only three firms on the Infirmary's subscription list; yet by 1814 there were 124, while overall a total of 227 firms appeared on the lists during the three decades covered by the case study's sample, the majority subscribing 2 guineas a year to the Infirmary. The sick poor of Bristol's eighteen parishes traditionally came under the care of Bristol's Corporation of the Poor and were treated in St Peter's Hospital, founded in the late seventeenth century.[22] Parishes outside the city itself began to subscribe to the Bristol Infirmary from 1789, and thirty-nine were listed as Infirmary subscribers in 1814. Keynsham was the first parish to subscribe, while the more distant parishes of Trowbridge and Frome began subscribing early in the nineteenth century. Five societies featured on the Bristol Infirmary subscription lists.[23]

Patronage of the Devon and Exeter Hospital in the late eighteenth and early nineteenth centuries was far closer to the stereotypical view of hospital patronage, with more than 99 per cent of its support arising from individual patrons, many of whom were of the nobility and gentry. As in Bristol, Exeter's Corporation of the Poor, formed to manage the poor of the twenty-two parishes and precincts comprising the city of Exeter, offered medical care to the city's parish poor in the workhouse infirmary and also paid apothecaries for treating the out-poor.[24] County parishes began to support the hospital in the 1780s, the first being South Molton, and ten parishes were listed as hospital subscribers in 1814.

Parish patronage was not unique to the hospitals of Bristol, Exeter, and Northampton in the late eighteenth century. Indeed, 'it was not unusual for parishes to take advantage of the facility of a hospital subscription'.[25] Citing the example of Manchester Infirmary, Geoffrey Oxley found that, between 1752 and 1837, prior to the formation of new Poor Law unions, 'seventy-seven parishes in Lancashire subscribed to the Manchester Infirmary for at least one year', but that only the most populous parishes,

Salford, Bury, Bolton, Oldham, and Manchester itself, remained subscribers for the whole of this period.[26] According to Joan Lane, fourteen of Worcestershire's parishes subscribed to the Worcester Infirmary in its foundation year, 1746–7. Its governors temporarily rejected parochial contributions after 1752 but the Infirmary had four south Warwickshire parishes as subscribers from the 1760s. Five Worcestershire parishes subscribed by 1787. In 1792 the governors again considered declining parish subscriptions as parishes were slow to pay, but by 1813 thirty-two parishes subscribed between one and 5 guineas each.[27] The Birmingham hospital had three Worcester parish subscribers from 1790 and seven Staffordshire parishes out of its total of eighteen parochial contributions,[28] and 'the Bedfordshire overseer's accounts contain numerous records of vestry resolutions to make annual donations to the Bedford Infirmary from 1803 onwards'.[29]

By comparison with other infirmaries, the number of parishes supporting Northampton's hospital seems strikingly large. A contributory factor was the hospital's policy of actively encouraging parish support. A statement, published in 1746, declared that

> As so many of the PARISHES have generously contributed for this PURCHASE [of the hospital building], it is much to be wished that they would follow the example of the parishes of Thorp, Kingsthorpe, Silverston, etc., etc., which join in the ANNUAL Subscriptions; the Advantages of which to PARISHES . . . is so very evident, that one cannot wonder it should not be a universal thing . . . The weekly expense of DRUGS for each Patient upon Average is about 9d . . . and the whole Accommodation of an In-Patient per week (upon an Average) with Drugs, Lodging, Diet, Attendance may be estimated one year with another at about 6s . . . so that as every In-Patient (one with another) is computed to stay in the Hospital about twelve weeks, the whole Expense an In-Patient must necessarily stand the Governors is £3 12s 0d . . . A clear Demonstration how much 'tis for the interest of the Parishes (considered as such) by their liberal and annual Contributions, to perpetuate this charity.[30]

The financial incentive is clear; a 2 guinea hospital subscription offered value for money. Protests that the sick poor might 'be as well taken care of in their own habitations as in an hospital' were countered by an explanation of the benefits 'which may be expected in lessening the poor's [sic] rate'.[31]

Historians writing on medical practice and the Old Poor Law have remarked that illness was a significant determinant of overall levels of poor relief and that cost-conscious overseers were anxious to find ways to reduce expenditure on the sick poor.[32] Poor Law overseers attempted to pare medical costs to a minimum and, as Hilary Marland has pointed out, they do seem to have been aware of the long-term advantages of providing effective medical relief, recognizing that a large short-term outlay on medical treatment could prevent sick or injured persons from becoming a permanent burden on the poor rate.[33]

While it was feasible for the more populous wealthier parishes to negotiate contracts with local surgeons for treatment of their sick poor, smaller rural parishes lacked access to medical practitioners. Kettering in Northamptonshire, for example, with a population of 3,011 in 1801,[34] contracted with Mr Wyman in 1797 to pay him £40 a year to provide medical assistance to the poor of the parish, other than those with smallpox, venereal disease or fractures, and pregnant women.[35] For smaller rural parishes, resort to local fringe practitioners might have been the only alternative to sending for a more distant (and therefore more costly) medical practitioner and paying him on an 'item of service' basis for visits, medicines, and surgery.[36] In the late eighteenth century, 'the continually increasing fees for doctors represented part of the burden parish overseers had to bear in a time of increasing costs for most necessities'.[37] In view of the evidence of increasing numbers of community hospital patrons, it must have been in the interest of parishes to have the opportunity to use their local hospital for their more difficult cases. The treatment of a parish patient in a hospital obviated parish expenditure not only on medical fees, medicines, and nursing attendance, but also on food and fuel allowances, rent and weekly doles.

However, the acceptance of parish patronage and the treatment of pauper patients by the voluntary hospitals was not automatic; it depended on each hospital's specific policy. The Radcliffe Infirmary at Oxford allowed the head officer of any society, parish, or township making a regular subscription the same privileges of recommending patients as a governor.[38] Wheatley was the first to take advantage of the scheme and 'by 1830, at least 80 Oxfordshire parishes – thirty per cent – were contributing to a special scheme, paying sums up to six guineas a year. In Berkshire thirty parishes joined – some twenty per cent'.[39] It has already been pointed out that Northampton's hospital actively encouraged corporate subscribers. A new and specific rule, included in the hospital's statutes of 1813, stated

> that Parishes may become Subscribers to this Infirmary; but that no Parish or Society subscribing less than two guineas per annum shall recommend an In-Patient; and that for every two guineas which such Parish or Society shall subscribe, it shall be entitled to recommend one In and four Out-Patients within each year.[40]

On the other hand, 'no paupers were to be admitted [to the Norfolk and Norwich Hospital], since it was felt that the workhouse inmates or those on outdoor relief already had access to medical facilities and treatment',[41] and the governors of the Devon and Exeter explicitly excluded parish subscriptions until the late eighteenth century.

The degree of parish patronage of voluntary hospitals in the late eighteenth century reflected the stance of each hospital's governors. Voluntary hospitals were each founded and developed independently. It appears that in cities where there was both a voluntary hospital and a workhouse infirmary, hospital governors saw no need to grant access to pauper patients from city parishes. But, from the 1780s, they were increasingly prepared to accept subscriptions from parishes outside their city boundaries. By contrast, governors of voluntary hospitals in county towns more readily accepted parish subscriptions. This can be seen as a reflection both of the geographical spread of hospital patronage and of the interests of hospital governors. In their policy towards parish patients, hospital governors were reacting pragmatically. Not only were they following their own interest as rate payers, trying to keep their fiscal burden within bounds, but they were also attempting to avert, or at least alleviate, the effects of poverty and sickness on local people.

Was self-interest or altruism the prime motive for firms to patronize hospitals? It is difficult to establish with any certainty why business partnerships and commercial firms began to patronize voluntary hospitals to an increasing extent from the late eighteenth century. Brian Abel-Smith took the view that 'employers subscribed to hospitals to gain the right to send any of their employees who were ill'.[42] This seems a plausible explanation. If skilled workers were ill or injured, it would make economic sense to have the means to expedite a workman's cure and return to the workplace, especially if the labour market was tight or the costs involved in training a replacement employee were high. The occupational profile of 'corporate' subscribers on Bristol Infirmary's lists was skewed towards partnerships and commercial firms which would have employed skilled manual labourers. Most were manufacturing and merchant firms, with bankers and accountants being in the minority.[43] However, it is not possible to provide from hospital patient records firm evidence to support the proposition that 'corporate' business firms subscribed to the Infirmary simply for the practical purpose of providing a cheap and efficient medical service for sick and injured members of the work force.

One contemporary's attitude towards 'community' support by business firms is illustrated in a letter written to a friend in 1771 by the Bristol Infirmary's treasurer, Richard Champion, in which he discussed the behaviour appropriate to a manufacturer:

> The manufacturer is exercising the Virtues of the Heart by Example. He finds employments for the Poor he cloaths He feeds He protects them. He Encourages the Industerous he rebukes the Sloathful, with the spirit of Charity he relievs the distress of His dependents and teaches them by his conduct to look upon him as a Father and their fellow Workman as their Brethren.[44]

Mary Fissell has taken the view that, for Champion, the hospital represented the natural outgrowth of his position as an employer – not just in the simplistic sense that the Infirmary would patch up his workers for him, but in the larger context of hierarchical social relationships defined by reciprocal obligation.[45]

The theory of paternalism centres around the concept that property has its duties as well as its rights. The motivations of the 'corporate' subscribers to Bristol Infirmary are by no means clear, especially since evidence from the hospital's subscription lists demonstrates that some proprietors or partners in business firms, listed in their 'corporate' capacity, also featured concurrently as individual subscribers to the Bristol Infirmary. Sufficient reason to subscribe to the hospital, whether as an employer or as an individual, or as both, could well have been paternalistic.

Growing 'community' support of hospitals by parishes and business enterprises is suggestive of a modification of philanthropic practice rather than of any radical change. However, the reasons for early support of voluntary hospitals by friendly societies are less clear. Does this support point to an emergence of self-help and the early development of mutual assurance by working-class members of friendly societies? Rose's Act of 1793 conferred various rights on friendly societies and their members, the Act's main aim being to encourage the formation of such societies so as to reduce the demand for poor relief.[46] It has been suggested that 'the working classes were driven to mutual help by insurance not because it appeared to them the most dignified way of securing medical help and funeral benefit, but because there was no other way of avoiding pauperization'.[47]

Although it is tempting to attribute hospital patronage by friendly societies to an initiative taken by the working classes, it is not clear whether these or 'Persons of Property' were the driving force. The Friendly and Humane Society of Daventry was one of the 'community' subscribers to Northampton's hospital. Its membership was restricted to those under 46 years of age who were resident in the parish of Daventry. An admission fee of 2s. 6d. was levied by the Society and subsequent membership fees were 1s. a month. The sum of 7s. a week was paid to members who were sick 'as long as the Affliction shall continue'. The society was established for 'Tradesmen, Mechanics, Labourers and other Inhabitants of the Parish of Daventry' so that they may

> secure to themselves and Families, a comfortable support, at a time when they stand in most Need of such Assistance, and have no other Means of providing for it, but by the dis-agreeable Recourse to the Parish: and to render the Benefit of this Society more extensively useful, many Persons of Property have entered themselves Members, without any Intention of receiving any Assistance, or taking any Advantage of it whatsoever.[48]

Thus at least one of the friendly societies which subscribed to Northampton General Hospital was not wholly funded by the labouring classes. It is likely that these societies involved a degree of upper-class patronage, control, and financial support, resulting in a combination of self-help with a large measure of paternalistic control and philanthropy. As with parishes and business firms, friendly societies paid a hospital subscription as a form of insur-ance. When sickness might last months or years, rather than days or weeks, the possibility of getting society members into hospital and cured, rather than being obliged to offer them protracted sick pay, must have been attractive.[49]

Sixteen friendly societies subscribed to Northampton's hospital during the decades sampled for this study, yet no such societies were listed as patrons of the Devon and Exeter Hospital. There were 412 friendly societies in Devon at the turn of the nineteenth century, compared to 169 friendly societies in Northamptonshire.[50] The acceptance of subscriptions from friendly societies depended upon the hospital governors' stance. The hospital at Exeter discouraged 'corporate' subscriptions. Those who received benefits from friendly societies were considered capable of paying for their care, either directly or through the society. The weekly committee of the Devon and Exeter rejected attempts by friendly societies to secure treatment through subscription for club members; subscriptions were returned in such cases.[51] Northampton Hospital's policy was more flexible and it is worth noting that eleven of the friendly societies which patronized Northampton's hospital were based in parishes whose overseers of the poor also subscribed to the hospital on behalf of their parishes. This geographical overlap seems to confirm that a possible motive for the involvement of 'Persons of Property' in Northamptonshire friendly societies was to control expenditure on the Poor Law by encouraging those workers who were able to do so to contribute to their own medical costs when sick.

The main point which emerges thus far is that patronage patterns were distinctive to each hospital. Each institution evolved in a different social context and sphere of influence. The patronage of the Bristol Infirmary strongly reflected its particular social milieu, that of the city's mercantile and industrial elites. Patronage of Northampton General Hospital, on the other hand, reflected the social milieu of the county's landed nobility and gentry and the difficulties faced by its agricultural labour force in a period of rising prices during the period of the Revolutionary and Napoleonic Wars.

Inquiry as to whether these 'corporate' patrons actually used their rights to nominate patients to the hospitals, how regularly they did so, and whether the patients recommended to the hospitals by 'corporate' patrons were different from those sponsored by individuals throws more light on the motivations of 'corporate' hospital patrons and on the recipients of eighteenth-century institutional medical care.

II

In order to investigate the mechanics of hospital patronage and to assess the characteristics of sponsors and hospital patients for three sample years, the names of patrons published in the annual reports of the Bristol Infirmary, the Devon and Exeter Hospital, and the hospital at Northampton have been cross-referenced with the names of recommenders listed in the hospitals' in-patient admission records. Those who recommended patients have been grouped into three categories: individual sponsors, 'corporate' sponsors, and the unidentifiable.[52] Patients admitted without sponsorship have been grouped into two categories: those described as 'cases admitting no delay' as accidents and emergencies, and patients admitted by the hospitals' honorary medical men or by the weekly committee.[53]

Only a small number of patients were actually admitted on the recommendation of community patrons. This is clear from Figure 5.2, which shows the numbers of patients admitted to each hospital, grouped by the category of the recommender.[54] Individual patrons sponsored the majority of patients; they recommended over three-quarters of all patients treated in the Devon and Exeter Hospital in each sample year but sponsored a diminishing proportion of those treated at Bristol Infirmary and an even smaller and decreasing proportion at Northampton's hospital. Accident cases, admitted without a letter of recommendation, clearly 'crowded out' patients sponsored by letters from

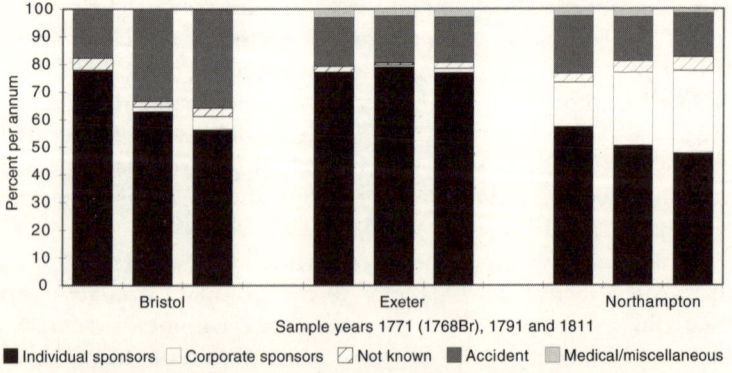

Figure 5.2 Percentage of in-patients by mode of admission to the Bristol Infirmary, the Devon and Exeter Hospital, and the Northampton General Hospital

subscribers and benefactors at Bristol Infirmary from the turn of the nineteenth century. By contrast, the proportion of beds taken up by accident cases admitted to the Devon and Exeter Hospital was steady and the proportion of accident cases treated at Northampton's hospital was falling.

However, the main point of interest highlighted by Figure 5.2 is the growing proportion of patients admitted to the North-ampton General Hospital on the recommendation of 'corporate' patrons. In 1811 over a quarter of in-patients were referred to the hospital by parish and friendly society subscribers. By contrast, the proportion of business firms and commercial enterprises recommending in-patients to the Bristol Infirmary was relatively negligible. Parish patients made up 16 per cent of in-patients admitted to Northampton's hospital in 1771, rising to 26 per cent in 1811. Those sponsored by Bristol firms rose from 1.5 per cent of in-patients in 1791 to 5.6 per cent in 1811.[55] If Bristol Infirmary's patrons were being deprived of the opportunity to use their rights of sponsorship by the growing numbers of in-patients admitted as accident cases, in the Northampton Hospital parish- and society-sponsored patients were growing in number at the expense of individual patrons' nominees.

Who were the patients who sought treatment in eighteenth-century hospitals?[56] Did 'community-sponsored' patients exhibit different characteristics from those sponsored by individual hospital patrons? Historians who have examined hospitals' patient records have all noted a bias in admissions towards men. Alannah Tomkins found that 53 per cent of patients admitted to the Salop Infirmary in 1755 were men.[57] Guenter Risse's study of the Edinburgh Infirmary found that men comprised 61 per cent of admissions during the decades 1770–1800.[58] Hilary Marland's work on the Huddersfield Infirmary for the year 1838–9 showed how much emphasis was placed on admitting those involved in the local economy: the majority of admissions were male (73 per cent) and young.[59] The gender bias towards male in-patient admissions was also common to all three hospitals in this case study; 67 per cent of all in-patients admitted to the Bristol Infirmary were men. Men comprised 58 per cent of admissions to the Devon and Exeter Hospital and 57 per cent to the hospital at North-ampton.[60] Separate analysis of accident and sponsored in-patients showed a different picture. As might be expected, a greater proportion of men than women were admitted to these hospitals as accident or emergency cases. Between two-thirds and three-quarters of all accident cases were male, which serves to confirm not only that men were more susceptible to accidents and more prone to seeking hospital treatment when injured but also that it is misleading to accept aggregate statistics. Much of the gender bias was a function of male accident cases.

The gender proportions of sponsored cases were more balanced: while male patients were predominant in the Bristol Infirmary, comprising 60 per cent of recommended in-patients in all three years sampled, the proportions of male and female patients recommended to the Devon and Exeter Hospital were almost equal, as they were at Northampton's hospital in 1791 and 1811. Only in 1771 were more female than male in-patients recommended to the hospital at Northampton. These observations can be taken to indicate a slight bias towards males seeking and obtaining a recommendation for hospital treatment, supporting the view that much emphasis was placed on the treatment and 'cure' of male 'breadwinners'. But they can also be interpreted as illustrating the long-suffering nature of women and a greater reluctance on the part of women to seek admission as in-patients. Evidence shows that more female than male patients were treated as out-patients. Hilary Marland found that women made up over 56 per cent of out-patient admissions to the Huddersfield Infirmary in the late 1830s, a similar proportion to those of the hospital in Northampton.[61] Probably women, especially wives and mothers, preferred to be 'casual attenders' rather than seek treatment as in-patients, since such treatment would absent them from the commitments of home and family.

The sex ratios of patients admitted on the recommendation of sponsors to each of the three hospitals in the case study are set out in Table 5.1. These figures confirm the male bias; women sponsored by individual hospital patrons were in the majority only in Northampton County Hospital in 1771, when 100 females were admitted for every ninety-four males. The proportionate increase in the numbers of male patients over the period is notable at all three hospitals, especially in the case of patients sponsored by firms and parishes to the Bristol Infirmary in 1811, when thirty-eight men and eleven women were treated as in-patients.[62] But there was little difference in gender bias between in-patients sponsored by individuals and those sponsored by 'corporate' sponsors. The male bias was clear in both cases.

Table 5.1 Sex ratios of hospital in-patients by recommender

	Year	Individual sponsor	Community sponsor
Bristol Infirmary	1768	137	100
	1791	141	167
	1811	158	345
Devon and Exeter Hospital	1771	109	–
	1791	120	–
	1811	125	200
Northampton General Hospital	1771	94	153
	1791	127	113
	1811	113	133

Whilst it might be thought that this bias reflects patient demand, in that men sought hospital treatment more frequently and successfully than women, there were other factors involved. Men's and women's wards were strictly segregated in the hospitals. It is possible that more beds were allocated to men than women and also that the 'turnover' of patients varied by gender. Moreover, it is not known how many were refused admission 'for want of room' or treated as out-patients, rather than being admitted to 'the House'. In the absence of sufficiently detailed records, all that can be said is that more men than women were admitted on the recommendation of hospital patrons, be they individual or 'corporate' subscribers, and that men were more likely to be employed in the local economy than women. The gender bias therefore could well reflect the economic motivation on the part of both the patients themselves and their sponsors.

The age distribution of in-patients treated in the three hospitals supports the contention that the majority of patients were men of working age. The average age of all male in-patients admitted to the Bristol Infirmary for the sample years 1768, 1791, and 1811 was 30.8 years. This was slightly lower than the average age of male patients treated by the hospitals at Exeter (34.2 years) and Northampton (33.2 years) in the sample years 1771, 1791, and 1811. Female patients were, on average, younger than male patients: average ages were 29.8 years in Bristol, 32 at Exeter and 28.4 at Northampton. In-patients on the books of these English hospitals were, on the whole, older than those treated in the

Edinburgh Infirmary in the same period. There the average age of the patients was 28.6 years, with women slightly younger (25.5) than men (32.7).[63]

Differences might simply be a function of the age structure and the sex ratio of the population in each region. However, more than 50 per cent of all patients listed in the case books of the Edinburgh Royal Infirmary were 25 years old or younger.[64] The admission registers of the hospitals in this study show a different picture with only about 40 per cent of in-patients being under 25 years old. When analysed by age group, the age distribution of in-patients at each hospital in this sample showed a similar pattern.[65] Accident cases were disproportionately young; for example, two-thirds of the 350 accident cases admitted to the Bristol Infirmary in 1791 were under 35 years old and, of these, ten were under the age of 7.

As with the analysis of gender, the inclusion of accident cases distorts the picture. Examination of the age-structure of hospital patients who were admitted with letters of recommendation showed that the greatest proportions of in-patients were in the 15–24 and 25–34 year age groups. The young and the elderly were a smaller proportion of the in-patient population admitted on the recommendation of sponsors. More light is shed on the motivation of sponsors when the age groups of in-patients are examined in terms of whether they were recommended by individual or 'community' subscribers.

Evidence from Northampton Hospital's patient records for 1771, arranged by recommender and by age group is set out in Figure 5.3.[66] The age distribution shows that the majority of parish-sponsored patients were either young, under 25 years old, or over 35. The relatively low proportion of parish patients in the 25 to 34 year age group is striking, as are the slightly greater proportions of young and old patients, a pattern which is repeated in Northampton General Hospital's in-patient sample for 1791. This pattern supports the argument that subscribing parishes used their sponsorship rights to alleviate the potential burden on poor rates. Furthermore, the pattern confirms that poor relief was closely linked with the life cycle, phases of poverty being particularly associated with childhood and old age and with the economic hardship faced by families at a stage when they had large numbers of dependent children not yet able to be net contributors to the household economy.[67] By contrast, 62 per cent

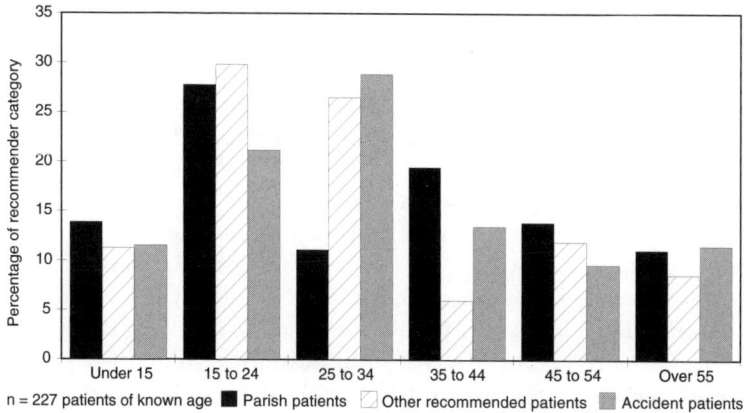

Figure 5.3 Northampton General Hospital, 1771: age group of in-patients
by recommender

of patients admitted on the recommendation of Bristol's business firms were in the age groups 15 to 24 and 25 to 34, hence of working age, indicative of the economic motive of business partnership and firm subscribers.

Whilst the hospitals had no upper age limit, they were reluctant to admit patients with chronic illnesses which were difficult to cure. Patients were admitted to the hospitals with a wide variety of ailments. A comparison of the diagnostic categories of in-patients sponsored by individual patrons and 'corporate' patients revealed few differences. Bristol Infirmary's patient admission records for 1811 showed that a higher proportion of in-patients, admitted on the recommendation of firms, suffered from pneumonia and phthisis, compared to other sponsored patients.[68] These patients might have contracted their diseases in the workplace. However, a higher proportion of patients admitted to Northampton's hospital in 1771 on the recommendation of parishes suffered from rheumatism when compared with those admitted on the recommendation of individual patrons,[69] an indication of parishes' use of their recommendation rights to refer those cases which, if not cured or at least relieved, were likely to become a long-term burden on the parish rates.

It seems that a hospital subscription did represent value for money to the friendly societies and parishes which took advantage of the rights of sponsorship attaching to their hospital subscriptions. Five friendly societies sponsored patients to the hospital at Northampton in 1811. One of these, the Society at Long Buckby, subscribed 2 guineas and referred two in-patients, who were discharged 'cured' after eleven and fourteen weeks' stay in the hospital. Sick pay for the same period would have cost the Society about £8. Recent research into the costs of medical care under the Old Poor Law in Campton, Bedfordshire, has demonstrated that the average cash payment made to individuals for occasional illness was 3s. a week. Some payments were as high as 10s. 6d. a week.[70] It therefore made economic sense for parishes to send their more intractable cases to hospital. The case of Hannah Merryweathers serves to illustrate the value of a parish subscription. In receipt of occasional parish relief from 1807 and of a parish pension, which varied between 3 and 5s. a week from 1813, Hannah was sent by the parish of Campton to the Bedford Infirmary in September 1814 where she stayed for five months. Against the cost of a 2-guinea subscription, the parish could set its avoidance of pension payments to support Hannah while she was in hospital, which might have ranged from £3 13s. 6d. to £5, and also of having to pay for her medicines, nursing, and fuel.

III

Voluntary hospitals offered a new locus of care for the treatment of the sick poor of eighteenth-century England and the 'community' increasingly cared for its sick poor in this new locus. While there is evidence to show that 'communities' – parishes, friendly societies and business firms – took advantage of the rights of sponsorship afforded by a hospital subscription, 'community' patronage of these charitable institutions was not uniform: it varied with its local context.

The emergence of parish patronage should be seen in the light of contemporary concern over the rising costs of the poor rate in a period of war and rapid monetary inflation. All areas of England and Wales experienced substantial rises in expenditure on the poor, both absolutely and in per capita terms, from the 1750s onwards, and 'the burthen of the poor's rate in proportion to the population was generally greatest in the most agricultural counties'.[71] David Eastwood's recent study has documented the overwhelming scale of rural poverty in late eighteenth- and early nineteenth-century Oxfordshire parishes, whose overseers' accounts showed an increasing number of poor relief claimants and an increase in per capita expenditure from £0.29 in 1776 to £1.03 in 1814.[72] He claims that 'the scale of poverty in Oxfordshire, when measured by numerical dependence on the Poor Law, was around 50 per cent greater than the national average, maintained by high rates of outdoor relief',[73] and that 'only by reducing their liability to support the poor could parishes hope to steady the underlying increase in local taxation'.[74] In the neighbouring agricultural county of Northamptonshire, as well as in other agricultural counties in the south of England, the acceptance of parish subscriptions by local hospitals and the use of these institutions by the 'community' of the parish should be seen as a pragmatic and rational attempt to check the escalating costs of the rate-funded poor.

By extension, financial support and use of this new locus of care by friendly societies within our three samples were greatest in Northamptonshire. There 'persons of property' were prepared to assist the artisan and labouring classes to help themselves through mutual assurance. For 'persons of property' this was another means of attempting to contain the rising costs of poor relief at the end of the eighteenth century. For the labouring classes, it was a prudent and logical means of obtaining medical treatment for a nominal sum, as well as a means of avoiding recourse to parish assistance, with the stigma of pauperization attaching thereto.

That the hospitals at Exeter and Bristol did not actively encourage the same type of 'community' patronage as the hospital at Northampton was largely due to both geographical and administrative differences. These south-western or western cities did not directly experience the problem of rural poverty, particularly marked in Northamptonshire, and medical treatment was available to the cities' parish poor under the auspices of their Corporations of the Poor. It is more difficult to account for 'community' sponsorship of hospital patients by business firm subscribers. Whilst it cannot be proven that employers subscribed to hospitals to gain the right to send any of their employees who were ill, it is likely that sponsorship by business firms was as much a manifestation of self-interest on the part of employers as it was an extension of traditional paternalism.

Policy-making was directly influenced by the aims, ideals, and perceptions of community of the lay philanthropists who were the hospitals' governors. This exploration of community sponsorship and the hospital patient has sought to demonstrate the degree of regional diversity among them, diversity which can only be fully understood when looked at in the wider context of the economic conditions of late eighteenth- and early nineteenth-century England.

NOTES

1 P. Langford, *A Polite and Commercial People: England 1727–1783* (Oxford, 1992), p. 134.
2 D. T. Andrew, *Philanthropy and Police* (London, 1989); J. Woodward, *To do the Sick no Harm: a Study of the British Voluntary Hospital System to 1875* (London, 1974).
3 R. Porter, 'The Gift Relation: Philanthropy and Provincial Hospitals in Eighteenth-Century England', in L. Granshaw and R. Porter (eds), *The Hospital in History* (London, 1989), p. 152; Langford, *A Polite and Commercial People*, p. 135.
4 K. Wilson, 'Urban Culture and Political Activism', in E. Hellmuth (ed.), *The Transformation of Political Culture in England and Germany in the Late-Eighteenth Century* (Oxford, 1990), pp. 174–5; A. Borsay, 'Cash and Conscience: Financing the General Hospital at Bath c. 1738–1750', *Social History of Medicine* 4 (1991), pp. 207–29; for the American case, see R. Stevens, *In Sickness and in Wealth: American Hospitals in the Twentieth Century* (New York, 1989), esp. pp. 26–7.
5 A. Wilson, 'The Politics of Medical Improvement in Early Hanoverian London', in A. Cunningham and R. French (eds), *The Medical Enlightenment of the Eighteenth Century* (Cambridge, 1990), p. 11.
6 Some hospitals restricted the number of patients each subscriber might nominate per annum. For a full explanation, see H. Hart, 'Some Notes on the Sponsoring of Patients for Hospital Treatment under the Voluntary System', *Medical History* 24 (1980), pp. 447–60.
7 P. Langford, *Public Life and the Propertied Englishman 1689–1798* (Oxford, 1991), p. 499, n. 258; for examples of 'community' support, see M. E. Fissell, *Patients, Power, and the Poor in Eighteenth-Century Bristol* (Cambridge, 1991), pp. 114–15; H. Marland, *Medicine and Society in Wakefield and Huddersfield 1780–1870* (Cambridge, 1987), pp. 172, 196.
8 E. A. Wrigley and R. S. Schofield, *The Population History of England 1541–1871* (London, 1981), pp. 183–4, 401–2; K. Snell, *Annals of the Labouring Poor: Social Change and Agrarian England 1660–1900* (Cambridge, 1985), pp. 23–49, 412–17.
9 D. Eastwood, *Governing Rural England: Tradition and Transformation in Local Government 1780–1840* (Oxford, 1994), p. 103.
10 Eastwood, *Governing Rural England*, p. 108.
11 I. Loudon, *Medical Care and the General Practitioner 1750–1850* (Oxford, 1986), pp. 231–5; A. Digby, *Making a Medical Living: Doctors and*

Patients in the English Market for Medicine, 1720–1914 (Cambridge, 1994), pp. 224–33. The terms of contracts varied but sums paid to parish surgeons tended to increase over the late eighteenth and early nineteenth centuries in line with inflation.

12 B. Abel-Smith, *The Hospitals 1800–1948* (London, 1964), p. 37.

13 S. Cherry, 'The Hospitals and Population Growth: the Voluntary General Hospitals, Mortality and Local Populations in the English Provinces in the Eighteenth and Nineteenth Centuries', *Population Studies* 34 (1980), p. 254.

14 Cherry, 'Hospitals and Population Growth', p. 251.

15 F. B. Smith, *The People's Health 1830–1910* (London, 1979), p. 252.

16 Marland, *Medicine and Society*, p. 63.

17 These hospitals were selected because comprehensive records survive, all were founded at about the same time, between 1737 and 1742, and they offer a socio-economic contrast. For details of records and MSS, see Amanda Berry, 'Patronage, Funding and the Hospital Patient c. 1750–1815: Three English Regional Case Studies', D.Phil. thesis (Oxford, 1995), pp. 272–3.

18 Each hospital's records are in the relevant local record office. Because of the length of hospital subscription lists and the volume of patient records, sampling was necessary. Computer datasets of patrons' details for each hospital cover the hospitals' financial years 1765–74, 1785–94, and 1805–14. Details of patrons recommending patients were linked to hospital admission records for all in-patient admissions for 1771 (1768 for Bristol Infirmary because of missing data), 1791, and 1811. See Berry, 'Patronage, Funding and the Hospital Patient', pp. 269–71.

19 The number of patrons of the Bristol Infirmary increased from 470 in 1765 to 1,473 in 1814. Patrons to the Devon and Exeter Hospital increased from 514 in 1765 to 616 in 1814. Patrons to Northampton's hospital increased from 286 in 1765 to 633 in 1814.

20 Parliamentary Papers, *Abstract of the Answers and Returns* to Population Act, 41 George III, 1800 (London, 1801–2).

21 G. E. Mingay (ed.), *The Agrarian History of England and Wales 1750–1850*, vol. 6 (Cambridge, 1989), p. 753.

22 E. E. Butcher, *Bristol Corporation of the Poor 1696–1898*, Historical Association (Bristol, 1972).

23 Berry, 'Patronage, Funding and the Hospital Patient', pp. 107–12. Many societies were ephemeral and few records survive.

24 C. Vancouver, *General View of the Agriculture of the County of Devon* (London, 1808, repr. Devon, 1974), p. 112.

25 G. W. Oxley, *Poor Relief in England and Wales* (Newton Abbott, 1974), p. 68.

26 Oxley, *Poor Relief*, p. 68.

27 J. Lane, *Worcester Infirmary in the Eighteenth Century*, Worcestershire Historical Society 6 (Worcester, 1992), p. 20.

28 Lane, *Worcester Infirmary*, p. 21.

29 W. E. Tate, *The Parish Chest: A Study of the Records of Parochial Administration in England* (3rd edn, Cambridge, 1969), p. 168.

30 Appendix to Rev Mr Henry Layng's *Sermon Preached in the Parish Church of All Saints in Northampton* (Northampton, 1746).

31 F. Marcus Hall, R. S. Stevens and J. Whyman, *The Kent and Canterbury Hospital 1790–1987* (Canterbury, 1987), pp. 6, 211.

32 For example, Fissell, *Patients, Power, and the Poor*, p. 106; Marland, *Medicine and Society*, p. 67; E. G. Thomas, 'The Old Poor Law and Medicine', *Medical History* 24 (1980), p. 6.

33 Marland, *Medicine and Society*, pp. 67–8.

34 Parliamentary Papers, *Abstract of Answers and Returns* to Population Act, p. 247.

35 S. A. Peyton (ed.), *Kettering Vestry Minutes*, Northamptonshire Record Society 6 (Kettering, 1933), p. 1.

36 See Loudon, *Medical Care and the General Practitioner*, ch. 11, esp. Table 27, for payments under the Old Poor Law to Bedfordshire parish surgeons in 1811, and Marland, *Medicine and Society*, ch. 3, for a discussion of Poor Law medical services.

37 Thomas, 'The Old Poor Law and Medicine', p. 8.

38 A. H. T. Robb-Smith, *A Short History of the Radcliffe Infirmary* (Oxford, 1970), p. 25.

39 Thomas, 'The Old Poor Law and Medicine', p. 4.

40 *Statutes and Rules of the General Infirmary at Northampton* (Northampton, 1813), p. 24.

41 S. Cherry, 'The Role of a Provincial Hospital: the Norfolk and Norwich Hospital 1771–1880', *Population Studies* 26 (1972), p. 295.

42 Abel-Smith, *The Hospitals*, p. 37.

43 The occupational profile of Bristol firms was traced through Bristol Directories for 1785, 1794, 1803, 1805, 1815, and the Bristol Poll Book, 1784.

44 Richard Champion was treasurer to the Bristol Infirmary between 1768 and 1778. Champion family letter-book, Bristol Record Office, 38083 (3), 29 September 1771, quoted in Fissell, *Patients, Power, and the Poor*, p. 78.

45 Fissell, *Patients, Power, and the Poor*, p. 79.

46 P. Gosden, *The Friendly Societies in England 1815–1875* (Manchester, 1961), p. 5.

47 H. Levy, 'The Economic History of Sickness and Medical Benefit since the Puritan Revolution', *Economic History Review* 1 (1944), p. 147.

48 *Rules and Articles to be Observed by the Friendly and Humane Society Established at Daventry, January 1779*, Northampton Record Office, D.9959, p. 3.

49 Marland, *Medicine and Society*, p. 196. These societies can be seen as precursors of the Hospital Saturday Fund, set up in the early 1870s; the fund collected a penny a week from workmen and, in return, secured admission tickets from hospitals to which it made contributions.

50 Parliamentary Papers, *Abstract of the Answers and Returns under Act 43 Geo 3 relative to the Expense and Maintenance of the Poor in England 1803–4* (London, 1804). The Abstract gives the number of persons belonging to friendly societies in Northampton as 6 per cent of the resident

population (which would have included children), compared to Devon's 9 per cent of the resident population.

51 Minutes of the Devon and Exeter Hospital Weekly Committee, 15 December 1763, quoted in W. B. Howie, 'Complaints and Complaint Procedures in the Eighteenth- and Early Nineteenth-Century Provincial Hospitals in England', *Medical History* 25 (1981), p. 354.

52 These were either illegible or indeterminate, for instance where the recommender in the patient records was a business firm but the patron listed as a subscriber was an individual with the same initials.

53 Patient admissions by the hospital's committee were unique to Northampton General Hospital in the sample.

54 Numbers of in-patients: Bristol Infirmary: 1768 = 1,147, 1791 = 1,050, 1811 = 1,066. Devon and Exeter Hospital: 1771 = 688, 1791 = 1,081, 1811 = 719. Northampton General Hospital: 1771 = 239, 1791 = 445, 1811 = 779.

55 Northampton parishes used their sponsorship rights roughly in proportion to their level of patronage. Bristol firms did not; cf. graph of corporate patrons as a percentage of all patrons in Figure 5.1, p. 130.

56 Cf. Fissell, *Patients, Power, and the Poor*; G. Risse, *Hospital Life in Enlightenment Scotland* (Cambridge, 1986).

57 A. Tomkins, 'The Experience of Urban Poverty: A Comparison of Oxford and Shrewsbury 1740–1770', D.Phil. thesis (Oxford, 1994), p. 171.

58 Risse, *Hospital Life*, p. 87.

59 Marland, *Medicine and Society*, p. 159.

60 These percentages represent the average of three sample years for each hospital.

61 H. Marland, 'Lay and Medical Conceptions of Medical Charity during the Nineteenth Century: the Case of the Huddersfield Dispensary and Infirmary', in J. Barry and C. Jones (eds), *Medicine and Charity before the Welfare State* (London, 1991), p. 159.

62 All 'community'-sponsored in-patients were resident in Bristol city parishes except for two seamen recommended by Price & Cross, Bristol shipbrokers and wharfingers.

63 G. Risse, 'Hospital History: New Sources and Methods', in R. Porter and A. Wear (eds), *Problems and Methods in the History of Medicine* (London, 1987), p. 188.

64 Risse, *Hospital Life*, p. 87.

65 Berry, 'Patronage, Funding and the Hospital Patient', pp. 221–8.

66 Parish patients = 36, other recommended patients = 151, accident patients = 52.

67 R. M. Smith, 'Some Issues concerning Families and their Property in Rural England 1250–1800', in Smith (ed.), *Land, Kinship and Life-Cycle* (Cambridge, 1984), pp. 68–72.

68 Some 18 per cent of the 49 in-patients admitted under the sponsorship of business firms compared to 12 per cent of the 601 patients admitted on the recommendation of individual sponsors.

69 Nine out of 38 parish-patients (23 per cent), compared with 13 out of 137 individual-sponsored patients (9 per cent).

70 The survival of Poor Law overseers' account books for parishes subscribing to the hospital at Northampton is patchy. I am grateful to Samantha Williams for information on the costs of Poor Law medical care in Campton, Bedfordshire. S. Williams, 'Poor Relief, Welfare and Medical Provision in Bedfordshire: the Social, Economic and Demographic Context, c. 1750–1850', Ph.D. thesis (Cambridge, forthcoming).

71 Mingay, *The Agrarian History of England and Wales*, pp. 763–4.

72 Eastwood, *Governing Rural England*, p. 135.

73 Eastwood, *Governing Rural England*, p. 145.

74 Eastwood, *Governing Rural England*, p. 168.

Part III

BEYOND THE ASYLUM: MENTAL HEALTH IN BRITAIN
c. 1700–1939

6

THE HOUSEHOLD AND THE CARE OF LUNATICS IN EIGHTEENTH-CENTURY LONDON[1]

Akihito Suzuki

I

The pattern of care and provision for lunatics in England went through a gradual but fundamental transformation between *c.* 1650 and *c.* 1850. The most remarkable aspect of the shift was the rise of the asylum, or specialist institution for the insane.[2] The increasing segregation of lunatics into asylums has been studied fairly extensively. Major works have concentrated on the twofold processes of the institutionalization of the insane and the creation of asylum-based specialized medicine, drawing a picture of more or less linear evolution from mixed institutions to mental hospitals. Michel Foucault's *Histoire de la Folie* is centred on the creation of the 'general hospital' which incarcerated the insane indiscriminately with the social outcast, emphasizing the role of the institution in the transformation of madness as an object of social policy and medical discourse.[3] Stimulated by Foucault, but largely critical of his conclusions, there is a body of increasingly sophisticated historical monographs dedicated to the study of individual institutions.[4] The role of the asylum in the making of the psychiatric profession and discipline has been studied in depth. Andrew Scull has examined the process through which English 'mad-doctors' transformed themselves into 'psychiatrists' to consolidate their position in the newly created asylum system and Jan Goldstein has charted the similar strategy of French alienists in a wider political and cultural setting.[5]

Although valuable in reconceptualizing the making of psychiatry as a political and institutional enterprise, those works have created a historiographical bias of concentrating on what happened within institutional walls and neglecting what took place *outside* the institution. This bias has recently been corrected, most notably by Michael MacDonald and Roy Porter.[6] In particular, there is now rising interest in the extra-institutional care of lunatics in the early modern period. Peter Rushton, Jonathan Andrews, and some others have examined the role of the family and the community to which the poor insane belonged.[7] These works on extra-institutional care have shown that, in seventeenth- and eighteenth-century England, the family was the primary locus of care for the insane poor, sometimes with the help of cash doles, nurses, or means of restraint provided by the parish. Only when domestic provision failed was recourse had to institutional care and confinement.[8] Influenced by the recent trend in the historical/anthropological study of early modern poverty and charity, the works by Rushton, Andrews, and others have supplemented earlier works which dealt almost exclusively with reformers, psychiatrists, and legislators, and have started to throw light on insane recipients of relief.[9]

These works have put us in a better position to look at the rise of the asylum in connection with what happened outside the institution. The aim of the present paper is to further the study of the interaction of institutionalization and extra-institutional care by examining under what circumstances the institutional threshold was crossed – or, in other words, how domestic and private provision for a lunatic failed. The major source on which this paper is based is the record of about 130 lunatics whose 'settlement' – right to reside in the parish – and right to poor relief was examined between 1735 and 1783 by the Poor Law officers of the parish of St Martin-in-the-Fields in the city of Westminster.[10] I have supplemented these sources with Quarter Sessions records of the County of Middlesex in the seventeenth and eighteenth centuries, as well as some from other counties, for this type of record contains more detailed and vivid description of the hardship caused by lunatics within their respective households.[11]

London in the mid-eighteenth century is particularly important in the history of the care of the insane, for it witnessed the growth of a new type of institutional provision, the private madhouse, some instances of which took not only well-off patients but also poor parish lunatics.[12] As Parry-Jones and Andrews have shown, parishes in and around London from the late seventeenth century onward kept and confined a significant number of parish lunatics in private madhouses, supplementing the limited provision of cheaper public charitable hospitals such as Bethlem Hospital and, from 1751, St Luke's Hospital.[13] St Martin-in-the-Fields made quite extensive use of this private institutional provision, as well as of Bethlem and St Luke's.[14] They utilized first 'Dr' Matthew Wright's madhouse at Bethnal Green (succeeded first by Mrs Wright and then by Thomas Cope) and from 1777 William Harrison's at Hoxton.[15] Between 1737 and 1783, 227 lunatics were sent from the parish workhouse to these private madhouses, and an unknown number of lunatics were sent there directly from their lodging places.[16] In 1748, it seems that around twenty lunatics from the parish were kept at Mrs Wright's house.[17] Long before the state-run asylum system came into existence, St Martin's, like many other London parishes, practised institutional segregation of the poor insane. By the early nineteenth century, the private madhouse at Hoxton boasted about 500 inmates: it was by far the largest asylum in England until beaten by the Middlesex County Asylum at Hanwell, which housed about 900 around 1840.[18]

For the growth of private provision for parish lunatics, three factors were necessary: (1) supply – entrepreneurial owners of private madhouses; (2) demand – parish Poor Law officers who would pay for having their lunatics kept there; (3) the basis of demand – poor lunatics who could not be contained within the realm of private care. This paper will investigate the third factor, by studying patterns in the breakdown of the domestic care for the insane poor. It has to be emphasized immediately that failure in domestic provision does not automatically entail the growth of the asylum. As Scull has rightly pointed out, the supply of institutional care for lunatics was not an automatic response to the rising demand for it, and he is certainly right in criticizing the naive functionalist view, which sees the asylum as spontaneously generating in the marsh of industrialized urban slums.[19] On the other hand, early asylums did not recruit their inmates chiefly by pulling lunatics out of their own self-sufficient households. If anything, the early asylums mainly coped with the lunatics who had already fallen out of their domestic realms and had already become public problems. Given that, it seems reasonable to ask whether there was any increase in the number of

155

lunatics who failed to be contained in their families, a phenomenon which *helped* people to discover lunacy as a special problem
and to legitimize the creation of institutional provision. Below
I should like to suggest some possible ways to tackle this question.

II

The problem inherent in looking at the ability of a family to
contain its insane member is that historians usually have to infer its
capacity from the evidence of its incapacity. This difficulty
is particularly serious when examining poorer families. Upper-
and middle-class families were likely to leave diaries, letters, and
memoirs which sometimes include accounts of the madness of
their relatives, or to ask for commission *de lunatico inquirendo* to
put their insane member under guardianship.[20] When poorer
lunatics were contained in self-sufficient or semi-self-sufficient
households, they were unlikely to leave any records.

There are, however, some cases which suggest a considerable
capacity to cope with its insane member on the part of the household of a poor labourer. For instance, the parish officers and
inhabitants of Hardington, Somerset, petitioned the Quarter
Sessions Court in 1627,

> asking for the release from danger of arrest of a poor man
> Lionel Grange for building a house for which they had given
> permission; he having [a] great store of children and lunatic
> wife, [whom] if he be sent to prison, they will be obliged to
> keep.[21]

Although Lionel Grange was a poor cottage labourer, this petition
suggests that the parishioners expected that he would be able to
keep his lunatic wife, as well as his children. In another case, a
petition was presented in 1657 by Edward Ffox in Nottinghamshire: 'his wife being very much distracted in her witts hath of late
pulled down part of his dwelling house wherein she was kept,
which by reason of his poverty he is not able to build upp'.[22] On
hearing the petition, the court just ordered that the house should
be rebuilt at the parish's expense. Despite Edward's poverty and
the wife's violence, it was still expected that, with this small aid
from public resources, he could keep the problem within the
private domain.

These cases suggest that the tie formed by marriage was important in containing the problem of lunacy within the domestic realm and that married lunatics were less likely to become a public problem than single lunatics. This assumption is supported by the cases from St Martin-in-the-Fields. Of 127 lunatics examined there, only twenty-eight of them (fifteen husbands and thirteen wives) or 22 per cent were married at the time of their first examination as chargeable lunatics. Of the ninety-nine 'single' lunatics, eighty had never married, twelve were widows, and seven were deserted wives.[23]

This low representation of married men and women in the chargeable lunatics was certainly due to economic factors. Marriage meant the capacity of the couple to earn an income high enough to form and sustain their own household.[24] Hence, generally speaking, the household of a married lunatic was likely to have a relatively higher income, larger savings, and other helpful resources, on which he or she could rely when insane. In 1657, the Middlesex Quarter Sessions Court ordered the parish officers of Hadley to pay Abigail, the wife of Ralph Note, 2s. 6d. per week for his relief when they learned that Ralph had been 'distracted in his mind and unable to gain his livelihood' for three months and that 'the said Abigail has been forced to hire people to watch him, for fear he shall do himself or others some mischief. *She has spent all her money and good[s] in seeking means for his recovery*' [my emphasis].[25] This case indicates that married people first tried to cope with the hardship of the lunacy of their spouses by drawing upon their private resources. The larger the resources, the better the chance of containing the problem within the family sphere.

Another factor, the emotional tie between the spouses, must have to a certain extent contributed to keeping a married lunatic within the household. The mental world of ordinary folk is, however, notoriously difficult to investigate, and the sources I have consulted do not allow any positive assessment of the strength of the emotional commitment to an insane spouse. Indeed, eight lunatic wives were in the end deserted, which suggests that one should not overestimate the affectionate bond in married couples.[26] Readiness to take on the burden of a disabled family member was probably weakened in a case of lunacy: the poor prognosis of the disease, the grim reality of attending a lunatic, and the lack of appreciative response from him or her might have lowered the emotional commitment.

In some cases of deserted lunatic wives, it is highly likely that their lunacy itself was the cause of their husbands' absconding. In 1743, Ann Metzer married Swithin Metzer, a journeyman tailor. In 1746, she was sent to a private madhouse by the parish officers of St Martin-in-the-Fields. Next year, when her right to poor relief was examined, she was still accompanied by her husband, and again sent from the workhouse to the madhouse. In 1752, we find her again in the workhouse of the same parish, pregnant but with her husband 'gone from her'.[27] Almost certainly Swithin was fed up with taking care of his chronically insane wife and the prospect of the further burden of the baby. The case of Elizabeth Hutchinson, the wife of Thomas Hutchinson, a glass-grinder born and apprenticed in Ireland, was indeed pathetic. She was 60 years old when she was brought to the parish workhouse. Perhaps in delusion, she stated that her husband Thomas then kept a house of £30 per year in Southwark. In fact, as John Godfrey, a local justice of the peace, testified a few days later, Thomas 'hath been gone from her about two months and he [Godfrey] has made search and enquiry after the said Thomas Hutchinson but cannot learn where the said Thomas Hutchinson is gone to'.[28] These cases support the picture of marriage in early modern London put forth by Vivien Brodsky and Peter Earle as 'a very fragile institution'.[29] The ratio of two deserted lunatic wives to every three non-deserted ones from St Martin-in-the-Fields seems to speak for itself, even when one takes into consideration the presumably large number of 'invisible' husbands who took charge of their lunatic wives without leaving any trace in the historical record.

I have elsewhere constructed an argument about gender imbalance in the capacity to cope with the lunacy of the spouse.[30] Mainly relying on the contrasting representations of lunatic husbands and wives in the Quarter Sessions Court, I have argued that lunatic husbands posed more serious problems than insane wives, because of the former's greater capabilities as breadwinners and greater threat of physical violence. The evidence from St Martin-in-the-Fields, however, controverts, or at least significantly modifies, the picture I have drawn. The image of a dependent wife who was helpless with her raging husband was more a product of rhetoric suitable for a petition, shrewdly tuned to the ears of paternalistic magistrates, than a faithful picture.[31]

It is true that there are some cases which suggest that a husband could more easily cope with a lunatic wife than vice versa. In 1746,

Martha Prat, a lunatic wife, was kept in the parish workhouse for about five months, during which time her husband paid 2s. 6d. per week for her maintenance, and Sarah Lamb, another lunatic wife, was taken out of the workhouse by her husband after about three weeks' stay.[32] The records from St Martin-in-the-Fields I have examined do not include any wife that contributed to the maintenance of her lunatic husband in the workhouse, nor any who took her lunatic husband out of an institution. Still, the ratio of lunatic husbands to lunatic wives brought to the parish officers was 15 : 13, showing little significant imbalance. When examining how lunatics of different familial positions gained their last 'settlement' (Table 6.1), I found no conclusive evidence that a husband could more easily cope with his lunatic wife in their domestic setting. The distributions of types of 'settlement' in the following three groups – (a) lunatic husbands, (b) husbands of lunatic wives, and (c) late husbands of lunatic widows – are almost the same. Yet the low average rent (a fairly reliable index of income) paid by the husbands of lunatic wives might indicate that a husband with higher income could have kept them from being a burden to the parish.

Table 6.1 Means by which 'settlement' gained

	Husbands	Wives	Widows
Rent above £10 p.a.	6	5	5
Average known rent	£31	£19 12s.	£36
Apprenticeship	4	4	3
Birth in parish	3	2	1
One year's service	2	2	0
Independent widow	–	–	3
Total	15	13	12

Another defect of my own earlier account is that it underestimates the contribution of women, especially that of working wives, to the household economy. A recent study by Peter Earle has shown that women without any gainful employment were a minority (30 per cent of his sample) in late seventeenth- and early eighteenth-century London.[33] As shown in Table 6.1, three widows earned their own 'settlement' (while they were sane) after the death of their husbands and their becoming chargeable under the Poor Law, two by domestic service and one by the business of milliner.[34] Ann Metcaff, a spinster linen draper, had supported herself well and resided in a house with a rent of £30 until she became insane and was sent to a private madhouse as a parish lunatic.[35] Since my sources are concerned only with the occupation and apprenticeship of the husband of a married couple, they 'hide' contributions by working wives. Indeed, there is a telling example from Middlesex Quarter Sessions records, which allows us to glimpse how a working wife could maintain and manage a lunatic husband. In October 1655, the Quarter Sessions Court ordered the withdrawal of the licence of Robert Gregory, victualler, for 'suffering disorders in their houses of the Lord's Day' and for refusing subsequent inspection. In December at the next session, the Court suspended the order, finding that 'the said Gregory is at some times distempered in his braine and that his wife is a sober and well-governed woman'.[36] Apparently, the justices thought that the sober wife would carry out both the business of victualling and that of managing her fitful husband.

Instead of an oversimplified model of a household sustained by a single male breadwinner, therefore, a more complex model which considers the earnings and spending of all the members of each household is necessary in order to understand the patterns in the breakdown of domestic care. As Andrews has perceptively pointed out, the life-cycle model is particularly helpful when examining the limits of domestic care of lunatics.[37] In some households in my sample, the burden of children seems to have aggravated the situation. Out of twenty-eight households with either a lunatic husband or a lunatic wife, twelve had at least one child. The strain of a new-born child seems to have been crucial: there were four households burdened with a baby under six months old.[38] Besides these cases, there are another four entries in the workhouse admission records which suggest the burden placed by a lunatic and a young baby on the family economy.[39]

There were several ways for a large family to cope with problems caused or aggravated by the existence of a lunatic. When Charles Cook found it difficult to keep both Grace his lunatic wife and Elizabeth their new-born child of five weeks, the father stayed with the child and committed his wife to the workhouse.[40] The case of the Conner family was more complex. Christian Conner was the wife of John Conner, who had once been a domestic servant with a comfortable £12 a year plus food and lodging. On 24 September

1745, the Conners were in great trouble and were sent to the workhouse, the wife having become insane with three children to maintain, aged 3 years, 2 years, and about 10 weeks respectively. Next day, John went out of the workhouse, leaving the rest of the family behind him, and Christian was sent to the private madhouse. The burden of a lunatic wife and three young children was apparently too heavy for him. After the baby's death two weeks later, however, Christian was discharged from the madhouse. Perhaps John might have found a way to support his family, the burden of which had become significantly smaller because of the death of the youngest child. The question was not only whether the wife was ungovernable, but also whether the family had the capacity to contain her.[41]

Despite its limitations and fragile nature, the tie formed by marriage still seems to have provided the most important support for those who became insane. The marriage tie was all the more important because the tie between parent and child, another bond in the nuclear family, does not seem to have contributed greatly to the domestic care of lunatics. In some cases, lunatic children seem to have suffered because of the blatant neglect of their parents.[42] The limited care lunatic children received from their parents was again, however, mainly due to problems pertaining to the life cycle. When a child was chronically insane or weak-minded from youth, his or her parents could and did look after it. When parents grew older and their income declined, it became harder for them to cope with the problem, for they were themselves having difficulty in making their living. This is exemplified in the petition of George Clark to Middlesex Quarter Sessions Court in 1719:

> In the year 1700 he was overseer of the parish of Thisleworth, which parish, being much in debt, did not reimburse the money due to him on the balance of his account, and he is now an aged poor man with a distracted daughter to maintain.[43]

Likewise, another father in Middlesex stated that he could not maintain his lunatic daughter and three children because he was 'aged sixty-six and much disabled by the dimness of his sight'.[44]

The sample from St Martin-in-the-Fields supplies some similar cases of the long-term care provided by parents, and its inevitable limitations. Although there is a case in which Thomas Chalmers, a

53-year-old smith and widower, discharged his lunatic daughter
Margaret from the private madhouse where she had been kept for
a year at the parish's expense, not every parent could afford such a
display of paternal or maternal concern.[45] Thomas Chandler, an
apparently chronic lunatic, had never been 'married nor bound
an apprentice . . . but always with [his father]'. In 1743, when
Thomas was 33 years old, his father, a yeoman, finally applied for
a place in Bethlem, perhaps finding it difficult to keep Thomas
any longer.[46] Moreover, some lunatic children found one of
their parents had already died at the time of their need. Of nine
lunatics whose parents appeared in their records, three had
widowed mothers.[47] In 1761, Sarah Summers, a widow, put her
daughter Ann to apprenticeship. Six months later, Ann 'went out
of her senses', was discharged from apprenticeship, and subsequently kept at the private madhouse as a parish lunatic.[48] Jemima
Dean, a widow, obviously found it beyond her power to cope with
Anne Dean, a lunatic daughter of hers, and Sarah Dean, Anne's
illegitimate child, whose father was unknown.[49] The lack of substantial support from the parents of lunatics was thus due more to
the incapacitating consequences of old age than to neglect or
unwillingness on the parents' side.

When it comes to the filial care of lunatic fathers and mothers,
reluctance rather than inability seems to have characterized cases
from my sample. There are five cases in which grown-up children
were involved in settling the problem of the lunacy of their parents,
and none of them invited the insane parents to their own households.[50] Philip Johnson, a 'glass flowerer' living in the parish of
St Martin-in-the-Fields, testified that he would remove his lunatic
father Jerom to the parish of St James, Piccadilly, where the
father had once gained 'settlement' by renting a house of £70
per annum.[51] John Eterneau, a leather breeches maker, had lived
in the parish of St Martin-in-the-Fields with his lunatic mother,
who had been widowed for twenty-four years. In 1774 he removed
her to the parish of St Anne, the place of her late husband's
'settlement'.[52]

As for the care provided by brothers and sisters, there is not
much evidence from my sample. Although we need further
research to confirm this point, it seems unlikely that brothers and
sisters invited their lunatic siblings to their own households for a
long-term stay without payment. When lunatics were provided with
long-term care by their brothers and sisters, the siblings almost

always received money either from the parish or from the property of the lunatics in question. Sometimes reimbursement did not entice the siblings to take care of the lunatics. When Elizabeth Baxter, a widow of some property, became insane in Yorkshire in the early seventeenth century, the parish found 'her kindred and friends utterly refusing to medle with her'.[53] This does not mean that people did not do anything to help their lunatic siblings. The helping hand of brothers and sisters could sometimes become generous: Ann Nott looked after her insane sister Jane Guyver at the house of her husband John for at least a year and a half. In the end, however, Jane was removed to the parish of St Paul Covent Garden, where she had earned 'settlement' by her own service.[54] The role of the siblings seems to have been mainly limited to providing short-term emergency help and initiating the necessary procedure for a more long-term 'settlement'. Thomas Achison, who was apparently chronically weak-minded and sometimes acutely insane, was first brought to his sister Isabella Clarke living in the parish of Covent Garden. She helped the parish to remove him to St-Martin-in-the-Fields, where Thomas was born, to be provided for at the workhouse.[55]

The limitations of domestic care for lunatics were, therefore, a part of that 'nuclear hardship' held to be inherent in early modern English society.[56] Support from extended kin outside the nuclear family was scarce, and children often did not help their lunatic parents after leaving the latter's household to form their own. The marriage tie, the core of the nuclear family bond, was the most important private resource one could rely on in time of need, and lunacy created no exception. Lunacy of a spouse, however, made the marriage tie more fragile, which was prone to breakdown at the desertion of one partner.

These conclusions lead us to a further question about local provision for lunacy. Namely, did local community ties and obligations mitigate the nuclear hardship created or exacerbated by lunacy? The same observation of short-term generosity that I have made above about siblings seems to be applicable to neighbourhoods. London in the eighteenth century had not yet witnessed the tendencies towards anonymity inherent in the growth of urban slums, and great concern was paid to maintain and promote the morality and harmony of the local community. A lot of people, whose relation to the lunatics in question is not stated in the records, offered lodging to them at the time of their examination, and some of them must have been generous neighbours. It is, however, quite understandable that their generosity towards a lunatic neighbour was limited.[57] Sometimes neighbours took the initiative in bringing a disorderly lunatic to the notice of public authorities. Several neighbours of Lot Beacham, a lunatic, reported to the parish officers that 'he is by lunacy so far disordered in his senses that he is dangerous to be permitted to go abroad having committed several acts of violence'.[58]

III

Above, I have examined the relative importance of ties between kin, especially between spouses and between parents and children. Next, the tie between masters and servants, which constituted the other major bond of the household in this period, should be examined.[59] Lunatic servants overwhelmingly dominate my sample. Forty-nine lunatics earned their last 'settlement' by a year's service.[60] The ratio of servants to the total of my sample is about 39 per cent, vastly exceeding the ratio of servants to the total population of London in this period, which is estimated to have been about 8 per cent.[61] Even if one considers that a West End parish, such as St Martin-in-the-Fields, was likely to have a higher proportion of domestic servants, still it seems safe to argue that lunatic servants posed a disproportionately large problem.

How can one explain this bias towards servants in the lunatic population? One cannot entirely exclude the possibility that servants in eighteenth-century London, coming out of rustic simplicity, engaged in psychologically demanding work and indulging in Metropolitan excitements, were more prone to madness than the rest of the population. There seems to be, however, a more straightforward and convincing explanation.

First of all, there was a change in the law. The 1697 amendment of the act regulating 'settlement' expanded the right to poor relief to include those unmarried persons who were hired for a year as servants, as well as those who had already been given the right by renting a tenement worth £10 a year or more, or being bound apprentice.[62] Now the parish had to provide for the lunatics who had earned their 'settlement' by a year's service.

Moreover, the position of the servants in their respective households was temporary and directly dependent on their ability to work. For obvious reasons, it is hardly imaginable that their masters, who dismissed servants for the slightest negligence of duties, would be prepared to maintain and keep their lunatic servants for a long period. There were six servants in my sample who had gained their 'settlement' by service to aristocrats.[63] Yet the majority of the lunatic servants in my sample had served in middle-class households, for example of two victuallers, a cabinet maker, an upholsterer, a peruke maker, and so on.[64] The life-style of middle-class masters and mistresses, especially their keen sense of economy in their household finance and their pursuit of domestic comfort, was totally incompatible with keeping an unproductive, disruptive, and sometimes dangerous lunatic servant.[65]

In some cases, lunatic servants dropped into the parish net immediately after they lost the job. In 1751, Peter Warren Esq. testified that 'Robert Combstock a lunatick was a yearly hired servt to this examinant . . . for the space of ten years at the yearly wages of £20 diet and lodging, quitted the same fourteen days ago'.[66] Yet Combstock's case is exceptional in that his lunacy was reported immediately after his quitting service. The median length of the period between the servants' quitting the service by which they earned 'settlement' and their being examined as lunatics, calculated from the twenty-nine cases in which the figure is available, is twelve months. Some of the servants became insane long after they quitted service, and some probably supported themselves by short service at other places or by other means.

It is reasonable to assume that fired lunatic servants did not become instantly chargeable to the parish. Being temporarily out of service was a part of life for domestic servants in eighteenth-century London, and they were often at pains to furnish themselves with a certain degree of 'cushion' for the time of unemployment.[67] Since the average wage of the twenty-seven lunatic servants whose wages are known is about £8, perhaps they could live for a short period on their savings after their dismissal.[68] Some fortunate lunatics could probably go on depending on the hospitality of their relatives, friends, and fellow servants. In 1777, Mary Smythee, a servant to 'Messr. Cox and Biddulph, bankers', stated that Elizabeth Smythee, her former fellow servant and probably a relative, quitted after four years' service. At the time of her examination, ten weeks after her losing the job, Elizabeth still resided at her former master's place, probably with the help of Mary.[69]

When servants became insane during their term of contract, their masters sometimes assumed responsibility for looking after them. In Hertford in 1662, Anthony Grey was ordered by the Quarter Sessions Court to keep Jeremiah Grey, his servant who had become insane, during the contractual term. When the contract expired, the servant was removed to his father's.[70] A similar example is found in my sample. In January 1760, Sarah Masterman, the wife of William Masterman, a cabinet maker, stated that Mary Masterman was a lunatic and 'was a yearly hired servant to the said Mr Masterman in Old Round Court for the space of two years at the wages of fifty shillings diet and lodging', and 'that she hath not quitted the said service'. In February, Mary was brought to the parish workhouse as a lunatic, but on the same day 'taken out by her mistress'. In the end, however, the Mastermans gave up looking after Mary and committed her to the workhouse five months later.[71]

The responsibility of masters during the term of contract was, however, not universally enforced. Mary Masterman bore the same family name as her master and was probably a relative, which almost certainly affected this rather rare display of care by a master. Martha and Robert Ashton, the mistress and master of Mary Desborough, were not as generous. Mary Desborough was committed to the workhouse as a lunatic on 3 November 1766. Next day, Martha testified that Mary 'hath been a yearly hired servant to this examinant . . . and continues with this examinant'. Yet there is nothing to indicate that the Ashtons paid for the maintenance of Mary either in the workhouse or at the private madhouse Mary was sent to in June next year.[72]

Reflecting the fact that domestic service attracted a lot of young immigrants to London, some servants in my sample came from the countryside.[73] Elizabeth Davis was a classic example of the tragedy of a poor country girl coming up to the town. She came to London from Shropshire when she was only 7 years old. She earned her 'settlement' by serving one Mr Snow in St Martin's for three years, which she left when she was about 21 years old. While she was subsequently serving one Mr Suage, a harpsichord maker, Hugh Mahoon, a journeyman lodging at Mr Suage's, 'had carnal knowledge of her body', and in 1735 she was brought to the workhouse pregnant with an illegitimate child of his. On the next occasion that she was brought to the workhouse, in 1737, she was found to be a lunatic and spent a good part of the following few years in the workhouse and the madhouse.[74] Sarah Humphreys is another example of an immigrant who became insane in London. She was born at Bridgwater in Somerset, and came to London in 1739 when she was 22 years old. She became a servant to Mrs Pembrook, an upholsterer, 'at the yearly wages of £3, diet, washing, and lodging'. She quitted the place around March 1741, after about a year's service. Half a year later, she was homeless ('hath no lodging') and was put into the parish workhouse. She left the workhouse, only to be readmitted a year later in September 1742. Three months later she was found so insane that she was sent to the private madhouse.[75] Although we do not know when her mental illness actually started, it seems likely that it was around the time of her losing her job and that it became worse during the period of unemployment and homelessness, the pattern we find quite often today.

The lunatic ex-servants who dominated my sample were, therefore, a part of the larger shift in demographic patterns and household structure in London in the eighteenth century.[76] London continued to grow in its population thanks to immigration, although the pace of growth became slower than in the sixteenth and early seventeenth centuries. The demand for domestic servants increased, for the upper and middle classes were employing a larger number of them for the purposes of making an ostentatious display on the street and of freeing the masters and especially mistresses from menial chores at home. Attracted by high wages, better living conditions, and the excitements of London, a large number of young men and a larger number of young women came to London to be domestic servants. Domestic service also provided a way to earn one's living for London-born people with limited resources. The demand for servants was high, the wages became higher, and, generally speaking, it was a good period for servants.

This large influx of servants into London households meant that there emerged a vulnerable sector in the primary locus of care of lunatics in the early modern period. The households to which the servants belonged offered very little protection when they became insane. Servants' membership of their respective households was directly dependent on their ability to work: when they became insane and unproductive, lunatic servants could not expect from the household the same extent of protection, care, and tolerance as was received by the members of the nuclear family, or, perhaps, even those of the extended kin. That their wages often included 'diet and lodging' made the situation worse: they lost accommodation at the very moment they were fired.[77]

From the viewpoint of the care of the insane, therefore, there was an inherent fragility in household structure in eighteenth-century London. Moreover, under the 1697 amendment of the law relating to 'settlement', the burden of taking care of this fragile population was put upon the shoulders of London parishes if 'settlement' had been earned by a year's service. This sector turned out to be by far the largest group in the lunatic population which the parish of St Martin's had to look after or cope with. Although one must guard against adopting the naive functionalist view of the 'spontaneous generation' of institutional provision for lunatics, I would like tentatively to suggest that a constant flow of lunatic servants was vital for the rise and growth of private madhouses in eighteenth-century London.

IV

Our present knowledge about the extent of the care of lunatics in extra-institutional and domestic settings is still limited, and we are not in a position to assess the role played in the rise of the asylum by changes affecting the household. A few things which deserve more careful attention, however, have emerged from the analysis above. Firstly, social structure, the rules of household formation, and the private ethos generated by these factors, greatly affected the extent of the private care of lunatics and the pattern of public care. Here, the pattern of care for lunatics in an early modern Japanese village provides a dramatic contrast. There, parents and children, extended kin group, and neighbours were expected to involve themselves in the care and management of lunatics to a much greater extent than were eighteenth-century Londoners. When a lunatic son escaped from his father's house to kill two villagers and himself, the father was punished severely for the neglect of his duty: half of the father's property was confiscated and he was expelled from the village.[78] Our understanding of the private provision for lunatics in England will benefit greatly from comparison with that in a society with a different social structure and rules of household formation.

Secondly, the capacity of a household to contain its lunatic members varied greatly because of various factors. Its financial situation, the stage in the life-cycle of its breadwinners and dependants, its emotional solidarity, and the structure of its membership, all affected the extent and the limit of the private and domestic resources available to its lunatic member. Another apparently important factor which does not appear in my sources is the way people utilized their domestic living space: whether the family could afford a separate room for its insane member, in which part of the house it kept the lunatic, and so on. These variables were crucial in turning a private problem into a public one, in bringing a lunatic 'hidden' in his or her own household to the notice of public providers of care and control. Further investigation into these issues will prove to be fruitful for our understanding of the rise of asylum in the late eighteenth century.

Thirdly, the problem of lunatic servants demands further attention. My research supports, although in an oblique way, Andrew Scull's thesis that the coming of a full capitalist market economy and 'commercialization of existence' prompted family and society to expel its insane and unproductive members eventually into asylums.[79] Servants' subsistence was directly dependent on the sale of their labour, and their position in their masters' households was a product of contract rather than custom in a Weberian sense. The cases from St Martin-in-the-Fields seem to indicate that the increase in demand for the public care of the insane in the eighteenth century was partly due to the growth of a vulnerable sector in the household, dictated by the logic of the contractual labour market.

NOTES

1 The research on which this paper was based was funded by the Japan Society for the Promotion of Science. My thanks go to JSPS. I am grateful to Jonathan Andrews and Roy Porter for their insightful suggestions on an earlier draft. The staff of the City of Westminster Archive have been extremely generous in their help.

2 The best survey of literature on the rise of asylum is R. Porter, 'Madness and its Institutions', in A. Wear (ed.), *Medicine in Society: Historical Essays* (Cambridge, 1992), pp. 277–301.

3 M. Foucault, *Histoire de la Folie à l'Age Classique* (2nd edn, Paris, 1972).

4 To mention only a few, A. Digby, *Madness, Morality and Medicine: A Study of the York Retreat, 1796–1914* (Cambridge, 1985); J. Andrews, 'Bedlam Revisited: a History of Bethlem Hospital c. 1634–c. 1770', Ph.D. thesis (London, 1991); C. Mackenzie, *Psychiatry for the Rich: a History of Ticehurst Private Asylum* (London, 1992).

5 A. Scull, *The Most Solitary of Afflictions: Madness and Society in Britain, 1700–1900* (New Haven, CT, and London 1993); J. Goldstein, *Console and Classify: the French Psychiatric Profession in the Nineteenth Century* (Cambridge, 1987).

6 M. MacDonald, *Mystical Bedlam: Madness, Anxiety, and Healing in Seventeenth-Century England* (Cambridge, 1981); and R. Porter, *Mind-Forg'd Manacles: a History of Madness in England from the Restoration to the Regency* (London, 1987).

7 A. Fessler, 'The Management of Lunacy in Seventeenth-Century England: an Investigation of Quarter-Sessions Records', *Proceedings of the Royal Society of Medicine* 49 (1956), pp. 901–7; P. Rushton, 'Lunatics and Idiots: Mental Disability, the Community and the Poor Law in North-East England 1600–1800', *Medical History* 24 (1980), pp. 34–50; J. Andrews, '"Mad and Poor, and Cannot Be Otherwise Provided For": Lunacy, Bedlam, and the Old Poor Law' (unpublished paper); A. Suzuki, 'Lunacy in Seventeenth- and Eighteenth-Century England: Analysis of Quarter Sessions Records', parts I and II, *History of Psychiatry* 2 (1991), pp. 437–56, and 3 (1992), pp. 29–44. See also an account of wandering lunatics in N. Hattori, 'The Pleasure of Your Bedlam: the Theatre of Madness in the Renaissance', *History of Psychiatry* 6 (1995), pp. 283–308.

8 Rushton, 'Lunatics and Idiots', p. 40; Andrews, '"Mad and Poor"'; Suzuki, 'Lunacy in Seventeenth- and Eighteenth-Century England', part I, pp. 440–51.

9 For recent directions in the study of early modern poverty, see R. Jütte, *Poverty and Deviance in Early Modern Europe* (Cambridge, 1994); S. Woolf, *The Poor in Western Europe in the Eighteenth and Nineteenth Centuries* (London and New York, 1986), pp. 1–46.

10 City of Westminster Library (hereafter WCL), MSS records of the parish of St Martin-in-the-Fields, 'Examination Books', F5027–F5067 (1 Aug. 1734–23 Mar. 1782); Workhouse 'Day Books', F4003–F4016 (3 Oct. 1737–15 July 1784).

11 Middlesex Sessions Books (hereafter MXSB) from 1638–1751 are available in typescript at the Greater London Record Office (hereafter GLRO). For the social historical background of eighteenth-century London, I have benefited from D. George, *London Life in the Eighteenth Century* (Harmondsworth, 1966); P. Earle, *The Making of the English Middle Class: Business, Society and Family Life in London, 1660–1730* (London, 1989), and *A City Full of People: Men and Women of London 1650–1750* (London, 1994).

12 W. Parry-Jones, *The Trade in Lunacy* (London, 1972); Porter, *Mind-Forg'd Manacles*, p. 141; Andrews, 'Bedlam Revisited', pp. 418–9.

13 Andrews, '"Mad and Poor"'; Parry-Jones, *The Trade in Lunacy*, pp. 8–9.

14 Private madhouses seem to have functioned as supplementary to Bethlem and St Luke's, used both before committal to the public hospitals and after discharge from them. See Frances Lewin's case (WCL F4004, 27 Nov. 1742 and 1 Jan. 1743) and E. Cornman (F4004, p. 556).

15 From the earliest extant Workhouse 'Day Book' from October 1737,

the parish sent its lunatics to 'Dr Wright's', and later to 'Mrs Wright's'. In 1755, the term 'Mr Cope' first appeared (WCL F4008, 9 Aug. 1755). In December 1777, churchwardens and overseers ordered the removal of 'the lunatics now at Mr Cope's . . . to Mr Harrison's at Hoxton' (WCL F2225, p. 70). Alexander Cruden was confined in Wright's madhouse. See A. Cruden, *Mr Cruden Greatly Injured* (London, 1739), pp. 2, 32.

16 For some examples of the lunatics who were sent directly to the private houses, see WCL F2225, pp. 39, 58, and 95. The important role of nineteenth-century workhouses in the care of pauper lunatics is discussed in P. Bartlett, 'The Poor Law of Lunacy: the Administration of Pauper Lunatics in Mid-Nineteenth Century England with Special Emphasis on Leicestershire and Rutland', Ph.D. thesis (London, 1993). For workhouses in the eighteenth century, see T. Hitchcock, 'Paupers and Preachers: the SPCK and the Parochial Workhouse Movement', in L. Davison, T. Hitchcock, T. Keirn and R. B. Shoemaker (eds), *Stilling the Grumbling Hive: the Response to Social and Economic Problems in England, 1689–1750* (Stroud, 1992), pp. 145–66; S. Macfarlane, 'Social Policy and the Poor in the Later Seventeenth Century', in A. L. Beier and R. Finlay (eds), *London 1500–1700: the Making of the Metropolis* (London, 1986), pp. 252–77.

17 WCL F4004, pp. 554–6, 'Lunatics at Mrs Wrights', listed twenty-nine lunatics, nine of whose entries said that they had been discharged or had died.

18 Porter, *Mind-Forg'd Manacles*, p. 141. In the parish of the Liberty of the Roll, there were several lunatics kept in the private madhouses at Kentish Town, Islington, and Bethnal Green, as well as Bethlem, St Luke's, and the parish workhouse. See WCL K346, Sept. 1799, Oct. 1799, Nov. 1801.

19 Scull, *The Most Solitary of Afflictions*, pp. 26–34; Porter, 'Madness and its Institutions', pp. 287–8.

20 R. Porter, *The Social History of Madness* (London, 1987); M. MacDonald, 'Lunatics and the State in Georgian England', *Social History of Medicine* 2 (1989), pp. 299–313.

21 E. H. Bates (ed.), *Quarter Sessions Records for the County of Somerset, 1607–1677*, Somerset Records Society 23–6, 4 vols (London, 1907–12), vol. 2, p. 46.

22 H. Hampton Copnall (ed.), *Notes and Extracts from the Nottinghamshire County Records of the Seventeenth Century*, Nottinghamshire County Records Committee (Nottingham, 1915), p. 122.

23 Out-and-out solitaries were, however, a minority among the 'single' lunatics. William Schwanberg was the only exception. According to his doctor Robert James (of powder and *Dictionary* fame), 'he is a foreigner . . . never gained any settlement in England neither has he any friends or relations or any goods, chattels or effects in England'. WCL F5036, p. 104; F4004, p. 554. Alexander Cruden, too, was a Scot immigrant with no immediate family in London. See Porter, *Social History of Madness*, pp. 126–35.

24 Recent studies of early modern marriage have been surveyed and

synthesized in K. Wrightson, *English Society 1580–1680* (London, 1982), pp. 94–104; R. Houlbrooke, *The English Family 1450–1700* (London, 1984), pp. 63–126.

25 GLRO MXSB, book 173.

26 Ann Metzer was accompanied with her husband at the time of her first examination, but deserted when examined for the second time.

27 WCL F5038, p. 255; F5042, p. 321; F4004, p. 556; F4005, 21 Oct. 1746.

28 WCL F5031, pp. 224, 229. It was often difficult to extract necessary and correct information about lunatics' 'settlement' from their own testimony. Frequently, a person who knew the lunatic in question well was called in. See also Andrews 'Bedlam Revisited', p. 434.

29 V. Brodsky, 'Widows in Late Elizabethan London: Remarriage, Economic Opportunity and Family Orientations', in L. Bonfield, R. M. Smith, and K. Wrightson (eds), *The World We Have Gained: Histories of Population and Social Structure* (Oxford, 1986), pp. 122–54; Earle, *A City Full of People*, pp. 164–5.

30 Suzuki, 'Lunacy in Seventeenth- and Eighteenth-Century England', part I, pp. 440–4.

31 The strategic use of elite ideology by the poor is discussed in S. Woolf, 'Introduction', in Woolf (ed.), *Domestic Strategies: Work and Family in France and Italy 1600–1800* (Cambridge, 1991), pp. 1–19.

32 WCL F4005, 6 June 1746; F4010, 3 and 27 June 1763.

33 Earle, *A City Full of People*, pp. 113–23.

34 M. Whitaker, WCL F5034, p. 103; F4003, pp. 520, 525; F4008, pp. 109, 113; Mary Combe, F5035, p. 208; Susanna French, F5032, pp. 258–9.

35 WCL F5040, p. 47.

36 GLRO MXSB, books 148 and 149.

37 Andrews, '"Mad and Poor"'.

38 John Page, WCL F5031, p. 92, F4003, 16 June 1739 WH lun (30); Thomas Baker, F5054, p. 294, F4010, 10 and 11 Oct. 1765; Grace Cooke and Christian Conner, see nn. 40–1 below.

39 WCL F4003, 22 July and 1 Oct. 1739; F4008, 2 June and 17 July 1753; F4008, 19 and 26 Feb. 1754; F4009, 11 Oct. and 23 Dec. 1759, and 1 Aug. 1760.

40 WCL F5049, p. 334; F4008, 17 and 18 May 1758.

41 WCL F5037, p. 38; F4004, 24 Sept. and 4 Oct. 1745 and p. 554. This example might suggest that recourse to institutional means was temporary and a part of the economy of makeshift for a poor family to cope with its insane member. Among the eleven parish lunatics from St Clement Danes, kept at Harrison's at Hoxton in August 1788, four were 'brought home' in a year and a half. See WCL B1248, Overseers' Order Book, 5 Aug. 1788 and Jan. 1790. For the priority given by Bethlem to 'ungovernable' lunatics, see Andrews, 'Bedlam Revisited', pp. 455–7.

42 The father of Mary Jones had failed in his business and ran away to Birmingham, leaving his daughter reduced to 'living by selling greens and fruit about the street'. Five years after, she was admitted to the workhouse as a lunatic. WCL F5033, p. 252; F4005, 11 Sept. and 6 Oct. 1746.

43 GLRO MXSB, book 777. Suzuki, 'Lunacy in Seventeenth- and Eighteenth-Century England', part I, pp. 446–7. For a similar example of domestic long-term care of a lunatic son, which was terminated by the death of the mother, see Andrews, 'Bedlam Revisited', p. 433, n. 80.

44 GLRO MXSB, book 158. See also the examination of Barnard Page over the 'settlement' of John Page, his lunatic son, with John's wife and two young children in WCL F5031, p. 92; F4003, 16 June 1739.

45 WCL F5064, p. 427; F4014, 7 and 11 Feb. 1778 and 20 Mar. 1779.

46 WCL F5035, p. 296. See also the cases of Hannah Poole, the daughter of Timothy Poole, in WCL F5028, p. 316.

47 Caroline Sechuson (29), WCL F5052, p. 345; F4010, 1 and 3 Mar. 1763; Ann Summers (16); Anne Dean (31).

48 WCL F5052, p. 203; F4010, 6 July 1762, 24 Aug. 1765.

49 WCL F5059, pp. 170–1.

50 Mary Whitaker (38), with a daughter Rebecca (17) then living at Bath, WCL F5034, p. 103; F4003, 24 Nov. 1741, 5 Dec. 1742; F4008, 12, 17 Mar. and 5 Apr. 1754; Thomas Holden (59) and his daughter Sarah Holden, F5050, p. 289; Jerom Johnson; John Eterneau; Ann Hedges. See, however, an affectionate concern expressed for his lunatic mother by a son, quoted in Andrews, 'Bedlam Revisited', p. 552.

51 WCL F5053, p. 403; F4010, 15 and 24 Nov. 1764.

52 WCL F5061, p. 430. James Hedges, a tin plate worker, also removed his mother Ann Hedges to the place of her own 'settlement', which she earned by renting a house of £14 p.a. (WCL F5056, p. 384).

53 Suzuki, 'Lunacy in Seventeenth- and Eighteenth-Century England', part I, pp. 448–9; *The Yorkshire Archaeological and Topographical Journal* 5 (1879), pp. 403–4.

54 WCL F5047, p. 166; F5049, p. 110. See also the example of Mrs Newby, matron of the lying-in hospital in London, who paid 4s. per week for keeping her sister at a private madhouse at Hoxton. WCL E981.

55 WCL F5029, p. 194; F5035, p. 407; F4004, 14 Jan. 1744.

56 For a general discussion of nuclear hardship, see P. Laslett, 'Family, Kinship and Collectivity as Systems of Support in Pre-industrial Europe: a Consideration of the "Nuclear-Hardship" Hypothesis', *Continuity and Change* 3 (1988), pp. 153–75; also P. Horden, S. Cavallo, this volume.

57 My research does not confirm John Walton's model of workplace-centred community solidarity as a significant resource for a lunatic to rely on. J. K. Walton, 'Lunacy in the Industrial Revolution: a Study of Asylum Admissions in Lancashire, 1845–50', *Journal of Social History* 13 (1979), pp. 1–21.

58 WCL F5055, p. 166. Likewise, Francis Pope was caught by a constable at four or five o'clock in the morning when wandering in lunacy. Next day, his brother-in-law took him out of custody (WCL F4004, 3 Oct. 1742).

59 P. Laslett, *The World We Have Lost – Further Explored* (London, 1983), pp. 1–8.

60 With the exception of Arthur Parry, who was reduced to being a workhouse inmate from having been a 'servant' in the capacity of clerk in the City with the handsome wage of £100 p.a. (WCL F5063, p. 331; F4013, 20 and 30 Sept. 1776), all of them were domestic servants. Besides these domestic servants, there are fourteen lunatics who were journeymen, twelve males, and two females. In Andrews' sample of 251 lunatics admitted to Bethlem (1694–1718), only three were servants. Andrews, 'Bedlam Revisited', pp. 523–4.

61 Earle, *A City Full of People*, p. 82.

62 G. W. Oxley, *Poor Relief in England and Wales 1601–1834* (North Pomfret, VT, 1974), pp. 20–1; P. Slack, *Poverty and Policy in Tudor and Stuart England* (London, 1988), pp. 194–5.

63 Mary Combe, WCL F5035, p. 208; Elizabeth Orme, F5042, p. 9; Mary Needham, F5053, p. 25; John Bryant, F5058, p. 373; George Jennings, F5059, p. 8; John Porter, F5059, p. 119.

64 WCL F5040, p. 289; F5047, p. 166; F5050, p. 450; E3234, p. 58; F5054, p. 222. There are in total eighteen servants whose masters' 'middle-class' businesses are known. The rest are: a distiller (F5040, p. 431), a grocer (F5037, p. 214), a stationer (F5032, p. 158), a glover (F5055, p. 255), a carpenter (F5030, p. 136), a piece broker (F5040, p. 381), a banker (F5064, p. 199), a paviour (F5035, p. 420), an attorney (F5043, p. 332), a cook (F5047, p. 226), a wineman (F5047, p. 108), a pewterer (B1179, p. 228), a painter (F5054, p. 211).

65 Earle, *The Making of the English Middle Class*, pp. 213–29. For committal of domestic servants by their masters in France, see Y. Ripa, *Women and Madness: the Incarceration of Women in Nineteenth-Century France* (Cambridge, 1990), pp. 55–6.

66 WCL F5042, p. 10.

67 J. J. Hecht, *The Domestic Servant Class in Eighteenth-Century England* (London, 1956), pp. 81–7; Earle, *A City Full of People*, pp. 128–9.

68 The median figure is £5, the average being pushed higher by the exceptional wage of 50 guineas earned by John Porter, a servant to the Duke of Argyle.

69 WCL F5064, p. 199; F4014, 29 Aug. 1777, 27 Sept. 1777 and 8 Oct. 1778.

70 W. J. Hardy (ed.), *Notes and Extracts from the Sessions Rolls 1581–1690*, Hertford County Records Society, 3 vols (Hertford: 1905), vol. 3, pp. 61–2; Suzuki, 'Lunacy in Seventeenth- and Eighteenth-Century England', part I, pp. 450–1.

71 WCL F5050, p. 450; F4009, 8 Feb. and 18 July 1760.

72 WCL F5055, p. 255; F4011, 3 Nov. 1766, 19 June 1767.

73 The records include information on the birthplace of an examinant only when he or she had earned 'settlement'.

74 WCL F5027, p. 335; F4003, 10 Dec. 1737, 16 June 1738, 12 Mar. 1739 and 1 Jan. 1740.

75 WCL E3234, p. 58; F5034, p. 7; F4004, 3 Sept. and 1 Dec. 1742. See also the case of Margaret Grifith, who came from Chester, in F5037, p. 214; F4004, p. 554; and that of Christian Cruckshank, an immigrant from Scotland, in F5030, p. 276; F4003 7 Dec. 1738, 20 Feb. 1739, etc.

76 See Hecht, *The Domestic Servant Class*; Earle, *The Making of English Middle Class*, pp. 218–29; Earle, *A City Full of People*, pp. 38–54, 123–30. For London's place in this period, see E. A. Wrigley, 'A Simple Model of London's Importance in Changing English Society and Economy 1650–1750', *Past and Present* 37 (1967), pp. 44–70.

77 There is no servant in my sample who received 'board wage'.

78 My account here is dependent on Genshiro Hiruta, *Hayari-yamai to kitsune-tsuki* [*Epidemics and Fox-Possession*] (Tokyo, 1985), a fascinating study of popular medical belief and practice in a village in early modern Japan.

79 Scull, *The Most Solitary of Afflictions*, p. 29.

7

FAMILIAL CARE OF 'IDIOT' CHILDREN IN VICTORIAN ENGLAND[1]

David Wright

I

Investigation into familial care of the insane in Victorian England lies in neglected land between three fertile fields of research: historical demography, the history of medicine, and the history of women's work. Historical demographers have traditionally examined fertility, nuptiality, and mortality and, in so far as they have investigated the affective relationships within and between families, these have been inferred from patterns of household formation.[2] Historians of medicine have explored various dimensions of individual mental hospitals,[3] the seemingly inexorable expansion of the asylum system,[4] the writings of eminent medical men,[5] and the struggle for professional dominance.[6] Treatment has tended to be narrowly defined as *institutional* treatment by a recognized medical elite. Historians of women's work have been most sensitive to issues of caring within the household, especially regarding children and the aged, but have shied away from issues of 'medical' care for disabled members.[7] Oral history studies have begun to uncover the exchange of caring duties between working mothers, but since this methodology was developed only in the 1970s, the historical period covered rarely predates the 1890s.[8]

Patterns of historical enquiry are always deeply immersed in the waters of contemporary interest or controversy. The history of care for those deemed 'insane' is certainly no exception. The critical re-evaluation over the last ten years of 'care in the community' for the mentally ill and mentally handicapped[9] has sparked historical interest in the relationship between the history of the family, the care of the 'insane', and the role of women's informal and unpaid work. This policy crisis, and a general disenchantment with the 'social control' approach to historical institutions, prompted Michael Ignatieff, the historian of Victorian penitentiaries, to re-evaluate custody and the 'deviant' in the light of the history of the family.[10] He challenged social historians to adopt a more dynamic approach to interpreting the relationship between familial and institutional 'social control'. Following his lead, Mark Finnane replied, in a prescient essay, that the family was the key to understanding the institutional committal of the insane in the nineteenth century: 'the asylum operated as a particular type of intervention in family life and the lives of those without familial context'.[11]

This new approach has begun to bear fruit. John Walton traced what he termed the 'casting out' and 'bringing back' of pauper lunatics, using, as his case study, the Lancaster pauper lunatic asylum. He argued that the county lunatic asylum was not the primary receptacle of 'casting out'; rather, it was merely the most extreme of a variety of options open to the family, options which also included boarding-out, confining a 'mad' relative within one's house or that of a relative, or illegally paying strangers to supervise a family member.[12] Charlotte MacKenzie, in her monograph on the private Ticehurst Asylum, noted that the Victorian rich had more options, including single confinement, home nursing, and 'exotic' trips abroad.[13] Nancy Tomes detailed how families adopted strategies of coping and caring for the insane prior to admitting relatives to the Pennsylvania Asylum; families resorted to the Asylum 'having exhausted all alternative forms of treatment'.[14] These historians, and others working on the early modern period,[15] have suggested that investigating the breakdown of the family system of care would lead to a greater understanding of the process of institutional committal.

This paper seeks to broaden the discussion of the nature of caring and treatment of the insane in Victorian England by studying problems posed by, and family strategies taken to cope with, 'idiot' children. It will investigate the pre-institutional experiences of 475 families of children admitted to the National Asylum for Idiots, Earlswood, the first purpose-built asylum for the education and treatment of idiot children in England.[16] It will *not* look at factors which influenced families to seek institutional care; rather, it will concentrate on the problems presented to the household economy by these children and on strategies families took to control and accommodate strange and deviant behaviour.

In doing so it will attempt to place the history of insanity within the context of patterns of care and kinship of the Victorian family outlined in other works and, particularly, the role of women and young daughters in the caring nexus of the household.

This paper argues that, despite the preoccupation of historians with the expanding asylum system, the nuclear family persisted as the primary locus of care for idiots throughout the nineteenth century. Secondly, reinforcing other evidence as to the relative responsibility of mothers and elder daughters for the care of the aged,[17] it argues that these individuals were primarily responsible for most of the 'caring' of idiot children. A strict gender division would, however, be misleading: fathers and sons had important roles to play, especially in the control of violent or disruptive behaviour within the household. Finally, the paper questions the widely held view that, amongst working-class households, reciprocal exchanges between neighbours and kin were as common as has been suggested by recent oral history.

II

The Asylums Act and Lunatics Act of 1845 have received attention primarily as the culmination of the medical profession's campaign to claim exclusive jurisdiction over the formal treatment of idiots, lunatics, or persons of unsound mind – the statutory definition of the insane.[18] This is no doubt an important theme in the history of medicine: licensed homes, hospitals, and asylums receiving insane persons were required to hire a medical man as chief institutional officer; certificates of insanity, the prerequisite for admission, had to be signed by medical practitioners; and the national inspectorate, the Lunacy Commission, was staffed partly by ex-medical superintendents of county asylums. But part of the cornucopia of statistics generated by the Lunacy Commission included returns of the insane kept 'at home' or 'with friends', signifying an informal market of care and treatment, largely outside the control of this national inspectorate. In 1859, the national returns indicated that 5,920 insane persons were 'residing with relatives or others', a number which the Lunacy Commissioners admitted was a gross underestimation.[19] Since legal or medical papers were not required by law for individuals kept with relatives, there are no documents with which to compare the care, diet, treatment, and use of restraint in the community with that in the formal asylum. Historians must rely on the accounts of middle-class diarists or the few insane themselves who later wrote about their experiences. However, it would be wrong to dismiss documents central to institutional committal as merely reflecting accepted and uncontested 'medical' observations. Indeed, as will be shown, two rarely used sets of admission documents may help uncover informal networks of care and supervision prior to institutional committal.[20]

The principal document for the purposes of this chapter is the Victorian Certificate of Insanity. The Certificate for non-pauper patients was a single, bifurcated sheet of paper, with duplicated sections for each of the two medical practitioners to fill in. After stating the date, his qualification, type of medical practice, and address, the doctor would classify the person as 'a lunatic, idiot or person of unsound mind', and then state his 'facts indicating insanity'. Below, he was obliged to fill out 'other facts indicating insanity communicated to me by others', and state by whom. Consequently, the second section usually read: 'Mother states . . . ' or ' . . . by the Father'; for example, 'the Mother[,] Mary Edward[,] states that he [her son] cannot dress himself and will play with fire and coal and cannot be left alone'. It is noteworthy, then, that the Certificates of Insanity allocated as much space to the comments of parents as they did to those of medical practitioners. In contrast to Certificates of Insanity for county pauper lunatic asylums, which were often signed by a handful of 'experts' associated with the institution, the Certificates for the Earlswood Asylum, a charitable institution, were filled in by local medical practitioners who were not 'experts' in medico-psychology. In theory, at least, this would make them less likely to 'override' comments of parents.[21] The format of the Certificates remained unchanged from 1853 to 1886, the period under study.[22]

The second admission document was an 'Order for the Reception of a Private Patient' (hereafter Reception Order), a document giving permission to the asylum superintendent to accept a patient under certain conditions.[23] These Reception Orders acted as 'medical' profiles of admissions, but nevertheless contain great quantities of 'social' and 'demographic' information about future inmates and the circumstances prior to their committal. For the purposes of this paper, four questions asked are relevant: the inmate's 'previous place of abode'; 'when and where previously under care and treatment'; 'duration of existing attack'; and 'whether subject to epilepsy'. In the case of idiot children, the Reception Orders were invariably signed by a guardian (usually the father) and the handwriting reveals that the information was usually filled out by him or her.

Since the address of the inmates at the committal is given on their respective Certificates of Insanity and Reception Orders, record linkage between these asylum admission documents of 1861, 1871, and 1881 and the family entries in the enumerators' schedules of the same year is quite straightforward.[24] Of the 203 families or kin admitting children in these census years, 134 (66 per cent) were located, giving additional information about the composition of the household, and specific detailed information about the informant. The results of the 475 families, including the 134 'linked' families, were analysed by means of a relational database. This technique of record linkage, therefore, gives the historian the best of both worlds – quantitative data on the composition of households, and rich, qualitative material revealing some affective and dependent relationships between household members and non-coresiding kin.[25]

One final word on the Earlswood Asylum and its inmates. The Asylum was built in 1853 near Redhill, Surrey, for the education and training of idiot children of the 'middle classes' and the 'respectable poor'. Inmates were admitted to the Earlswood Asylum on three payment statuses: *elected* patients, who were admitted free of charge for a fixed five-year period; *reduced* fee-paying patients, who were admitted at a subsidized rate; and *private* patients, who paid at least the £50 per annum required for non-subsidized institutional care. Consequently the occupations given by male guardians included illiterate unskilled labourers, members of the Labour Aristocracy, clerks and grocers, and a handful of private, fee-paying patients. This variety of socio-economic background was matched by a wide distribution across England and Wales and a reasonable balance between children previously living in villages, small market towns, and urban centres. The Asylum admitted twice as many boys as girls and the population grew from 200 to close to 500 inmates in the 1870s. The average age of admission (by yearly cohorts) varied between 9 and 11 years and the length of stay varied between five and seven years.[26]

III

An analysis of the 'linked' families strongly suggests that the environment of caring for idiot children seems to be the household of the parents. Eighty-four per cent of children were present in their household on census night.[27] The *type* of household seems to be overwhelmingly that of the nuclear family: 85 per cent of these linked households were primary coresiding families without kin.[28] These 'snapshots' of residential patterns are complemented by information from the Reception Orders indicating the duration of coresidence: the overwhelming majority of idiot children had been indicated as 'always at home' or 'always lived with parents'. Previous institutional stay for any child of the sample years was rare: apart from the 10 per cent of all sample children who were readmissions to Earlswood, only 5 per cent were indicated as having *ever* stayed in a hospital or another asylum. This reinforces other more fragmentary evidence of 'national' or 'regional' studies which suggest that the insane, including idiots, were most likely integrated members of a primary family prior to institutional committal.[29]

What of the 'missing' 16 per cent of children – those not in their households on census night? One might logically assume some sort of Poor Law supervision; however, the Earlswood Asylum did not accept any pauper patients. These absent children, consequently, must have been boarded-out or out-nursed in the informal economy of care and supervision which so vexed the Commissioners in Lunacy.[30] Here, the 'previous treatment' category of the Reception Order fills in some missing information. Henry Markley had been boarded-out by his father, a Hackney butcher, with 'friends' in the 'recent past'.[31] Similarly, Fleming Brook, a shopkeeper in Castleford, Yorkshire, had his ten-year-old daughter, Kate, 'out-nursed' for three years before her admission to the asylum, despite the fact that Fleming Brook had a 'general servant' enumerated in his household.[32] It should be noted that these twenty-one families with 'missing' children range across the occupational spectrum. There also does not appear to be any gender specificity to boarding-out.[33]

As for the few extended families, these types of household appear often in cases where one of the parents of the child had died. Thus Thomas Kendrick, a 33-year-old 'cigar maker', lived with his widowed sister who had, according to the 1871 schedule, two 'imbecile sons', one of whom had a habit of setting his clothes on fire.[34] Jane Aldridge, a widow 'housekeeper' in the Horsham census of 1871, cared for Eva, her 13-year-old idiot daughter, whilst living with two brothers, one of whom was 'deaf and dumb from birth'.[35] These extended families imply, as has been suggested elsewhere, that widows and widowers adopted strategies of household formation in 'critical life situations', specifically the integration of an unmarried kin of the opposite sex.[36] Thus, although lodgers were present in a mere 17 per cent of *all* 'linked' households, this frequency doubled in cases of households headed by a widow or widower.

Caring within the household by those listed as servants was an option for better-off families. Henry Frayling who, as a Clerk to the Lord Chief Justice, would have been firmly in the middle ranks of society, admitted his son, Henry, after the death of his wife in 1871. Prior to his wife's death, two 'temporary nurses' were enumerated in his household, presumably with responsibility for the boy.[37] The Fraylings were one of fifteen families with servants who were also listed as 'nurses' in the occupation column of the census. More problematic is the existence of a further forty-three households (30 per cent) with domestic servants listed as 'general servants' in the occupation column. These individuals were mostly single or pairs of servants in families headed by small shopkeepers and clerks. Michael Anderson has suggested that these individuals, as well as 'unoccupied' female residents and lodgers, would have been available for general caring responsibilities, but their precise role in the caring and supervision of idiot children is not at all clear from the certificates. If they did assist in caring, then their assistance was probably ancillary.[38] It almost goes without saying that families headed by agricultural labourers, drovers, shepherds, and other unskilled workers had no recourse to servants.

IV

The picture which emerges, then, is an environment of caring which centres on the primary coresiding family. If this is accurate, how can we more firmly determine *who* was doing the caring within the household, and what dimensions this caring took? In line with most general surveys of women's unpaid work within the household and 'prescriptive' ideologies of the mother-as-carer,[39] the primary responsibility of caring for idiot children seems to have fallen disproportionately on mothers and elder daughters. The first set of evidence for this stems from the testimony given to the local medical practitioners. While the father tended to sign the Reception Order, it was disproportionately mothers and sisters of the patient who, in the Certificates of Insanity, retold stories of household dependence, disruption, and deviance. Of the certificates in which the informant is given, doctors noted the testimony as coming from the mother in 51 per cent of certificates, compared to 20 per cent as from the father. Similarly sisters outnumbered brothers nearly three to one.[40] This reinforces the perception that, even in poorer families, there were 'understood' responsibilities: the father as head of the household signed the Reception Order; mothers discussed issues of caring for dependent members. This does not mean, however, that caring was exclusively a female domain: there are too many examples in the certificates of brothers and fathers intervening to control violence or aggression. It was, however, disproportionately the prerogative of mothers and daughters.

Ellen Ross has argued that the years of 6 to 12 were 'caretaker' years, when the daughter or son was responsible for running errands, child-minding, and ancillary domestic assistance.[41] The frequency with which brothers and sisters were used as carers depended upon the nature of the mother's employment. If she was required to be absent at certain times of the day or for parts of the year, then the other children were expected to step in and take over.[42] Sisters were often mentioned as assisting in feeding the dependent child – an easy enough task if the receiver obliged, but shrieks and violent behaviour could greet those feeding uncooperative siblings. As Diana Gittins has demonstrated, caring often fell to elder daughters who had not been released into the 'formal economy' or marriage.[43] Thus Emma Offer, a 30-year-old unmarried governess still living with her parents, told a certifying practitioner how her 14-year-old sister, Adele, was 'not able to dress herself, [or] able to cut up her own food [and was] incapable of taking care of herself'.[44] This may well be an example of how even grown women, if still unmarried and residing with their parents, owed 'allegiance' as carers for members of that household.[45]

The second most commonly cited problem was associated with dressing. Sarah Roberts of Notting Hill noted her son's inability to dress himself and his being 'entirely dependent on the help of other persons'. His two older brothers may have helped, but since they were employed outside the household as clerks, it is more likely that the mother attended to most of his needs.[46] Many children unable to dress themselves would have been subsumed under the more general category of 'not being able to care for themselves'.

Toileting and general 'hygiene' represented the third area to which the onerous duties of caring had to be directed. The brother of Henry Brooks informed the local practitioner that Henry had been unable to 'hold his urine or faeces for going on eight years',[47] and others complained of the constant 'soiling of bed and dress' requiring extra washing duties.[48] Some idiot children 'made known their wants by screaming', at which time certain unnamed family members had to render assistance.[49] Families of the middle classes spoke delicately of their son's or daughter's 'inattention to the calls of nature'. One mother recounted the problems of toileting by saying that her daughter, when requiring 'relief of the bladder or bowels', would in the street ask strangers to 'unfasten her drawers'.[50] Families could do little but improvise. Alfred Wand stated that because his son had a tendency to 'pass urine involuntarily', a 'receptacle' was kept constantly at hand.[51]

Assistance in feeding, dressing, and toileting represented direct intervention of family members, often at specific times of the day, and was, no doubt, hindered by the incapability of many of these children to 'make known their wants' or 'understand any question'. Caring, however, often included an informal supervisory role. The ubiquity of fire and coal in the homes of all social classes presented a challenge to families needing to keep a watch over the erratic and, at times, unpredictable behaviour of a member. Some children were guilty of 'playing with fire' or 'putting things into the fire'; others had a habit of injuring themselves by either setting fire to their clothes or directly burning themselves.[52] Mary Blagrove seems to have suffered from the stresses of such supervision. A 'glazier's wife' in Reading, she had not only to watch over her daughter Mary, who was 'constantly getting into the fire and coal', but also to care for two other children described as idiots in the Certificate of Insanity and as 'dumb from birth' in the 1861 Census.[53] This required family members to keep the child away from the hearth or, in another case, from laying his hands on Lucifer matches. The possibility of the child's 'carrying the fire' to different parts of the home had obvious dangerous consequences.[54] Clare Banner testified to the doctor that her sister once took a lighted branch from the fire up into her bedroom and crawled under the bed.[55] Even the habit of lighting paper, ostensibly for amusement, would be enough to cause families grave concern. As with 4-year-old Louisa Adams, the daughter of a farm bailiff in Fletching, Sussex, such an indifference to the danger of fire could require 'constant care and watching' by one or more members of the family.[56] These issues, however, were not entirely novel: as Akihito Suzuki notes in his study of institutional committal of the insane in early modern London, the concern over fire or arson revealed by families petitioning Quarter Sessions animated discussion about insanity and family care for hundreds of years.[57]

Uncontrollable 'excitability' could also pose particular problems to families. Mrs Barker stated that Edward was 'of a very excitable temperament, and is obliged to keep knives and other instruments out of his way'.[58] Children tore clothes, ripped the bindings off books, spilled boiling water on others or on themselves, threw knives randomly, upset chairs, broke furniture, hid under beds with burning articles, and performed 'all sorts of mischief' not further defined in the Certificates. The complete Certificate for James gives one the impression of the range of 'mischief' detailed to the first local medical practitioner consulted:

1 He is never quiet, he is always crowing like a cock or barking as a dog;
2 He tears his clothes to pieces, cuts up all the apron strings and boot laces he can get;
3 He has thrown the school keys, hammer and hard bill down the privy;
4 He throws anything he can get at at any person or thing to which he takes a disliking;

and to the second practitioner:

He runs away all day without his clothes if he can get away. He strangled a rabbit . . . because it bit him when feeding it. Took a lighted branch from the fire into the bedroom and crawled under the bed with it. Requires constant care to prevent his doing improbable acts of mischief.[59]

As many mothers and fathers testified, vigilance was the only recourse. With demands on the time from the family, it is not surprising that many, like George Wheeler, a gardener from Hammersmith, complained to medical practitioners that the rest of the family were obliged to keep watch constantly over his daughter.[60] Mothers complained to their doctors that their idiot children would eat anything – rotten apples, dirt, coal – or that they would feed turpentine to unsuspecting baby siblings.[61] Lucy Pinchard, a widow from Exeter, admitted to the certifying medical practitioner that her 9-year-old son 'requires constant watching, giving more trouble than a baby'.[62]

Behaviour usually described as 'spiteful' or 'passionate' included biting, slapping, and pushing other children or the mother. In these cases, those charged with caring were also prime targets for injury. When Alfred Curters, a 'clerk in Holy Orders' presented his 18-year-old daughter, Ellen Curters, to his local medical practitioner in Dover, he testified that Ellen had 'shown a strong propensity to injure her own brothers and sisters'. It is notable that Ellen is the eldest of the four siblings in the enumerator's schedule, suggesting a possible problem for families with violent or aggressive children but no older child in the household to intervene.[63] Even 'occasional' or 'threatened' violence could force families to take pre-emptive action such as restraint or confinement within the home. A quotation from one case of inspection by a Commission in Lunacy gives an example of home restraint:

> The cottage, externally and internally, was in a state of great dilapidation, and presented an aspect of extreme poverty. The Idiot is about six years of age; and of the other children living with their parents, five in number, the youngest is now only eight months old. The parents appeared to be very respectable and kindly disposed, but obviously not in a position properly to maintain and take care of their poor Idiot Child, who, on account of her restlessness and violent agitation, and for her own protection, had been during the past two years kept in restraint day and night. . . . When seen by the Visiting Commissioner she was lying in a cradle crying out and beating her head and face, and with her arms, legs, and body confined by bands.[64]

Exceptional investigations like these tend to suggest, as Mark Finnane has implied in his work on post-famine Ireland, that restraint could be as much a device in poorer households as in formal mental institutions.[65]

Approximately one-tenth of the Reception Orders note the presence of epileptic fits.[66] Caroline Diplock of Southampton testified to the local practitioner that her 'deaf and dumb' son, Henry, remained in a 'disturbed' state after 'constant' fits and would slap his elder sister.[67] The seizures themselves varied enormously in frequency and severity – 'four or five times a day', 'twice a day', 'daily', 'frequent', 'once a week'. The 'prostration of mind', 'falling', or general state of 'mental torpor' which came in the aftermath of a seizure necessitated watching day and night.[68] One mother alluded to the injuries sustained by her child because of losing consciousness and falling during an 'attack'.[69] It was for the treatment of epilepsy and not for the general mental disability of the child that local medical practitioners were called in periodically to prescribe medicines or special diets. Stephen Ward, a chemist and druggist from Leicester, had his epileptic son treated at home by a Dr Jackson.[70] In these cases, names and addresses of individual practitioners were listed under the 'previous treatment' column of the Reception Orders. Included are local surgeons, surgeon-apothecaries and parish doctors.[71] Sometimes a visit to the home was followed by out-patient 'treatment' at a local infirmary or dispensary, the Cheltenham, Bristol, and Clapham Dispensaries all receiving future inmates of Earlswood when they were younger. More specialized treatment at the London Epileptic Hospital or the Children's Hospital on Great Ormond Street was rarer and tended to be short, often no more than a few months.[72] The vast majority of responses to the question of whether the prospective inmate had ever been under 'previous treatment' gave simply 'never' or 'only under parents', reinforcing the point made earlier that the family was the primary locus of care for idiocy.

V

So far this discussion has detailed caring, control and supervision of idiot children within the physical confines of the household – but what of the division between household and neighbourhood? It has often been implied that, in the absence of asylum treatment, the insane were free to wander about the community unchecked. This implication seems to have been made by historians as a rhetorical foil for the incarceration of the insane in purpose-built institutions, rather than as an accurate description of how communities responded to aberrant and unsocial behaviour. Many relatives detailed previous experiences of their son's or daughter's wandering from home and getting lost. Henry Markwick, a carpenter from Brighton, stated that his 17-year-old daughter, 'cannot be left alone; if left alone would stray away and could not find her way back again',[73] and there are a few testimonies of children's straying or getting lost, and staying out overnight.[74] John Twiddy had a habit of wandering into other people's houses; so too did Walter Price, who was often found in a neighbour's bed.[75] Twelve-year-old Thomas Carney would run naked through the street of St Pancras, London, 'without evincing any shame'.[76]

More seriously, family members feared that the child was not capable of perceiving danger. Besides being 'unable to be left alone for any time', John Evington, according to his father, 'has always evinced a strong desire to run into the Humber'.[77] One young woman told the doctor that, 'if a horse, carriage or cart was coming quickly along the road she [her sister] would not draw to one side to get out of danger', while another boy actively endeavoured to 'throw himself under the wheels of carriages' passing by.[78] As a consequence, one infers from the Certificates of Insanity, that houses themselves became informal 'asylums', outside which the child was not allowed to go unattended. On the other hand, there are many cases of children's being sent to a parish, 'ragged', or national school (and often being sent home). Some certifying medical practitioners alluded to instances of coming into contact with the idiot children in the neighbourhood. One such child, James Cox, seemed to have been a frequent caller at this local doctor's home: 'frequently following after me and telling me to go and see persons, saying they have sent [him] when such is not the case, coming to my door and asking for victuals, after he has had sufficient at home'.[79] And in only one of six instances of neighbours testifying in the Certificates of Insanity, community members of Shrivenham confirmed the 'strange occurrences' witnessed by the medical practitioner of one local idiot.[80]

VI

The permanence of idiocy was a crucial factor in differentiating it from lunacy.[81] It also had important implications for the patterns of caring within the household. The Reception Orders queried the 'duration of attack', a question which was conceived, presumably, with lunatics in mind. Nevertheless, parents interpreted it in one of two ways: the duration of epileptic fits or the duration of the disability. In the latter case, most simply said: 'always been an idiot', or 'idiot from birth'. Some Certificates of Insanity allude to a deteriorating condition – 'been worse of late' – but the fragmentary nature of these descriptions precludes any conclusion that in many of these cases things were getting worse. In fact, parents were frustrated by the stasis and the day-in day-out caring while their other children, and their neighbours' children, grew up and assumed their responsibilities in the natural life-cycle of their respective families.

The implications of the permanent dependence were noted by contemporaries. John Conolly, a famous champion of non-restraint and member of the Earlswood Board of Governors, alluded to the changing nature of care over the life-cycle of the family, when describing the 'typical' poor family seeking admission for their child at the asylum:

> You will find it [the child] in winter placed by the fire, and in summer by the door, seated in a little chair, or lying in a little bed . . . It cannot dress itself, nor feed itself, nor feel itself in any way . . . The matter of admiration is, that this imperfect little creature, which only entails privations upon them, is still to them an object of even peculiarly tender solicitude . . . [they] seem to love their afflicted brother or sister more than they love each other. They watch it, they protect it from danger, they try to amuse it, they draw it about, and they give it some of their own little portions of food. With increased stature and strength, however, the necessity of labour comes upon them. One by one they go from home, and support themselves. The poor imbecile alone remains and becomes an even heavier burden to its father and mother when years are gathering over them.[82]

Conolly's sentimental portrayal of the typical Earlswood family was designed as much to elicit contributions to the asylum as to depict the crisis of caring within the household. Yet it does raise issues of caring over the lifespan of the family and of how the responsibilities changed as siblings grew older.[83] Space does not permit a more detailed discussion of the importance of the family life-cycle to the problems of caring. Suffice to say, however, that a crisis of care in the family could well be predicated upon certain demographic features such as the absence of elder children in the household. It also calls into question the notion of one care-giver. It is more likely that, as the family 'aged', and as daughters and sons left the household to marry or take up paid employment, the duties of caring may well have been transferred from one sibling to another. This, naturally, raises the question, as Conolly hinted above, of what the ageing parents did with an 'adult idiot', still dependent on them for care. The importance of life-course transitions and the ability of households to adapt to changing economic circumstances need to be more fully investigated. Historians of caring would do well to look at two other developments: the decline in fertility and the rise of compulsory elementary education. Both of these factors must have had a profound impact on the availability of children during their 'caretaker' years and, hence, on the ability of these children to assist in caring for dependent and disabled family members.[84]

VII

Within the history of medicine and the history of the family, two debates persist about the care of the insane and the care of dependants: to what extent did formal medical institutions replace the family as society's response to the problem of insanity, and to what extent was caring for dependent family members restricted to the 'autonomous' nuclear family?[85] Victorian households constituted the primary locus of care for idiots both prior to, and in lieu of, institutional confinement. Previous institutional treatment and long-stay confinement were both rare. Boarding-out and out-nursing did occur, across class divides, but this research suggests that they represented a minority of cases. Widowed families tended to combine with kin in the household to fulfil the role of the absent or dead parent: caring by kin when primary families were intact seems the exception rather than the rule.

A common complaint about the analysis of enumerators' schedules is that they overemphasize the importance of the household at the expense of kin and neighbourhood networks.[86] Similarly it is a possibility that the process of testifying during the certification of idiocy (and insanity) downplayed the role of local caring networks, and that these admission documents, like the census schedules, exaggerate the importance of household members in the 'mixed economy of welfare'. On the other hand, there were no restrictions or specifications as to who should testify to the local medical practitioner. Nowhere on the Certificate of Insanity does it state that the informant had to be the guardian or even a member of the household. Considering the overwhelming preponderance of household members in the process of certification and committal, it is possible that the idyll of the benevolent working-class neighbour sharing in the burden of care, which has been highlighted by recent oral histories, may be somewhat exaggerated.

A second qualification about using Certificates of Insanity, Reception Orders, and census schedules to understand the complex matrix of care in an industrializing society is that the admission records testify to the problems of families who would eventually seek an institutional solution to their problem. Thus, like early modern Poor Law accounts, these records are biased in favour of the *failures* of family care, rather than the successes. Consequently, it is possible to speculate that the picture of those families seeking institutional confinement may be biased toward those household units who had few kinship supports.

Thirdly, the nature of the certificates is such that problems of care are intermixed with the 'indications of insanity' required by law. Thus they are not intended explicitly to describe patterns of care and supervision in the past. This being said, the linkage of traditional demographic sources, such as the census schedules, and the more nuanced and flexible 'medical-administrative records' provides a multi-dimensional approach which can both reveal aggregate results and highlight interesting individual cases. Since these admission documents were required by law for all patients admitted to all types of asylum – private, charitable, and pauper – they provide rare insights into problems posed by, and strategies used to cope with, insane relatives across class divides.

Much remains to be researched, especially how caring varied over time, by class, geographical location, and family life cycle. To explore these variables, regional or local studies of care and supervision will probably be much more effective in understanding the 'complex web' of caring than 'national' studies such as the one undertaken in this paper. Furthermore, it is paramount that historians investigate more thoroughly the patterns of *discharge* from formal institutions rather than focusing almost exclusively on the admission process. It is only by examining the ex-inmate's

191

reintegration (or lack thereof) into the community that historians will begin to demystify the asylum as a 'museum' of madness, and understand the formal institution as only one part of a larger life-long strategy families used to care for dependent members in the Victorian era.

NOTES

1 The author would like to thank the Royal Earlswood Hospital (formerly the National Asylum for Idiots, Earlswood) and the Surrey Record Office for kind permission to quote from the hospital records.

2 M. Anderson, *Family Structure in Nineteenth Century Lancashire* (London, 1971), esp. ch. 6; P. Laslett, *The World We Have Lost – Further Explored* (London, 1983); P. Laslett and R. Wall (eds), *Household and Family in Past Time* (Cambridge, 1972); E. A. Wrigley (ed.), *Nineteenth Century Society: Essays in the Use of Quantitative Methods for the Study of Social Data* (Cambridge, 1972); L. Bonfield, R. M. Smith, and K. Wrightson (eds), *The World We Have Gained: Histories of Population and Social Structure* (Oxford, 1986). Cf. Cavallo, this volume.

3 Monographs on individual asylums are too numerous to mention. Notable books, however, are: R. Hunter and I. MacAlpine, *Psychiatry for the Poor: 1851 Colney Hatch Asylum – Friern Hospital 1973, a Medical and Social History* (Folkestone, 1974); A. Digby, *Madness, Morality and Medicine: a History of the York Retreat, 1792–1914* (Cambridge, 1985); C. MacKenzie, *Psychiatry for the Rich: a History of Ticehurst Private Asylum, 1792–1917* (London, 1992).

4 A. Scull, *Museums of Madness: the Social Organization of Insanity in Nineteenth Century England* (London, 1979), and *The Most Solitary of Afflictions: Madness and Society in Britain, 1700–1900* (New Haven, CT, and London, 1993); D. J. Mellett, *The Prerogative of Asylumdom: Social, Cultural and Administrative Aspects of the Institutional Treatment of the Insane in Nineteenth Century Britain* (London, 1982).

5 R. Hunter and I. MacAlpine, *Three Hundred Years of Psychiatry, 1535–1860* (London, 1963); F. Alexander and S. Selesnick, *The History of Psychiatry: an Evaluation of Psychiatric Thought and Practice from Prehistoric Times to the Present* (New York, 1966); V. Skultans, *Madness and Morals: Ideas on Insanity in the Nineteenth Century* (London, 1975), and *English Madness, Ideas on Insanity, 1580–1890* (London, 1979).

6 A. Scull (ed.), *Madhouses, Mad-Doctors and Madmen: the Social History of Psychiatry in the Victorian Era* (Philadelphia, 1981); W. F. Bynum, R. Porter, and M. Shepherd (eds), *The Anatomy of Madness: Essays in the History of Psychiatry*, 3 vols (London, 1985–8).

7 L. Tilly and J. Scott, *Women, Work and Family* (London, 1978); J. Lewis, *Women in England, 1870–1950: Sexual Division and Social Change* (Brighton, 1984); J. Lewis (ed.), *Labour and Love: Women's Experience of Home and Family 1850–1940* (Oxford, 1986), and its 'twin' volume, A. John (ed.), *Unequal Opportunities: Women's Employment in England,*

1800–1918 (Oxford, 1986); E. Roberts, *Women's Work, 1840–1940* (London, 1988); J. Rendall, *Women in an Industrializing Society: England, 1750–1880* (Oxford, 1990); P. Hudson and W. R. Lee (eds), *Women's Work and the Family Economy in Historical Perspective* (Manchester, 1990).

8   E. Roberts, *A Woman's Place: an Oral History of Working Class Women, 1890–1940* (Oxford, 1985).

9   A. Scull, *Decarceration: Community Treatment and the Deviant, a Radical View* (2nd edn, Oxford, 1984); A. Scull and S. Cohen (eds), *Social Control and the State: Historical and Comparative Essays* (Oxford, 1988); F. M. L. Thomson, 'Social Control in Modern Britain', in A. Digby and C. Feinstein (eds), *New Directions in Economic and Social History*, vol. 1 (Basingstoke, 1989), pp. 182–95; HMSO, *'Better Off in the Community?': the Care of People who are Seriously Mentally Ill*, Health Committee, First Report, vol. 1 (London, 1994); *The Report of the Inquiry into the Care and Treatment of Christopher Clunis* (London, 1994). Cf. Thompson, this volume.

10   M. Ignatieff, 'Total Institutions and Working Classes: a Review Essay', *History Workshop Journal* 15 (1983), pp. 172–3.

11   M. Finnane, 'Asylums, Families and the State', *History Workshop Journal* 20 (1985), p. 135.

12   J. K. Walton, 'Casting Out and Bringing Back in Victorian England: Pauper Lunatics, 1840–70', in Bynum, Porter, and Shepherd (eds), *The Anatomy of Madness*, vol. 2, pp. 132–46.

13   MacKenzie, *Psychiatry for the Rich*. See also, for the role of family in the committal process in New South Wales, S. Garton, *Medicine and Madness: a Social History of Insanity in New South Wales, 1880–1949* (Kensington, Australia, 1988), pp. 31–2, 47, 98.

14   N. Tomes, *A Generous Confidence: Thomas Story Kirkbride and the Art of Asylum Keeping, 1840–1883* (Cambridge, 1985), pp. 103–8.

15   P. Rushton, 'Lunatics and Idiots: Mental Disability, the Community, and the Poor Law in North-East England, 1600–1800', *Medical History* 32 (1988), pp. 34–50; A. Suzuki, this volume.

16   These years are: 1856, 1861, 1866, 1871, 1876, 1881, 1886.

17   Roberts, *Women's Work*, pp. 169–81; E. Ross, 'Survival Networks: Women's Neighbourhood Sharing in London before World War I', *History Workshop Journal* 15 (1983), pp. 4–27; E. Ross, 'Labour and Love: Rediscovering London's Working-Class Mothers, 1870–1918', in Lewis, *Labour and Love*, p. 85. For a contemporary perspective, see J. Lewis and B. Meredith, *Daughters who Care: Daughters Caring for Mothers at Home* (London, 1988).

18   Scull, *Museums of Madness*, pp. 163, 172, ch. 5.

19   Parliamentary Papers, *Fifty-fourth Report of the Commissioners in Lunacy to the Lord Chancellor* (London, 1900), vol. 37, p. 89.

20   All the medical Certificates of Insanity and Orders for the Reception of a Private Patient for the Earlswood Asylum are located in the Surrey Record Office (SRO) under the title 'Admission Papers' (SRO 392/21) and bundled by year of admission. Hereafter, references to Certificates of Insanity and Reception Orders will be given by name of inmate and year of admission.

21 I shall hereafter refer to the individuals giving testimony to the local medical practitioner as 'testifiers' or 'informants'.

22 Certificate Sched. (A) No. 2, Sects 4, 5, 8, 10, 11, 12, 13. In 1887, the Idiots Act required only one medical signature for the certification of idiots.

23 Order for the Reception of a Private Patient, Sched. (A) No. 1, Sects 4, 8. There were separate forms for the Pauper Reception Orders and Private Reception Orders.

24 The author is grateful to R. M. Smith for suggesting this technique. For a similar exercise in the linkage of hospital admission records and the census enumerators' schedules, see M. Dupree, 'Family Care and Hospital Care: the "Sick Poor" in Nineteenth-Century Glasgow', *Social History of Medicine* 6 (1993), pp. 195–212.

25 Hereafter, when 'linked' households are being cited, the reference will include the Reception Order and the Certificate of Insanity and then the Public Record Office reference number (series RG) for the enumerator's schedule of that household.

26 D. Wright, 'The National Asylum for Idiots, Earlswood, 1847–1886', D.Phil. thesis (Oxford, 1993), chs 2, 3, 8.

27 Of the 134 households located: 107 children were present, twenty-one were not present, and six were families whose children were admitted before census night and therefore excluded from this calculation.

28 Out of the 134 linked households, the numbers are: sixty-two (50 per cent) Primary Coresiding Families (PCF); fifty-one (35 per cent) PCF with at least one non-relative present; eighteen (13 per cent) Extended Coresiding Families (ECF); four (3 per cent), two non-related coresiding families. Taken from those admitted to Earlswood between the day of the census and the end of that calendar year regardless of whether the child was present or not. Households were defined, in line with common demographic practice, by including all individuals listed between respective 'heads' of households, excluding visitors. The similarity to Anderson's 1 per cent sample of the 1851 census is striking: Anderson found (for 1851) 50 per cent PCF, 28.4 per cent PCF with at least one non-relative of the head present, 17.8 per cent ECF. M. Anderson, 'Households, Families and Individuals in 1851: Some Preliminary Results from the National Sample from the 1851 Census of Great Britain', *Continuity and Change* 3 (1988), pp. 421–38.

29 M. Finnane's case study of 133 Admission Warrants for the Omagh District Asylum in Ireland revealed that 80 per cent were living with their nearest relative in a 'nuclear family'. Finanne, *Insanity and the Insane in Post-Famine Ireland* (London, 1981), p. 132. See also J. Saunders, 'Quarantining the Weak-Minded: Psychiatric Definitions of Degeneracy and the Late-Victorian Asylum', in Bynum, Porter, and Shepherd (eds), *The Anatomy of Madness*, vol. 3, p. 274.

30 'There is the strongest ground', declared the Commissioners in their Fourth Annual Report, 'for believing that a much larger number of persons of unsound mind are, in point of fact, deprived of their personal liberty, and kept under care and control as single patients

for hire or profit than the returns made to this office would otherwise indicate . . . ' Parliamentary Papers, *Fourth Report of the Commissioners in Lunacy* (London, 1850), vol. 23, p. 372.

31 Certificate of Insanity and Reception Order for Henry Markley, 1871; PRO, RG 10/317, 76a–77. See, however, for skilled artisans, the example of Alfred Wilden, the son of a blacksmith, who was boarded-out prior to his admission to Earlswood in 1886.

32 Certificate of Insanity and Reception Order for Kate Brook, 1871; RG 10/4639, 8.

33 The numbers are: six from families of unskilled labourers, three from skilled labourers, five from clerks and small shopkeepers, two from the professional classes, one from a widow family, and four from families where the father's occupation was not listed. Twelve boys and nine girls were 'missing', reflecting the larger number of boys admitted to the asylum.

34 Certificate of Insanity and Reception Order for Frederick Everitt, 1871; RG 10/535, 23.

35 Certificate of Insanity and Reception Order for Eva Aldridge, 1871; RG 10/1097, 77–8.

36 Anderson, *Family Structure*, pp. 144–6, Table 41.

37 Certificate of Insanity and Reception Order for Henry Frayling, 1871; RG 10/710, 55a.

38 Anderson, *Family Structure*, p. 74; E. Higgs, 'The Tabulation of Occupations in the Nineteenth Century Census with Special Reference to Domestic Servants', *Local Population Studies* 28 (1982), pp. 58–66.

39 Roberts, *Women's Work*, ch. 3; Rendall, *Women in an Industrializing Society*, ch. 2.

40 The testimony of *either* grandparents *or* neighbours *or* 'friends' occurs in less than 5 per cent of all certificates in which an informant's relationship to the idiot child is given.

41 Ross, 'Labour and Love', p. 85.

42 For an example of how caring duties of daughters in a rural setting could vary seasonally, see P. Horn, *Victorian Countrywomen* (Oxford, 1991), p. 26.

43 D. Gittins, 'Marital Status, Work and Kinship, 1850–1930', in Lewis, *Labour and Love*, p. 264.

44 Certificate of Insanity for Adele Offer, 1881; RG 11/736, 104a–5.

45 Gittins, 'Marital Status', p. 250.

46 Certificate of Insanity and Reception Order for William Roberts, 1871; RG 10/46, 10.

47 Certificate of Insanity for Henry Brooks, 1861.

48 Certificate of Insanity for Wilfred Bucknall, 1866.

49 Certificates of Insanity for John Evington and William Feesey, 1876.

50 Certificate of Insanity for Mary White, 1881.

51 Certificate of Insanity for Alfred Wand, 1881; RG 11/3157, p. 17a.

52 Certificate of Insanity for Thomas Woodcock, 1871, Clamida Smalls, 1856, or Frederick Everitt, 1871. 'Mary Ann Ashfield of 58 Russell St Bermondsey says that Emily Lewis had several times burned herself,

"yet will go and burn herself [again]"'. Certificate of Insanity for Emily Lewis, 1866.

53 The 1861 Census did not ask for the enumeration of idiots, imbeciles, or lunatics. This began in 1871 in response partly to the belief, as witnessed above, that idiot children were being returned as 'dumb'. My own research of future inmates of Earlswood suggests, however, that the labelling of 'idiot' children as 'dumb' was relatively uncommon. This research uncovered only two such cases out of a possible thirty-six. See Wright, 'Earlswood', ch. 7.

54 Certificate of Insanity for Ethel Watkins, 1886.

55 Certificate of Insanity for Amy Banner, 1866.

56 Certificate of Insanity for Louisa Adams, 1856.

57 Suzuki, this volume.

58 Certificate of Insanity for Edward Barker, 1871.

59 Certificate of Insanity for James Cox, 1861.

60 Certificate of Insanity for Alice Wheeler, 1881.

61 'His mother informs me that he puts everything which is given him into his mouth'. Certificate of Insanity for William Figg, 1876.

62 Certificate of Insanity for George Pinchard, 1881.

63 Certificate of Insanity for Ellen Curters/Curtis, 1861; RG 9/546, 114.

64 Parliamentary Papers, 'Report of the Visiting Commissioner to the House of a Village Shoemaker at Haracott, near Barnstaple, Barnstaple Union', *Nineteenth Report of the Commissioners in Lunacy* (London, 1865), vol. 21, p. 48.

65 Finnane, *Insanity*, pp. 141, 155–6.

66 This figure is lower than one might expect and is due to a policy of the Asylum Board of Governors to limit the numbers with high rates of epileptic fits because of the extra demands these placed on staff.

67 Certificate of Insanity and Reception Order for Henry Diplock, 1871; RG 10/1189, 146a–7.

68 The Commissioners in Lunacy recommended night attendants for all lunatic asylums because of the number of deaths of epileptics who, after having a seizure in the middle of the night, had suffocated themselves. Parliamentary Papers, *Twenty-Eighth Report of the Commissioners in Lunacy* (London, 1874), vol. 27, p. 36. See also Certificates of Insanity for Frederick Timbers, 1876, and William Jacobs, 1886.

69 Certificate of Insanity for Alfred Wand, 1881. See also James Baker, 1886.

70 Reception Orders for John Lees, 1861 and Stephen Ward, 1881.

71 See, for example, Reception Orders for Ellen Curters/Curtis, 1861, William Cooke, 1866, Gertrude Harding, 1871.

72 Reception Orders for Emily Lewis, Mary Shee, Willliam Taplin, 1866; Robert Campbell, 1871; Charles Wallis, 1871; Louisa Wheeler, 1881; Mary White, 1881. Jones Jones, admitted to Earlswood in 1866, 'on 1st attack was taken to the Dispensary at Wrexham for a short period'. Reception Order for 1866.

73 Certificate of Insanity for Henry Markwick, 1871.

74 Certificate of Insanity for Ephraim Day, 1861.

75 Certificate of Insanity for Walter Price, 1866.

76 Certificate of Insanity for Thomas Carney, 1856.
77 Certificate of Insanity for John Evington, 1876.
78 Certificate of Insanity for Benjamin Harrow, 1856.
79 Certificate of Insanity for James Cox, 1861.
80 Certificate of Insanity for Ephraim Day, 1861.
81 The 1845 Lunatics Act defined an idiot in the following manner. 'Every person whose mind from his birth by a perpetual infirmity is so deficient as to be incapable of directing him in any matter which requires thought or judgement, is in legal phraseology *an idiot.*' This definition was eventually widened to include also those who were idiot from sickness and infirmity 'from an early age'. 'Every person *qui gaudet lucidis intervallis*, and who sometimes is of good and sound memory, and sometimes *non compos mentis*, is in legal phraseology *a lunatic.*' C. P. Philips, *The Law Concerning Lunatics, Idiots and Persons of Unsound Mind* (London, 1858), pp. 1–2.
82 John Conolly, lecture to a Cambridge meeting, as quoted in J. Clarke, *A Memoir of John Conolly* (London, 1869), pp. 124–5.
83 Gittins, 'Marital Status', p. 264.
84 D. Gittins, *Fair Sex: Family Size and Structure 1900–39* (London, 1982), p. 52; Lewis, 'Introduction', *Labour and Love*, pp. 3–11.
85 For two recent contributions to these debates, see, respectively, A. Scull, '*Museums of Madness* Revisited', *Social History of Medicine* 6 (1993), pp. 3–23, and B. Reay, 'Kinship and the Neighbourhood in Nineteenth Century Rural England: the Myth of the Autonomous Nuclear Family', *Journal of Family History* 21 (1996), pp. 87–104.
86 G. Levi, 'Family and Kin: a Few Thoughts', *Journal of Family History* 15 (1990), 567–78.

8

COMMUNITY CARE AND THE CONTROL OF MENTAL DEFECTIVES IN INTER-WAR BRITAIN

Mathew Thomson

I

The history of caring has traditionally concentrated on the role of institutions, but historians of the nineteenth and twentieth centuries are also beginning to recognize the importance of care provided outside of institutions by the family, neighbourhood support networks, and formal agencies such as the Poor Law.[1] This 'care in the community' has always, in numerical terms, been the dominant form of care. On the other hand, it is also recognized that during the nineteenth century provision of institutional care began to dominate policy; reflecting this domination, the capacity of hospitals, reformatories, asylums, and workhouses expanded rapidly and the proportion of the British population in institutions peaked in the census of 1911.[2] Unsurprisingly, therefore, historians of late nineteenth- and early twentieth-century social policy have concentrated on care provided inside rather than outside of institutions. As a consequence the historiography of care in the community remains detached from histories of the emergence of 'community care' as policy. There has been a vigorous debate over the timing of, and rationale behind, this policy shift from institutional to community care; in particular, and of primary relevance to this essay, there has been heated debate over the emergence of community care for the mentally disordered. The shift has been variously attributed to therapeutic advance, a liberal critique of incarceration, or a cost-cutting manoeuvre in response to a crisis of welfare capitalism.[3] Where historians are in agreement

198

is that the transition occurs in the post-World War II period, probably in the late 1950s.[1] There is widespread acceptance of Titmuss's assertion that the first official use of the term 'community care' was in the report of the 1954–7 Royal Commission on Mental Illness and Mental Deficiency.[5]

This is simply not correct. The term was used thirty years earlier, ironically in part of the very area where Titmuss later located it – the care of mental defectives. Not only did the language of 'community care' emerge in the inter-war period, but so too can the policy shift to community care be located in this period. On reflection, it is unsurprising that community care emerged just as the peak of institutionalization receded. It could be argued that a shift away from the institution (though not perhaps the language of 'community care') can be observed across a wide spectrum of care in the 1920s and 1930s: the shift from the workhouse back to provision of forms of outdoor relief such as public assistance or unemployment benefit; the emergence of clinic treatment for infants and mothers; and the provision of after-care for a group such as the tuberculous. As Simon Goodwin has pointed out, although the total number of people in hospitals for the mentally disordered continued to rise throughout the inter-war period, as a proportion of the whole population the residential figure peaked in 1930 at 3.57 per thousand – twenty years before the assumed turning point towards community care.[6] An exploration of mental deficiency policy can provide a bridge between our understanding of care in the community and the emergence of 'community care' as policy. This essay will first briefly review the language which was used to describe early community care of mental defectives, the numbers in such care, and the nature of this care and its relationship to institutional care; secondly, it will explore the reasons for the emergence of community care as policy; and finally, it will examine the limitations of early community care.

'Community' and 'care' are notoriously difficult terms to define; combined together into 'community care' they are doubly so.[7] There are three ways we might choose to define community care. The first simply rests on location – care in the community, as opposed to the institution, provided by either state or family.[8] The second is care in the community where provision at least partly involves the state. The third is care in the community provided, again at least partly, by the state but which is also explicitly defined as 'community care'. A further variant on each of these three definitions is whether they reach the standards of ideally defined notions of 'community' and 'care'. My interest here is not on the first, location-dependent definition, but on the second and third definitions which rest on the involvement of the state. The difference between the second and third definitions rests on terminology; it may also however indicate a difference in degree, in maturity, and in the extent to which community care provision was explicitly conceived as policy. Community care for mental defectives in inter-war Britain straddled the second and third definitions: the term 'community care' began to be used, however the practice which this term described was in operation before the development of the term itself. The essay will examine whether this new terminology denoted anything more than a change in language.

II

Although the term 'community care' was used in inter-war mental deficiency policy, it was not the most common term applied to formal care of defectives in the community. In its annual report of 1929 the Board of Control, the government department overseeing mental deficiency policy and administration, advocated in its annual report: 'day centres should form an integral part of each Authority's scheme for the care and supervision of defectives living in the community'.[9] The following year the term 'community care' itself was used in the Board's annual report: 'it is clear that society cannot afford to segregate defectives who are in other respects fit for community care merely to prevent them from marrying'.[10] During the 1930s the use of the term became common in the policy recommendations of the Board. There are two possible explanations for the emergence of the new term: either community care policies were introduced for the first time in the early 1930s, or pre-existing, but otherwise named, community care practices began to adopt this title. I would suggest that the latter was the case. Well before the common use of 'community care' there were other terms in use which carried much the same meaning. The term 'after-care' went back to the late nineteenth century at least, when it was applied to the provision of care and monitoring of children leaving special schools and assistance for the mentally ill leaving hospital. After-care was superseded by the term 'supervision', which became the more common way to refer to care in the community under the Mental Deficiency Act in the 1920s. The generic terms 'care' and 'visiting' were also used for the work which would subsequently be termed community care. In summary, it is clear that the term 'community care' was used in the inter-war period from at least the start of the 1930s; moreover the practices which this title described can be traced back to at least the late nineteenth century.

The case for arguing that community care policies can be located in the inter-war period rests, not simply on terminology, but also on scale. It has been argued that the Mental Deficiency Act was a failure in terms of implementation and eugenic control; this view is based on the limited success of segregation by the early 1920s and the assumption that calls for sterilization reflected the failure of segregation.[11] I do not want to go into this debate here, except to say that limited institutional provision in the early 1920s is not surprising considering the set-back caused by the outbreak of war soon after the passage of the Act, and to mention that by the late 1930s almost 50,000 people were in institutions for mental defectives – surely not a mark of clear failure.[12] What I want to stress here is that the reach of the Act was even greater than this, for by the end of the 1930s a further 40,000 were under 'statutory supervision', almost the same number were under 'voluntary supervision', and another 5,000 were under 'guardianship' orders. Thus, the number of defectives in community care was twice that of those in institutions, almost 100,000 by the end of the 1930s.[13] Since community care aimed to provide control just as much as care, assessments of the limited reach of the 1913 Act are in need of revision. More importantly, in terms of the present argument, the numbers under community care by the end of the 1930s – about 100,000 – are surely of a scale to force reassessment of the idea that community care policies only emerged in the second half of the century.

Having demonstrated that a significant number of mental defectives were placed under what was termed 'community care', the only way left to deny the existence of community care during the inter-war period would be to argue that community care of defectives did not, qualitatively, deserve this title. This is a highly problematic argument; for it is based on the assumption that there is an ideal type of community care, when in fact community care has been notoriously difficult to define. The differences between inter-war and later twentieth-century forms of community care seem to me, not to invalidate the former's status, but to illumine the development of the latter.

The most common category of community care for defectives was what was termed 'supervision'. Supervision referred to the status of the defective. It also referred to a style of care, though other forms of care such as occupation centres and home teaching might be provided alongside supervision for defectives under supervision orders. The official case history of a defective would start with 'ascertainment'. To be ascertained defectives had to come before the mental deficiency authorities for some reason, such as recommendation by teachers, doctors, or parents, or detection by workhouse or penal authorities. The mental deficiency authorities then had to prove the defective, intellectually, to be feeble-minded, imbecile, or idiot from birth or early age and, socially, to be in need of care or control. Once 'ascertained' the defective was 'subject to be dealt with' and would be placed either in an institution or under some form of community care, usually supervision. Supervision was chosen if the home situation of the defective was deemed adequate in terms of care and control, though sometimes it was simply because there was no space available in institutions. Supervised defectives were visited at regular periods. There was probably wide variation in the timing of these visits. The Board of Control recommended that visits be 'at least once a month and more often if the defective is likely to get into difficulties'.[14]

It is difficult to reconstruct the nature of the supervisory visits.[15] The reports from the visitors concentrated on an evaluation of the standard of home care, the economic status of the family, the physical and moral environment of the home, the hereditary history of the family, and the behaviour of the defective; from this evidence alone it seems that the visits were primarily supervisory in style – a monitoring of whether home care was adequate. The tone of the reports and recommendations also indicates that the visits served a controlling function: visitors used the threat of institutionalization to pressurize families into controlling and caring (thus strengthening the proposition, raised above, that the scope of segregatory influence under the Act has been underestimated). It is more difficult to establish what sort of care was provided under supervision. This may be, in part, because the provision of advice and sympathy are less likely to be recorded in the most common form of evidence, the legalistic visitors' reports.

The Board of Control advocated that 'success depends almost entirely on the personality of the supervisor. Unless supervisors have the social qualities which will enable them to become the trusted friends of the families they visit, very little good will be effected'.[16] One wonders how common it was for supervisors to become 'trusted friends'? Undoubtedly the official and monitoring style of supervision must have reinforced the social distance between visitors and clients. However, to families in distress from the problems of caring, official recognition and advice from those who had been trained in the area and brought with them a scientific explanation of mental deficiency may have been of comfort.

Where one can be more certain about the limitations of care is the provision of material welfare; one would expect some documentation of aid and since there is none we can assume that care stopped short here. In fact, visitors often performed the roles of 'rent collectors': visiting families whose members were already in institutions and threatening them with fines if they failed to make contributions towards support.[17] Some of the supplementary services linked to supervision were more evidently of material assistance to the recipients. For instance visitors attempted to place defectives in employment, seeking out sympathetic employers for sheltered work or establishing occupational centres. Such schemes provided some supplementary income to aid family care, relieved the rest of the family from their caring roles, diverted the energies of defectives from potential misconduct, and aimed to train the defectives for non-sheltered employment. The number of defectives registered at occupation centres peaked in 1939 at about 4,200.[18] Occupation centres were more common in towns where the density of population made it viable for a sufficient number of defectives to visit a centre daily or several times a week. In rural areas different types of community care developed: for instance, home teachers visited families who lived too far from a special school for their defective child to attend on a daily basis.

Community care did not end when the defective entered an institution: as noted above, the 'case history' remained on file and visitors continued to visit the family, partly to collect contributions towards the cost of care, but also to monitor any improvements in home condition which might justify a return to the community. A second form of community care was guardianship, which placed defectives under a different legal status from supervision. Guardianship had been intended as the main form of community care under the 1913 Act but never extended on the scale of supervision, rising steadily but reaching only about 5,000 by the end of the 1930s. Ascertained defectives were placed under the legal responsibility of guardians who provided the defectives with a home and sometimes employment and, in return, were paid a guardianship fee.[19] The final main form of community care, licensing, emerged out of institutional care. Defectives were granted extended leave from institutions on the condition that they keep to the regulations of a licence. Under licence they would again come under the supervision of visitors. Ideally, if the conditions of the licence were kept to, the defective would be released from the conditions after a set time – often several years – though in reality licences were often extended.[20]

The role of the licence in bridging the gap between institution and community, like that of supervision carrying the threat of institutionalization into the community, indicates the close relation between community and institutional care; the two were not diametrically opposed but overlapping strategies, linked in a common aim of care and control and developing in a dialectical process.[21] Ideas of community were present in institutional care: the model of a colony was used in establishing a community of defectives; accommodation in a 'village' of 'villas' or 'cottages' rather than hospital blocks was intended to create a rural, communal, healthy, and simple atmosphere which would suit defectives and might even socialize them and train them in craft work so that they could return to visit the outside community. Within the institution a system of boy-scout or girl-guide-like rewards and punishments was set up to regulate the patient population through cultivation of a 'community' spirit. Rewards extended from 'parole' within the institution and grounds, to leave from the institution to the outside community, to residence in hostels located outside but nearby the institution.[22] Likewise one can see community care adopting institutional models: this is most strikingly the case with the occupational centres which adopted the workshop model developed in mental deficiency institutions. Significantly, those involved in community care did not develop an ideological critique of the institution; community care was seen as a supplement, not a replacement, extending the reach of provision out from the institution into the community.

In summary, institutional and community care were not yet opposites. On the contrary, at least in terms of mental deficiency, it seems that to universalize the polarized model which emerged in the polemics of the era of 'decarceration' is to run the danger of obscuring the full history not only of community but also of institutional care. It is recognized that the sort of community care provided for mental defectives in inter-war Britain was not that of an ideal model – if such a model exists – of care by the community and cut off from the system of institutional care. However, community care was a formalized system of care, provided by the state, and located in the community and, therefore, surely qualifies under any reasonable definition of community care policy.

III

As argued above, the practices which came to be described as community care predated this terminology and can be traced back to before the 1913 Act. The question remains, however, of why such practices gained the support of the state and were implemented on such a scale during the inter-war period? The first and central reason is that community care provision was used to compensate for the shortfall in institutional space. Building of specialized mental deficiency colonies and hospitals was delayed by war and then the building of working-class housing, a priority of post-war reconstruction. By the mid-1920s the majority of county and borough authorities still lacked a mental deficiency institution.[23] The Board of Control, somewhat ambivalently, encouraged supervision as 'better than nothing'.[24] Although institutional provision improved, total accommodation continually lagged behind that level recommended as necessary: for instance in 1927 the Board asserted that the number of defectives in institutions should have been at least one per thousand of the general population, but lamented that thirty-three local areas reached a level of 0.5–1.0 per thousand and forty-four authorities fell below the level of 0.25 per thousand.[25] Not only could community care be an alternative to institutional care, but it might also serve a preventive purpose. As early as 1922 the Board argued that if young defectives were made to visit community occupation centres, 'the regular occupation and training afforded by this form of supervision will tend to decrease the number of cases who will ultimately have to be sent to institutions'.[26] The publication of the Wood

Report on mental deficiency in 1929 highlighted the inadequacy of institutional care; the Report claimed that the defective population was larger than previous estimates – 10.49 per thousand, rather than the 1908 estimate of 4.6 per thousand – and that there was a dull and backward population on the 'borderline' of mental deficiency who also needed care and control.[27] The Board acknowledged that 'since the publication of the Report of the Wood Committee there has been a growing realization that the public care and protection of the majority of mentally defective persons must be organised outside institutions and colonies'.[28]

Alarm over the inability to provide comprehensive segregation for an expanding population of defectives revived the eugenic issue. A debate emerged over whether sterilization of defectives should be introduced.[29] There were also suggestions of a law to prohibit marriage by and to defectives. The campaign for sterilization has attracted considerable attention from historians; what has been less commented on is the relation of this policy to the community care system: it was hoped that sterilization would provide an alternative form of eugenic control to segregation and thereby relieve pressure on the institutional system, but, since sterilized defectives were still deemed a potential social and sexual danger as actors or victims, release was only safe if the sterilized defectives could be supervised in the community.[30] Thus, it was, in part, the existence of a community care system which drew the government to consider sterilization: 'it is clear that society cannot afford to segregate defectives who are in other respects fit for community care merely to prevent them from marrying'.[31]

For political reasons sterilization was not introduced. However, the shortage of institutional space continued; problems were exacerbated by falling institutional death rates, the accumulation of long-term chronic cases, and added pressure on mental hospital space arising from the new out-patient clinics for the mentally ill set up under the 1930 Mental Treatment Act. In reaction, the Board advocated the removal of defectives, either sending them to another type of institution or back to the community: 'it should be the aim of Local Authorities to reduce to a minimum the number of defectives who need to be retained permanently in institutions'.[32] Licensing of defectives was one solution to the problem. The Board advocated that all institutions should aim to match the figure, achieved by three leading colonies, of 10 per cent of patients on licence.[33] For the more able type of defective, licences could be used as a form of trial with a view to discharge. In accord with this philosophy, the colony model was recommended as the ideal institutional design by the 1929 Hedley Committee Report.[34] The new strategy was summed up by the Board in their 1932 Report: 'colonies are now looked upon as training schools, and one of the justifications of their position is the number of stabilised defectives that they can return to the community'.[35] By 1936 the Board was also recommending that licences be applied to less able but non-dangerous defectives: 'those who are unfit for discharge but who can properly be permitted to remain in community care on licence from the institution'.[36]

Community care policies were also attractive for economic reasons. Since community care services were often provided by voluntary organizations and by women it was relatively cheap for local authorities to contract out community care work. Not only did this save the cost of building institutions and the upkeep and staffing of institutions, it also provided the local authorities with a ready-made network of agencies to perform the time-consuming tasks of administering the Act, and ascertaining and supervising defectives.[37] Money was also saved by the state as it utilized the national headquarters of the Central Association for Mental Welfare to serve as a vital information and training bureau to coordinate the development of community care practice. Even the more expensive forms of community care were, the Board argued as early as 1924, far cheaper than institutional care.[38] Such thinking was encouraged by the assault on public expenditure in the early 1930s: 'the restriction of capital expenditure makes it all the more important that local authorities should develop fully all methods of community care . . . In comparison with institutional care the cost involved is small'.[39] In summary, the coincidence of economic crisis in 1930–1, the publication of the Wood Report in 1929, and the added pressure on resources from the Mental Treatment Act of 1930 placed great strain on the mental deficiency system. Although the community care policies which emerged as a result of this crisis were not new, the adoption of the term at this point in time is surely symbolic of a maturation of community care as deliberate, rather than improvised, policy.

The limitations of institutional space and parsimony are both negative reasons for the emergence of community care. There were also some positive reasons for its adoption. Community care was seen, not simply as a second-best alternative, but also as a supplement to extend the reach of the Act to groups who did not need institutional care or to those who could not easily be institutionalized under the regulations of the Act.[40] Of particular concern were children who came under the remit of the Board of Education and could be lost sight of before they became the responsibility of the Board of Control. As the latter Board argued in 1924,

> the keynote of the Mental Deficiency Act is 'continuous care' and our experience shows us that a break in care and supervision, especially in early youth or adolescence, has led to periods in prison or in poor law institutions which is harmful to the defective and renders him far less amenable to discipline and kindly control when he at last finds his way to an institution or a colony for defectives.[41]

To understand the positive appeal of community care in inter-war Britain we also have to consider contemporary ideas of community. Evident in the language of community care were concerns over the instability of the community. On the one hand, there was a fear that the breakdown of family networks of care, the changing nature of work, and the complications of life in the urban community, in a sense created the problem of mental deficiency, leaving a growing proportion of the more simple, but previously non-problematic, sufferers as unable to cope without outside aid. As the Board of Control expressed it: 'the more complicated the social fabric becomes the greater the need of the defective to have a place found in it for him. . . . The defective must be fitted for his environment and the environment adapted to the defective'.[42] On the other hand, there was also a concern that the defectives themselves were a threat to the very fragility of the community, as a direct danger through crime and sexual deviance, as a long-term danger through their poor genetic stock, and in a less direct sense as an economic drain on the resources of the community. The attraction of community care also stemmed from contemporary ideas of citizenship. For instance, the supervision, training, and reform of defectives, and the ever-broadening definition of 'social inefficiency' reflected concern to mould 'good', 'healthy', and 'efficient' citizens to populate a self-governing community. Finally, the provision of community care on such a scale was only possible because it was (wo)manned by battalions of volunteers; this provision of care, for a section of the population deemed as non-citizens, was itself very much a product of an era dominated by ideas of community responsibility and active citizenship.[43]

IV

Although there was good reason for the adoption of community care in inter-war Britain, growth slowed in the later 1930s: guardianship never reached more than 5,000 during the inter-war years, licensing did not substantially expand, and voluntary-run occupation centres fell from about 150 in 1931 to around sixty by 1939.[44] Most important of all, the use of community care as a route towards eventual discharge from the institution remained too low in scale to cause a significant impact, with only about 500 defectives discharged each year by 1937.[45] To help explain this stagnation I will consider two areas: firstly, the problematic nature of community care, and secondly, the changing welfare environment.

Turning to the first of these factors, the limited expansion of community care in inter-war Britain can be traced to the fundamental ambiguity within the 1913 Mental Deficiency Act – that care should be provided to protect the defective from the community, yet also to protect the community from the defective.[46] The first side of this equation, protection of the defective from the community, reflects a mistrust of the community from which the defectives came – a mistrust which pervades the reports of visitors to the working-class homes of defectives.[47] This lack of sympathy for indigenous community care meant that supervision within the community would usually be seen as a second-best alternative rather than a replacement of institutional care. The second side of the community care equation, protection of the community from the defective, was used by community carers to advocate their importance in the alarmist wartime and post-war atmosphere, when there was concern that uncontrolled defectives would spread venereal disease, be a eugenic danger, and cause havoc as delinquents.[48] But such a rationale would ultimately prevent expansion of community care, for supervision, though a definite infringement on the liberty of the defectives and their families, could never maintain comprehensive control; in fact, when studied in detail, supervision can be shown to be a process of negotiation, albeit one based on an inequality of power, between visitors and families. Inevitably, therefore, defectives under community care did occasionally commit offences and the public scandals which resulted made the authorities cautious about liberalization. This helps to explain the limited growth of licensing.[49] Similarly, the growth of guardianship was held back by concern over the inadequacy of control and a reluctance to make parents or families into guardians, even though the financial aid available through this form of care would have been an invaluable aid to home care.[50] Finally, instead of licences being used as a stage towards discharge they tended to be extended indefinitely so that defectives could be reinstitutionalized rapidly and easily if they again became the subject of social concern.[51]

The second problem with the inter-war conception of community care was the failure to address the social and economic conditions of the community. For, under the Mental Deficiency Act, defectives were defined, not only according to hazy intellectual criteria, but also in terms of social efficiency – that is the ability of the defective or the defective's family to be self-supporting. In an era of economic depression and high unemployment this social construction of the problem was crucial. However, community carers continued to blame poor home conditions on the inadequacy of the parents and were loath to provide any type of aid to improve the material conditions of the defective's community.[52] In terms of material aid, the ideal of providing assistance to the less advantaged in order to make them 'active citizens' was unsuited to a group who were permanently disadvantaged. The entry of psychiatric ideas into community care did not remedy the unwillingness of proponents of community care to address social needs: it led to a focus on the individual rather than the community, to an interest in psychodynamics within the family which often perpetuated the blaming of mothers and could even be manipulated to address traditional concerns over self-help.[53]

The problems of community care were also rooted in the changing welfare environment of the 1930s. I have already attributed the rapid early growth of community care to the savings this enabled. I will now show why it is no contradiction to use the economy also to explain subsequent decline. Once community care services became established they tended to be taken over by the local authorities who saw voluntary groups as an unnecessary complication to administration and sometimes as a threat to the roles of local officials.[54] The number of local voluntary associations for the care of mental defectives fell from over fifty in 1930 to about forty at the end of the 1930s.[55] This process was hastened by the changes in funding brought about in 1930 by the Local Government Act, which replaced the system of annual central grants to match local expenditure on individual services, by five-year block grants for all services. This made the extent of funding which was being devolved to voluntary groups far more obvious. Many local authorities reacted by amalgamating mental deficiency services into their public health departments.[56] Placed alongside other higher profile services, provision for mental defectives suffered.

The second change in the welfare environment was that voluntary community carers began to professionalize: they became employees of the local authorities, trained and qualified, and armed with the trappings of psychiatric expertise. This process was slow, but, with professionalization, employment of community carers became more expensive, thus destroying the original attraction to the authorities. In the long run the inadequacy of training facilities and funding for training would be crucial in holding back growth of community care.[57]

The third key change in the welfare environment has already been touched upon in the discussion of citizenship – an expansion of concern from the problem of mental deficiency to the mental health of the normal population. The transition was linked to the changes in the welfare environment already discussed: the amalgamation of mental deficiency services with public health had encouraged concern to expand to a wider population, while the psychiatric training of social workers meant that they lost interest in the incurable defective and moved to jobs which dealt with the curable and the more 'psychiatrically interesting'.[58]

V

In conclusion, I hope that this essay has shown that, for mental defectives at least, one can talk about community care as already existing in the inter-war period – well before the emergence of community care is usually dated. It may be the case that mental deficiency is an exception. On the other hand, the implication of this study is that in searching for an ideal type of community care and a particular terminology one may be ignoring a hidden pre-history of community care. Just as recent work has revealed the continuities in the history of care in the community, it seems likely that there is far more continuity than previously realized in the history of community care as policy.

Through looking back at this earlier model of community care, post-1945 developments can be placed in new perspectives. Firstly, the rapid growth of inter-war community care would seem to indicate that the mixed welfare environment of these years, where the central state, local government, and voluntary organizations interacted and overlapped, may be fertile ground for community care. On the other hand, there were also underlying weaknesses in this mixed welfare system: the retreat from the interventionist and segregationist policies of the early twentieth century, and the devolution of responsibility for care to local government and voluntary organizations was a cost-cutting manoeuvre which in the long term would stifle the maturation of community care.

Secondly, the inter-war example indicates that community and institutional care should not necessarily be seen as separate. In this respect the division between hospital and social services under the NHS may have been particularly damaging to the care of a group such as defectives whose needs lay on the border between caring and curing.[59] Inter-war community care emerged as a way to overcome the limitations of institutional care, not to replace it.[60] The interplay between the institutional and community spheres indicates that it may be wrong to see the 'era of institutionalization' as a disjunction in the history of care. Although processes of state expansion, bureaucratization, and professionalization were creating a more definite division between institutional care and community care, a surprising degree of fluidity remained and there were significant continuities with the forms, style, and mix of informal and formal care developed over several centuries of the Poor Law welfare system.

Thirdly, I do not want to appear to eulogize the inter-war system, for, as I have shown, the notion of 'care' is heavily dependent on the values of the providers and in the inter-war period was inextricably linked to the desire to control the behaviour of defectives and their families. A blindness to the shaping of the problem of mental deficiency by socio-economic factors, and the desire to impose an ethos of 'self-help', prevented care from extending to the provision of material aid.

The fourth point which emerges is the tendency for resources to shift from the incurable and chronic, who cannot defend their needs, to the health of the normal population. In this respect the inter-war existence of specialized government departments and voluntary groups was an advantage in targeting resources at the defective; though this must be balanced by doubt as to whether such services and groups would have emerged if the defective had not originally been perceived as a danger.

Finally, the inter-war example indicates that the failure to address the material conditions of the community and to cooperate with indigenous community carers can severely limit the ability to provide effective care.

NOTES

1 Work on the role of women in the modern period points to the continuing importance of informal family and neighbourhood care, for instance: J. Lewis (ed.), *Labour and Love: Women's Experience of Home and Family 1850–1940* (Oxford, 1986); E. Ross, 'Survival Networks: Women's Neighbourhood Sharing in London before World War I', *History Workshop Journal* 15 (1983), pp. 4–27.

2 Though, as Jose Harris points out, and as this essay will explain, 'such a figure masks the fact that official thinking was moving simultaneously in quite contrary directions', *Private Lives Public Spirits: A Social History of Britain* (Oxford, 1993), p. 218.

3 The historiography is vast and at times vitriolic. For opposing sides of the debate see: A. Scull, *Decarceration: Community Care and the Deviant – A Radical View*, 2nd edn (Cambridge, 1984), and G. Grob, 'Marxian Analysis and Mental Illness', *History of Psychiatry* 1 (1990), pp. 223–30. New perspectives emerge in S. Goodwin, *Community Care and the Future of Mental Health Service Provision* (Avebury, 1990), and 'Community Care and the Mentally Ill in England and Wales: Myths, Assumptions and Reality', *Journal of Social Policy* 18 (1989), pp. 27–52.

4 Here, even Scull and Grob agree. New light is cast on the emergence of 'open door' policies in the 1950s, including mention of earlier precedents, in L. Clarke, 'The Opening of Doors in British Mental Hospitals in the 1950s', *History of Psychiatry* 4 (1993), pp. 527–51. Joan Busfield has discussed the development of forms of community care for the mentally ill in the 1930s but recognizes that this was on a small scale: *Managing Madness: Changing Ideas and Practice* (London, 1986). In contrast to the extensive literature on the mentally ill there has been little attention to the mentally defective. The best account of community care services is M. Rooff, *Voluntary Societies and Social Policy* (London, 1957), pp. 79–169.

5 For instance, A. Walker, 'The Meaning and Social Division of Community Care', in A. Walker (ed.), *Community Care: the Family, the State and Social Policy* (Oxford, 1982), p. 15. R. Titmuss, 'Community

213

Care – Fact or Fiction?', in R. Farndale and H. Freeman (eds), *Trends in the Mental Health Services* (London and Oxford, 1963), pp. 221–5.

6 Goodwin, 'Community Care and the Mentally Ill', pp. 43–4. Although Goodwin points out the earlier trend away from institutional expansion and discusses the limitations of the community care policy of the 1950s, he does not reveal the development of many of the 1950s community care practices in the care of mental defectives during the inter-war years. This missing factor may help to make sense of the surprisingly limited discussion of the policy shift in the 1950s – the policies were already accepted and in practice.

7 For explorations of the terms: M. Bulmer, *The Social Basis of Community Care* (London, 1987); R. Plant, *Community and Ideology* (London, 1974); E. and S. Yeo, 'On the Uses of "Community": from Owenism to the Present', in S. Yeo (ed.), *New Views of Cooperation* (London, 1988), pp. 229–58.

8 A broad definition of the state is taken, to include central and local government and coopted groups employed by the state and thereby given 'statutory authority'. But, because the role of the state is so important in differentiating between my definitions of care in the community and community care as policy, I will concentrate on evidence from central government to prove that community care was a policy of the state.

9 *Board of Control Annual Report [BCAR] for 1929*, p. 61 (all such reports were published by HMSO, London, usually in the following year).

10 *BCAR for 1930*, p. 71.

11 This literature is now fairly extensive and this is not the place to discuss it with any justice. The view of segregation as a failure, judged by figures for the early 1920s, can be found in H. Simmons, 'Explaining Social Policy: the English Mental Deficiency Act of 1913', *Journal of Social Policy* 11 (1978), pp. 387–403. On sterilization emerging due to limitations of segregation as a eugenic policy: J. Macnicol, 'Eugenics and the Campaign for the Voluntary Sterilization in Britain between the Wars', *Social History of Medicine* 2 (1989), pp. 147–70.

12 For a fuller discussion: M. Thomson, 'The Problem of Mental Deficiency in England and Wales, c. 1913–1946', D.Phil. thesis (Oxford, 1992).

13 Statistics are compiled from Annual Reports of the Board of Control; they are collected in Thomson, 'Problem of Mental Deficiency', Graph 4. III, p. 130.

14 *BCAR for 1923*, p. 47.

15 For a more detailed analysis see: M. Thomson, 'Family, Community, and State: the Micro-Politics of Mental Deficiency', in D. Wright and A. Digby (eds), *From Idiocy to Mental Deficiency: Historical Perspectives on People with Learning Disabilities* (London, 1996), pp. 207–230.

16 *BCAR for 1923*, p. 47.

17 Thomson, 'Problem of Mental Deficiency', pp. 224–61.

18 Rooff, *Voluntary Societies and Social Policy*, p. 126.

19 For a discussion of this type of care under the 1913 Act: *BCAR for 1923*, pp. 50–4.

20 *BCAR for 1932*, pp. 64–5.
21 For a more detailed exploration of this interaction see M. Thomson, 'Sterilisation, Segregation, and Community Care: Ideology and the Problem of Mental Deficiency in Inter-war Britain', *History of Psychiatry* 3 (1992), pp. 473–98; and A. Scull, 'The Asylum as Community or the Community as Asylum', in A. Scull, *Social Order/Mental Disorder* (London, 1989), pp. 300–30.
22 Thomson, 'Problem of Mental Deficiency', pp. 84–121.
23 Only about twenty, compared to around eighty by the end of the inter-war period. For more details see Thomson, 'Problem of Mental Deficiency', pp. 95–103.
24 *BCAR for 1927*, p. 49.
25 *BCAR for 1927*, pp. 42–3.
26 *BCAR for 1922*, p. 47.
27 *Report of the Interdepartmental Committee on Mental Deficiency, 1925–9* [*Wood Report*], 3 vols (London, 1929).
28 *BCAR for 1930*, p. 59.
29 Macnicol, 'Campaign for Voluntary Sterilization'.
30 Such moral concerns had restricted support for sterilization at the time of the 1913 Act: D. Barker, 'How to Curb the Fertility of the Edwardian Unfit: the Feeble-Minded in Edwardian Britain', *Oxford Review of Education* 9 (1983), pp. 197–211.
31 *BCAR for 1930*, p. 76.
32 *BCAR for 1933*, p. 65.
33 *BCAR for 1932*, p. 64.
34 *Colonies for Mental Defectives: Report of the Departmental Committee* (*Hedley Report*) (London, 1931).
35 *BCAR for 1932*, p. 66.
36 *BCAR for 1936*, p. 55.
37 Thomson, 'Problem of Mental Deficiency', pp. 122–49.
38 *BCAR for 1924*, p. 72.
39 *BCAR for 1931*, pp. 13–14.
40 E. Fox, 'Modern Developments in Mental Welfare Work', *Eugenics Review* 30 (1938), p. 165.
41 *BCAR for 1924*, p. 76.
42 *BCAR for 1934*, p. 11. A similar problem was recognized as lying behind the growing problem of senility: 'there is a change in the habits of the population, due partly to housing difficulties and partly, perhaps, to the weakening of family ties, with the result that there is a greater readiness to seek institutional treatment for elderly patients who would formerly have been nursed at home'. *BCAR for 1930*, p. 8. For a more detailed discussion of the issue of family responsibility, Thomson, 'Problem of Mental Deficiency', pp. 245–52.
43 The model of active citizenship was typified by the National Council of Social Service: M. Brasnett, *Voluntary Social Action: a History of the NCSS, 1919–69* (London, 1969). For a more detailed discussion of community and citizenship in relation to mental deficiency see Thomson, 'Sterilisation, Segregation, and Community Care', pp. 488–93.

44 Rooff, *Voluntary Societies and Social Policy*, p. 126.
45 *BCAR for 1937*, p. 55.
46 *Mental Deficiency Act, 1913* (3 & 4 George V, cap. 17).
47 For instance Mrs Emmett in *Central Association for Mental Welfare Annual Conference Report for 1926*, p. 54. For a more detailed discussion of the interaction between community carers and families, see Thomson, 'Family, Community, and State'.
48 Public Records Office (PRO), Kew, Ministry of Health File (MH), 51/691, Central Association for the Care and Control of Mental Defectives (CACMD) to the Ministry of Reconstruction, 24 Oct. 1917; *CACMD Annual Report for 1918–19*, p. 16.
49 *BCAR for 1923*, p. 60; *BCAR for 1924*, p. 80.
50 *BCAR for 1923*, pp. 49–51; *BCAR for 1926*, pp. 53–4.
51 *BCAR for 1929*, pp. 65–72.
52 There is some sign of an ambivalent recognition that aid was needed (though no sign of significant provision): *BCAR for 1933*, pp. 66–7.
53 E. Harrison, 'The Changing Meaning of Social Work', in A. Halsey (ed.), *Traditions of Social Policy* (Oxford, 1976), p. 96; S. Brown, 'Methods of Social Case Workers', in F. Bartlett, M. Ginsburg *et al.* (eds), *The Study of Society* (London, 1939), pp. 379–401; M. Cosens, 'Psychology and Social Case-Work', *Charity Organisation Quarterly* n.s. 7 (1933), pp. 63–73.
54 *Public Health* 37 (1924), pp. 301–2.
55 These figures are compiled from the Annual Reports of the Central Association for Mental Welfare (CAMW); see Thomson, 'Problem of Mental Deficiency', p. 128.
56 S. Wormald, 'Mental Deficiency under the Local Government Bill, 1928', *Mental Welfare* 10 (1929), pp. 1–4; PRO, MH 58/70.
57 Such limitations on expansion were highlighted during World War II but not acted upon: C. Blacker, *Neurosis and the Mental Health Services* (London, 1948), pp. 92–100.
58 E. Fox, 'Modern Developments in Work for Mental Defectives: a Historical Survey', *CAMW Annual Conference Report for 1934*, pp. 44–59.
59 M. Thomson, 'Social Policy and the Management of the Problem of Mental Deficiency in Inter-War London', *London Journal* 18 (1993), pp. 129–42.
60 This would support Goodwin's conclusion that community care policies served to expand, rather than contract, psychiatric services: 'Community Care and the Mentally Ill', pp. 45–7.

Part IV

CHILDREN AND THE ELDERLY IN THE TWENTIETH CENTURY

9

SAFEGUARDING THE HEALTH OF THE COMMUNITY

Maternal and infant welfare services in four London boroughs 1902–1936

Lara Marks

I

In recent debates over health and welfare provision, 'community care' has become a key concept, especially in relation to provision for the elderly, the infirm, and the mentally and physically disabled. Yet what is meant by this concept and how it is to be implemented, is continually being contested. Such difficulties of definition are not unique to the present crisis in social policy. Some of the earliest debates concerning 'community' and health care also surrounded the development of maternal and infant welfare services in the early twentieth century. These services were among the first state measures in health and welfare, and were as strongly influenced by particular concepts of 'community' as are the health care policies being formulated today. None the less, while present policies are largely being enacted against a background where welfare is increasingly being farmed out to the voluntary sector, those of the past took place at a time when the reverse was happening – when the state was beginning to take a more active role in the provision of welfare.[1]

The health of the infant and of coming generations lay at the heart of this initiative, as is most clearly seen in the Inter-departmental Committee on Physical Deterioration (1904). The falling birth rate, predictions of population decline, and the persistence of high infant mortality at a time when other mortality levels were declining, all added to governmental anxiety. Health, particularly that of infants, was no longer an individual responsibility, but was linked to the welfare of the nation.[2]

219

Mothers, as the 'reproducers' of the nation, also had a special place within this discourse.[3] They were seen as having an important duty to the 'community', just as the 'community' was seen as having a particular duty to mothers. None the less, it was unclear which 'community' mothers were supposed to serve and who was responsible for helping them perform their role – was it their family or society as a whole? This was left vague not only by male politicians and social reformers arguing that mothers should take more responsibility for the care of future citizens, but also by female social activists.[4] The ambiguity was apparent in the state measures taken in maternal and infant welfare during the years 1902 to 1936. While state funding of maternity and infant welfare services increased greatly, the policies pursued still emphasized the primary responsibility of mothers in the care of their infants and the family. Maternal and infant welfare facilities were, moreover, not comprehensive, and were largely dependent on the policy of the local authority where mothers resided as well as on the services of local voluntary agencies. This meant that, while much of the legislation for maternal and child welfare in the years 1902 to 1936 grew out of national concerns, many of the social tensions which emerged on a local level were vital determinants of how such provision was implemented.

The aim of this paper is therefore to explore the ways in which the notion of 'community' was locally negotiated in the economically and socially diverse London boroughs of Hampstead, Kensington, Stepney, and Woolwich, and to see what practical effects this negotiation had on the development and justification of maternal and infant welfare schemes.

While integrally part of the wider metropolitan community of London, Hampstead, Kensington, Stepney, and Woolwich each had their own distinct socio-economic and political characteristics and could be considered communities in themselves united within their formal geographical and political boundaries. In all four boroughs the rich and the poor tended to be segregated from each other, with the poor generally subject to the highest levels of overcrowding. This was most marked in the case of Kensington, where the disparity in wealth and poverty was greatest. Within Kensington most of the richer residents lived in large houses or great blocks of expensive flats in the south of the borough, while those who were much poorer dwelled in the north, where some of the most notorious slums of London were located.[5] Such differences in residential patterns were a powerful component in determining local social relations and networks. On the surface it might be assumed that those neighbours who came from the same socio-economic status were more likely to share a sense of common identity and solidarity. Indeed, Ross has shown that in many working-class neighbourhoods of London poverty could draw residents together through informal networks of mutual assistance and the sharing of limited resources. As Ross points out, however, while poverty could act as a unifying force, it could also divide people. Sharing tap water and toilets, for instance, did not always promote the most harmonious relationship between neighbours.[6]

However, there were some perceptible neighbourhood relationships and networks which might be identified with the dominance of the particular classes in each area. This had important implications for the political affiliations of each borough and its responses to welfare provision. In Hampstead and Kensington, attitudes towards welfare were largely influenced by the fact that the poorer residents were confined to domestic service and isolated from other workers. They were also fewer in number than the middle class and greatly dependent on their richer neighbours for employment. This generated paternalistic relationships. One advantage the poor in Kensington had over those in Hampstead was that they were greater in number, which made it more difficult for the rest of the borough to ignore their plight. Such social relations sharply contrast with those of Woolwich and Stepney, which had an overwhelming majority of working-class population who thus enjoyed more cultural and political autonomy than those living in Kensington and Hampstead. In both Stepney and Woolwich the shared experience of poverty was an important political force which drew on the notion of mutual assistance developed at the more localized level of the street and the neighbourhood. Sharing between neighbours and friends was therefore taken as a crucial underpinning for larger collective provision by the borough as a whole.

II

Welfare provision, particularly for mothers and their infants, was not only dependent on the class dynamics and social relations of each area. The presence of women within the council chamber and other positions of power was an important force in making these issues a high priority within each borough. Yet the degree to which women could influence maternal and infant welfare policies was greatly dependent on the general political outlook of the area, and the way in which the provision of services was divided between municipal and voluntary sectors. What was at stake was how the health of the nation or the 'community' could be protected and enhanced. Despite this common aim, however, the boroughs differed in the tactics they adopted to achieve it.

In all the boroughs the maternal and child welfare policies were intricately tied up with those being developed at a national level. Under the Maternity and Child Welfare Act of 1918 local authorities were required to create specific committees for administering maternal and infant welfare. Local councils and voluntary institutions could also apply for governmental grants to provide paid midwives, health visitors, infant welfare centres, day nurseries and milk and food for necessitous mothers and infants. Implementation of the 1918 Act varied enormously between councils and regions. Some new schemes were developed under the Act, but many of those which did emerge stemmed from voluntary activities of the nineteenth century.[7] Voluntary organizations, often supported by local government grants, continued to play a vital role in the provision of maternal and infant welfare into the inter-war period. The extent to which they did so was, however, highly dependent on the precedent for such work in each individual borough.

Table 9.1 summarizes the different types of maternal and infant welfare service that were provided in each borough. Significantly, municipal provision, particularly of infant welfare clinics, appeared first in Woolwich. This was partly attributable to the strong representation of the Labour Party on its council from early on, but was also essential in an area where there were very few middle-class residents to undertake philanthropic work in this field. Woolwich had only one voluntary infant welfare centre which had emerged at the relatively late date of 1914. By contrast, Stepney had an abundance of voluntary maternal and infant welfare agencies. Part of this stemmed from the weakness of the Labour Party during the years before the war, as well as the strong tradition of philanthropy in the area. Added to this was a profusion of charitable Jewish and Irish Catholic maternal and infant welfare services that had been developed for the large Irish and Jewish

Table 9.1 Health levels, demographic profiles, and the types of maternal and infant welfare provision in the four boroughs

	Hampstead	Kensington	Stepney	Woolwich
Mortality patterns	High maternal mortality	Varying maternal mortality	Very low maternal mortality	Varying maternal mortality
	Low infant mortality	Highest infant mortality in London	High infant mortality	Low infant mortality
Women of childbearing age, 1921 (% of total population)	33%	32%	25%	24%
Children aged 0–4 years, 1921 (% of total population)	5.7%	6.5%	9.9%	9.2%
Borough Council's estimated expenditure on maternal and child welfare per child aged 0–4, 1922–3	13s. 2d.	7s.	17s.	£1 4d.
Voluntary/municipal provision of maternal and infant welfare services	Voluntary	Voluntary	Voluntary and municipal	Municipal

Table 9.1 cont.

	Hampstead	Kensington	Stepney	Woolwich
Coordinating bodies	Hampstead Council of Social Welfare	Voluntary Advisory Committee – coordinated by council	Voluntary bodies and council	Council
Strengths	Health Institute – multiple services – TB, maternal and infant health services Pioneer specialist obstetric provision by council for maternity emergencies	Mother and Baby Clinic with medical treatment from 1910 – run by Women's Labour League Birth control clinic 1924 Good ante-natal care Good domiciliary midwifery provision	Good obstetric care from voluntary maternity hospitals Abundance of Infant Welfare Centres Good ante-natal provision Immigrant communal provision	Milk depot Municipal Infant Welfare Centres from 1906 British Hospital for Mothers and Babies (voluntary)

immigrant population living in East London.[8] Such a large number of voluntary agencies rendered council initiative far less important than in Woolwich. In the 1920s, with the rise of the Labour Party, these charitable enterprises did not disappear; rather they were incorporated alongside the municipal provision.

Voluntary organizations also tended to dominate maternal and infant welfare services in both Hampstead and Kensington. This was largely due to the presence of a large upper and middle class in these boroughs which could sponsor and work for such ventures. The Hampstead Council for Social Welfare (HCSW) was a major promoter of voluntary work in this field. Originally established under the direction of Thomas Hancock Nunn in 1902, it provided an administrative body for bringing together independent societies and parish relief programmes, and in later years initiated co-operation between voluntary and state activities.[9] No comparable body existed in Kensington, but in 1921 voluntary maternal and infant welfare organizations were linked up through the establishment of an Advisory Body, constituted by representatives of all the voluntary infant welfare centres in the borough. Under this Body the infant welfare centres came largely to be seen as an extension of the borough council, although they were run by voluntary agencies. Alongside it were also a number of pioneering services, such as the Labour Party's Mother and Baby Clinic and the North Kensington Women's Welfare Centre established by Margery Spring-Rice and a number of other key women activists.

III

It would therefore seem that while Woolwich was unusual in its early municipal provision of services, this was counterbalanced in the other three boroughs by their prolific voluntary services. What differentiated the boroughs more were the *perceptions* that the political pressure groups and residents attached to their local community, and their beliefs about how they should provide for the poorer constituents, particularly mothers and infants. These differences were manifested not only between the boroughs, but also between the different political parties and grassroots pressure movements within each neighbourhood. They were shaped by the kind of citizen or 'community' each political party or movement drew its support from. While the Labour Party was primarily concerned with the poorer residents and was more likely to prioritize the funds and welfare provision of the neighbourhood in their favour, the Municipal Reform Party more closely identified with the rate payers, seeing their interests as taking precedence in deciding the level of welfare services.[10] Such differences could partly be seen in the expenditure that each of these parties was willing to allocate to the municipal provision of maternal and infant welfare services per child aged 0–4 years in 1922–3.[11] As Table 9.1 shows, this tended to be much greater in the poorer boroughs where the Labour Party had a stronger hold than the Municipal Reformers.

Different parties therefore appealed to two very distinct groups of voters, which entailed contrasting notions of 'community' and of who should be protected. A more nuanced concept of community, and one which was prominently promoted by Hancock Nunn and the HCSW, was that which conceived of community within the framework of civic spirit. This emphasized the need for a community in which everyone, both rich and poor, would have a part to play in the provision of welfare services. Stress was laid on the strength of neighbourly ties between 'active, earnest, loving men and women, each contributing individual effort to a common aim', which would not only alleviate the condition of the poor but also raise the standards of the whole community.[12] Such views were not dissimilar to those put forward by many within the Labour Party in Woolwich, which called for 'the cultivation of the civic spirit so that it will find its highest expression in social service for the community'. As members of the party said, 'we want a walk "Round the Borough" to bring us pride in the sight of smiling bairns, living under conditions which give opportunity for full development of brain and body'.[13] From this it would seem that the Labour Party in Woolwich shared the vision of community expressed by the HCSW. Indeed, there were links between the HCSW and Woolwich Labour activists.

None the less, the HCSW and Woolwich Labour Party differed widely in the ways in which they interpreted this concept. One of the prime aims of the HCSW was to foster a sense of community which would unite all classes. This was to be partly achieved by the promotion of greater social service and voluntary work among the middle class, whose good works in this area it was hoped would eliminate some of the evils of poverty, preserve the humane approach in welfare provision, and prevent the growth of revolutionary discontent. Such ideals were not shared by Woolwich Labour Party activists, who saw voluntary work as paternalistic and unsympathetic to the poor, and as maintaining the inequalities within society. Their ideal was that the poor should have greater opportunity to be heard, either through voting or by standing in elections for the borough council and other local government bodies. From early on the Labour Party encouraged the notion that everyone within Woolwich, as in the nation as a whole, was part of a 'community', and as such had a right not only to participate in the decision-making process but also to demand certain welfare and social benefits from that 'community'.[14]

Different concepts of 'community' were also articulated by women's organizations, who made the needs and demands of women a central component in their vision of 'community' and their campaigning efforts. A central part of this vision was the idea that women, because of their different roles from men and their experiences as wives and mothers, had an important part to play in the well-being of a 'community'. But opinions varied greatly about which women were to be included under the category of 'community'. Labour Party women, such as Ethel Bentham and Marion Phillips in Kensington, were much more likely to ally themselves with working-class women than with politically conservative women whose activities were directed more towards raising the equality and conditions of women of property. In this context, therefore, 'community' was not a single concept, but one which was greatly affected by class considerations and political outlook.[15] This was particularly apparent in the different solutions socially and politically active women adopted for the particular problems women faced and in their approaches to maternal and infant welfare provision. While Labour Party women asserted the need for more state provision, calling for better housing and higher incomes as well as more comprehensive state maternal and infant welfare services, this was not a strategy supported by more conservative women, who saw voluntary initiative and self-help as the answer.[16]

IV

The remaining part of this paper examines how these different visions of community could contrast with each other as well as overlap, and on how this process affected the provision of *milk depots* and *birth control* as just two examples of maternal and infant welfare services in the four boroughs.

An important consideration is the ways in which the specific health trends of each area, particularly maternal and infant mortality, shaped the priorities each borough gave to the services it would provide. As Table 9.1 indicates, partly reflecting their greater density of population and worse problems of overcrowding and poverty, infant mortality was much higher in Kensington and Stepney than in the two other boroughs. Maternal mortality, which was less sensitive to socio-economic conditions, was much more variable between the boroughs. Stepney showed some of the lowest rates of maternal mortality both in London and nationally, and this can partly be attributed to its very good charitable maternity facilities, which seemed to have outweighed the socio-economic disadvantages that many of the women experienced in the borough.[17]

V

One of the most burning questions in the early twentieth century was the persistence of infant mortality. Yet, despite the gravity of concern the problem generated, no consensus existed as to how it might be solved. Some of the fiercest arguments over this issue can be seen in Kensington, which had the highest rate of infant mortality in London. Indeed, many within the borough were appalled by the problem. In 1902 Orme Dudfield, Medical Officer of Health for Kensington, summed up these feelings when he reminded his readers that 'quite apart from general considerations as to the future of the Empire and the like, this in a West London borough more particularly, ought not to be tolerated by the borough itself'.[18] None the less, while many shared Dudfield's horror at the high rates of infant mortality, seeing it as ruining Kensington's prosperous reputation in the rest of the capital, battles raged over how it was to be eliminated.[19] One of Dudfield's suggestions was to set up a municipal milk depot and municipal crèches. Yet such a proposition did not meet with universal approval. Indeed, many within the borough regarded municipal provision, as one newspaper editor put it, as the first step towards 'municipal trading in a peculiarly insidious form' and an evasion of responsibility on the part of the individual.[20]

While in Kensington the conservative majority prevented the

establishment of a milk depot, this was not the case in Woolwich, where one was set up in 1906 as the result of the election of the Labour borough council in that year. The milk depot in Woolwich followed the example of those that had been established else-where, providing milk for necessitous nursing mothers and those infants whose mothers were unable to breast-feed, as well as infant consultations and health visiting.[21] One of the chief aims of those organizing the depot was to provide modified germ-free milk at the same price as ordinary milk, and thus affordable by the very poor. The policy was seen as crucial since about half of the parents of those infants in the borough who could not be breast-fed lacked the means to purchase modified milk; they were forced to use the cheaper condensed milk, which often caused infantile diarrhoea.[22] In 1908 it was estimated that about 19 per cent of the infant popu-lation in Woolwich were being hand-fed.[23] The depot was therefore not serving a small minority. Within months of opening it was reporting a rapid increase in numbers and was obviously supplying a public need.[24] 328 infants were being supplied with milk, approx-imately 12 per cent of the infant population of the borough.[25] A great majority of their parents would not otherwise have been able to feed their children sufficiently.[26] Woolwich was unusual in that it supplied milk to the family's doorstep.[27] In common with other depots it also had an extensive health visitors' scheme and established infant consultations for infants to be weighed and checked by a medical officer. Thus the depot was also encouraging the education of mothers in infant rearing and feeding.[28]

While the establishment of the milk depot in Woolwich partly arose as a result of pressure from the Labour Party within the council chamber, and can therefore be seen as a triumph for the more radical political forces in Woolwich, its existence was never secure. Soon after the depot appeared the Labour Party lost its majority on the borough council to the Municipal Reformers, one of whose aims was to shut down the depot. Echoing the sentiments expressed in Kensington, they argued that the depot was merely a form of 'municipal trading' which was too expensive to run and a waste of rate payers' money. The depot was forced to economize. This had repercussions for the ways in which mothers were charged. Any mother who fell behind on her payments, even if only for a week, was denied supply from the clinic. In 1908 the strict application of this rule led to the withdrawal of milk from many infants.[29] The depot was a costly business involving not only the purchasing of milk, but also the daily collection and cleansing of bottles. By 1909 it was costing between £400 and £500 a year. After attempts to have the depot taken over by a private firm failed, it was finally closed in 1909.[30]

While the more conservative lobby finally had the upper hand in Woolwich, both in restricting the extent to which the very poor could be provided with the service and in shutting the depot, it encountered much opposition within the borough. This can most clearly be seen in the debates that followed the depot's closure. These illustrate the very different perceptions and demands that surrounded the provision of welfare services as a whole. Numerous letters of objection were sent to the council from individual mothers, as well as the Women's Labour League and various trade union associations and radical working-men's clubs. Such protests signified the widespread grassroots support for the depot and concern for maternal and infant welfare provision.[31]

The main argument put forward by the Municipal Reformers for the closure of the depot had been that it covered only a small proportion of infants and was therefore an inefficient use of the council's resources.[32] Others claimed, however, that the depot had been a popular service, and had provided for nearly half of the infant population in the borough who were hand-fed.[33] Indeed, they stressed that such a service was important even if it had saved only one infant life within the borough. This was the view put forward by the mothers themselves, the Labour Party, the chief Medical Officer of Health, and Alice Gregory, the honorary secretary of the British Hospital for Mothers and Babies.[34] For these campaigners the question was not one of saving rate payers' money, but rather one of long-term investment in the health of the whole borough and ultimately the future of the nation.

VI

The struggle over the provision of the milk depot in Woolwich and Kensington indicates the tension between interest-parties that was inherent in the politics and policies surrounding maternal and child provision in these years. One matter which also attracted particularly heated controversy was the provision of *birth control*.[35] What is most interesting about the struggle over such provision was that both protagonists and antagonists justified their stand on the grounds of protecting the future and the health of the nation.[36]

Within the Labour Party and among other socialist circles, attitudes to birth control were not clearly delineated by class or gender. Some of the strongest advocates of birth control came from a number of working-class women's groups and the Workers' Birth Control Group (established in 1924). Much of their campaign was aimed at continuing the momentum generated within the Women's Sections of the Labour Party to pressurize the Minister of Health into allowing for the provision of birth control within maternal and infant welfare centres. This they justified on the grounds that birth control was already widely available to those who could afford to pay for it. In this context birth control was viewed as a right and something which should not be left to voluntary private clinics.[37] Many of their arguments also stressed state provision of birth control as a matter which affected the 'physical and mental constitution of the community'.[38] Many women in the Labour movement saw contraception as a class issue; something which should be free to all women, a means of ending the oppression of motherhood and the high maternal mortality caused by numerous abortions.[39] Nevertheless this was not a view shared by all Labour women. Ethel Bentham for instance opposed such provision on the grounds that it would subject women to more oppression by husbands.[40] Similarly some Labour women, alongside other male Labour supporters, saw birth control as a 'side issue' which did not tackle the more important need to alter the 'distribution of wealth and the means of life'.[41]

What was at stake was whether state funding for contraception would enhance or undermine the welfare of the nation. Opponents of state-funded birth control were quick to see such a measure as fuelling an even faster decline in the national birth rate and hence depleting a population whose maintenance was seen as crucial to the nation's military and economic strength in the rest of the world. Much of their concern derived from the fact that the birth rate had halved from slightly over 36 per 1,000 in 1876, when it stood at its peak, to 17 per 1,000 in 1927, and was predicted to fall even more.[42] Advocates of birth control, however, saw it as a means of securing better health for women and their infants and hence of enhancing the future of the nation. Many promoters of birth control stressed that it enabled women to space their families, and thus improve both their health and their capacity for reproduction.

231

The provision of birth control within state-funded maternal and child welfare centres raised the question of the extent to which the state could intervene in areas which were often seen as purely private matters. Central to this was also the degree to which such provision conflicted with religious beliefs. Should birth control be encouraged by the state in the interests of safeguarding the health of the wider community regardless of religious considerations? Of the four boroughs, Stepney and Kensington are particularly good for examining these questions and highlight the complexities involved in the provision of birth control clinics and the different approaches that were adopted.

Advocates of birth control were particularly powerful in Kensington, where the third birth control clinic in the country was established under the auspices of the Society for the Provision of Birth Control Clinics.[43] Known as the North Kensington Women's Welfare Clinic (NKWWC), it was founded on the premises evacuated by the mother and baby clinic established by the Women's Labour League. Yet the provision of birth control in Kensington cannot be linked solely to the activities of the ranks of Labour women. Indeed, those who were most active in pushing for such provision came not from Labour women (who were not unanimously in favour of birth control), but from those who mixed in more politically conservative circles. This can be seen from the founding members of the NKWWC, including Margery Spring-Rice who had ties with the Liberal Party.[44] Beyond the clinic other supporters of birth control included Miss Pennefather, who was a Municipal Reform councillor from 1922 and chairman of the Maternal and Child Welfare Committee in the 1930s.[45] Much of the pressure within Kensington from these women and those involved in the NKWWC stemmed from the strong tradition of the women's movement in Kensington, which put the rights of women high on the agenda. Yet it would be a mistake to see these efforts as solely the result of the suffragette movement. During the inter-war years many birth control groups found little sympathy nationally from middle-class and upper-class membership of feminist organizations.[46]

The degree to which Margery Spring-Rice and others succeeded in prioritizing birth control within the borough can be seen from the fact that in 1926 Kensington became the first council in London, and the second in the country, to campaign for changes in the laws governing contraception so as to enable it to be provided through infant welfare centres run by local authorities. This was justified on the grounds that it would guarantee greater continuity of care and enable women to be served by those who knew their backgrounds.[47] The Ministry of Health, however, opposed such a measure on the grounds that birth control was not in the remit of the infant welfare centre. Those women needing contraceptive advice for medical reasons were, it argued, to be referred to a private practitioner or hospital. When in 1930 the Ministry finally allowed local councils to provide birth control information, Kensington Council was quick to point out the limitations of the Ministry's guidelines. Provision was restricted to married women and to cases where further childbearing would be dangerous to the health of the mother.[48] Such stringencies meant that the number of maternal and infant welfare clinics that offered birth control advice remained small. By 1937 only ninety-five of 423 of these centres had opened birth control clinics.[49] Many within Kensington Council felt that provision should be available to all women, and be provided on social and economic grounds as well as medical ones.[50]

A deputation sent in 1934 from the council and the North Kensington clinic to the Ministry of Health illustrates the ways in which many within the borough felt about such provision. One of the premises of the campaign for greater access to birth control was that it was an issue which affected the whole life of the borough and the future of the nation. For those leading the deputation, birth control was not just a matter of preventing the unnecessary deaths of mothers and infants, who were the key to the next generation, but was a means of limiting state intervention on a grander economic scale.[51]

Birth control was seen therefore as a much cheaper option than other social welfare measures. Indeed, for those leading the deputation, birth control was an issue intertwined with the conditions prevailing in North Kensington, which many feared would undermine the borough's reputation and also fuel revolutionary fervour for greater state intervention. This contrasted with the demands made by those involved in the Labour Party, who saw the provision of free contraception as something which should supplement, rather than be an alternative to, state help in areas such as family allowances and cheaper housing.[52] In this way the rhetoric surrounding health and the future of the nation was intricately bound up with state intervention and policy decisions which were tied to perceptions of the needs of the neighbourhood. Birth control was also seen as one of the answers to Kensington's very high rate of infant mortality.[53]

In Stepney the debate about birth control was very different, and more heavily influenced by religious considerations. The strong presence within the borough of Irish Catholic immigrants and their children made the municipal provision of birth control a contentious issue. During the 1920s grassroots Catholic organizations within Stepney were particularly active in opposing birth control.[54] Fearing that public institutions were about to be given public money to offer birth control advice, the Catholic community sent a circular to the Ministry of Health in 1925 calling on it not to do so.[55] In 1927 a voluntary birth control clinic was, however, established in Stepney, prompting a heated discussion within the council chamber. Some councillors such as Miriam Moses, who was Jewish, called for municipal provision of contraceptive information for poor mothers, arguing that they should have it available in the same way as rich people. However, while Miriam Moses saw this as a question which should not be determined by religion, those who opposed municipal provision thought religion paramount and regarded the topic of contraception as one which should not even be discussed by the council.[56] The strength of opposition within the council and in the borough can be measured by the resolution that was passed in 1929, which forbade council workers to provide information on birth control, arguing that the practice was not only 'probably illegal' and against the public policy of the Ministry of Health, but also 'highly offensive to the religious beliefs and conscientious opinions of many inhabitants of the borough'.[57] Yet while the resolution in 1929 showed the council to have a certain consideration for the residents it was serving, this changed in 1931 when the council accepted the Ministry of Health's new ruling that contraceptive information should be made available through maternal and child welfare centres to those women for whom childbearing would be dangerous.[58] Clearly what was at stake was not only the type of resident the Council saw itself as serving, but also the degree to which it was bound by central policy from outside the borough.

VII

The concept of 'community' thus played a variety of roles in shaping maternal and infant welfare in the early twentieth century. Its meanings were intricately bound up with the social relations of neighbourhood and the perceptions a variety of people attached to their entitlements. With increasing state provision of welfare, a new sense of communal responsibility was emerging which drew the concept of 'community' closely together with the notion of what the state should provide. Yet the extent to which this change affected the provision that was made depended greatly on a complex number of factors. The ways in which the notion of 'community' was perceived and used depended greatly on the social and economic circumstances of particular areas, as well as on their political and social networks and gender relations.

In the richer and more politically conservative boroughs such as Hampstead and Kensington the sense of community was more strongly associated with the needs of the rate payer. Any welfare and health services that were provided in these areas were restricted accordingly. This can be seen not only from the limited expenditure that these boroughs were willing to allow for services, but also from the hostility that was aroused in trying to establish a service that would be municipally funded, as in the case of the milk depot in Kensington. By contrast, the poorer and more politically radical boroughs, such as Stepney and Woolwich, had a greater sense of a community that was focused on the needs of the poor and not the ratepayer. This was reflected in the large amounts of money that they were willing from early on to allot to municipal services which were seen as crucial for the majority of its residents.

None the less, even within the boroughs the concept of who constituted the community and whose needs should be served was under continual negotiation. This can be seen in the case of the establishment of the milk depot in Woolwich, where both the rhetoric and the provision of services were contested in terms of the interests of the poor and the ratepayer. As the case of birth control shows, the battle-lines were drawn not only between the rate payers and the poor, but also on religious and ethnic grounds. Further, any policies carried out in each borough were greatly influenced by national policies and interests as much as by local neighbourhood relations and political affiliations. Thus, Stepney, which initially resisted the provision of birth control on the grounds that it would offend some of its Irish Catholic residents, by later years was providing such services as a result of the relaxation of national policy which began to legitimate birth control provision.

NOTES

1 Fuller discussion and documentation of much that follows will be found in L. Marks, *Metropolitan Maternity: Maternal and Infant Welfare Services in Early Twentieth Century London* (Amsterdam, 1996).
2 A. Davin, 'Imperialism and Motherhood', *History Workshop Journal* 3 (1978), pp. 9–66.
3 See for instance the inaugural address by John Wheatley (MP) in *Third English Speaking Conference on Infant Welfare* (London, 1924),
4 J. Lewis, *Women and Social Action in Victorian and Edwardian England* (Aldershot, 1991), Introduction and Conclusion.
5 H. Llewellyn Smith *et al.*, *The New Survey of London Life and Labour*, vol. 6 (London, 1934), p. 427.
6 E. Ross, 'Survival Networks: Women's Neighbourhood Sharing in London before World War I', *History Workshop Journal* 15 (1983), pp. 4–27. See also J. White, *The Worst Street in North London: Campbell Bunk, Islington, Between the Wars* (London, 1986), ch. 3.
7 F. Prochaska, 'A Mother's Country: Mothers' Meetings and Family Welfare in Britain, 1850–1950', *History* 74 (1989), pp. 379–99; A. Summers, 'A Home from Home: Women's Philanthropic Work in the Nineteenth Century', in S. Burman (ed.), *Fit Work for Women* (London, 1979), pp. 33–63.
8 L. Marks, 'Irish and Jewish Women's Experience of Childbirth and Infant Care in East London, 1870–1939: the Responses of Host Society and Immigrant Communities to Medical Welfare Needs', D.Phil. thesis (Oxford 1990), especially chs 4 and 8; and L. Marks, *Model Mothers: Jewish Mothers and Maternity Provision in East London, 1870–1939* (Oxford, 1994).
9 M. Moore, 'Social Work and Social Welfare: the Organization of Philanthropic Resources in Britain 1900–1914', *Journal of British Studies* 16 (1977), pp. 98–102.
10 See for example *Kensington News and West London Times*, 25 Feb. 1910, p. 2.
11 Summary of replies received by Shoreditch Borough Council for the Financial Year 1922–3 to assess the provision of milk supplies. In Tower Hamlets Local History Library, Stepney Maternal and Child Welfare (MCW) Committee Minutes, 12 June 1922, p. 75; *Census for England and Wales* (1921), table 13.
12 *Hampstead and Highgate Advertiser*, 20 June 1912, p. 3.
13 *The Pioneer*, May 1922, p. 5.
14 *The Pioneer*, 8 April 1921, cited in D. Weinbren, '"The Peace Arsenal"

Scheme: the Campaign for Non-Munitions Work at the Royal Ordnance Factories, Woolwich after the First World War', Ph.D. thesis (London, 1990), p. 165.

15 Cf. C. Collins, 'Women and Labour Politics in Britain, 1893–1932', Ph.D. thesis (London, 1991), pp. 386–9.

16 *Hampstead and Highgate Advertiser*, 12 Feb. 1921, p. 6.

17 This is explored in greater detail in Marks, *Metropolitan Maternity*.

18 *Kensington News and West London Times*, 17 Oct. 1902, p. 5.

19 *Kensington News and West London Times*, 24 June 1904, p. 5; 28 Nov. 1913, p. 6; cf. Greater London Records Office, Hampstead, Medical Officer of Health (MOH) *Annual Report* (A/R) for 1906, p. 36; *Hampstead and Highgate Advertiser*, 5 Dec. 1912, p. 3.

20 *Kensington News and West London Times*, 4 July 1902, p. 5; 17 October 1902, p. 5; 5 Nov. 1907, p. 6; 9 May 1913, p. 6.

21 D. Dwork, *War is Good for Babies and Other Young Children: a History of the Infant and Child Welfare Movement in England 1898–1918* (London, 1987), pp. 101–23.

22 Woolwich MOH, A/R 1906, pp. 82–3.

23 Woolwich MOH, A/R 1908, p. 149.

24 Greenwich Local History Library, Woolwich Council Minutes, 23 Nov. 1906, p. 101.

25 Woolwich MOH, A/R 1908, p. 149.

26 Woolwich Council Minutes, 17 June 1910, p. 577.

27 Woolwich MOH, A/R 1906, pp. 84–5.

28 Woolwich Council Minutes, 5 July 1905; 23 Nov. 1906, p. 101; 11 Oct. 1907, pp. 897–8; 9 Oct. 1908, pp. 822–3; 17 June 1910, pp. 576–7; Woolwich MOH, A/R 1906, pp. 82–95; 1907, pp. 87–8; 1908, pp. 149–50; 1909, pp. 114–15.

29 Woolwich MOH, A/R 1908, p. 150.

30 R. B. Stucke (ed.), *Fifty Years History of the Woolwich Labour Party 1903–1953* (London, 1953), p. 14; Woolwich MOH A/R 1910, p. 108; Woolwich Council Minutes, 15 March 1910, p. 378.

31 Woolwich Council Minutes, 20 April 1910, p. 426; 23 May 1910, p. 454.

32 Dwork, *War is Good for Babies*, pp. 116–22.

33 Woolwich Council Minutes, 17 June 1910, p. 582.

34 *The Pioneer*, 2 Nov. 1906.

35 Collins, 'Women and Labour Politics in Britain, 1893–1932', pp. 281–2.

36 *The Labour Woman*, 1 March 1924, p. 34.

37 *Report of the Conference on the Giving of Information by Public Health Authorities*, April 1930 (Fawcett Library, East London University, 362.82).

38 *The Labour Woman*, 1 July 1925, p. 123, and 1 March 1926, p. 88.

39 R. A. Soloway, *Birth Control and the Population Question in England, 1877–1930* (Chapel Hill and London, 1982), pp. 284, 296.

40 Collins, 'Women and Labour Politics', pp. 281–2; J. Lewis, *Women in England 1870–1950* (Brighton, 1986), p. 32; J. Lewis, *The Politics of Motherhood: Child and Maternal Welfare in England, 1900–1939*

(Beckenham, 1980), pp. 196–200; A. McClaren, *Birth Control in Nineteenth-Century England* (London, 1978), pp. 61, 215–8; Letter from Isabel Peterkin to Lucy, 15 Oct. 1976, in papers relating to Mary Middleton and Margaret MacDonald Baby Clinic and Hospital (National Museum of Labour History, Manchester, Box BAB 429).

41 *The Labour Woman*, 1 May 1924; 1 Oct. 1926, p. 151. For a fuller discussion of the conflict over birth control within the Labour Party see Collins, 'Women and Labour Politics', pp. 281–90.

42 N. E. Himes, 'The Present Status of Birth Control in England', unpublished MS. 4 (Francis Countway Library, Boston, MA, BMS C77 Box 85, f. 903).

43 E. H. Martyn and M. Bird, *The Birth Control Movement* (London, 1930), p. 18; Soloway, *Birth Control*, pp. 192–5.

44 Soloway, *Birth Control*, pp. 259, 291.

45 *Kensington News and West London Times*, 3 Nov. 1922, p. 3; 23 Oct. 1925, p. 5; and *North Kensington Citizen*, Dec. 1931.

46 Soloway, *Birth Control*, p. 298.

47 Kensington Local History Library, Kensington Council Minutes, 27 July 1926, p. 359; 6 March 1934, p. 164.

48 Stepney Maternal and Child Welfare (MCW) Committee Minutes, 14 April 1931, p. 38.

49 Lewis, *Women in England*, p. 33.

50 'Kensington Public Health Survey' (1932); letters between Kensington Council and Ministry of Health, 25 Feb. 1931; 17 March 1931; 24 Feb. 1931; 15 April 1931; 13 Feb. 1934 (Public Record Office (PRO), MH 52/177); Kensington Council Minutes, MCW Committee, 24 Feb. 1931, p. 183; 6 March 1934, pp. 165–6; 24 July 1934, pp. 346–7.

51 Notes from Deputation to Ministry of Health from North Kensington Women's Welfare Clinic, 1 June 1934 (PRO, MH 52/177).

52 *North Kensington Citizen*, July 1937, p. 1.

53 Notes from Deputation to Ministry of Health from North Kensington Women's Welfare Clinic, 1 June 1934 (PRO, MH 52/177).

54 M. M. Thornely, 'A Record of the Catholic Women's League. Union of Catholic Mothers', 19 May 1935, p. 19 (Westminster Diocese Archive file: Hi 2/951).

55 *Magazine of the Sacred Heart*, Sept. 1925, pp. v–vi. See also *The Tablet*, 9 April 1921, p. 475; 5 Aug. 1922, p. 187; 28 Oct. 1922, p. 579; 29 Nov. 1924, p. 701; 13 Dec. 1924, pp. 812–3.

56 Stepney MCW Committee Minutes, 15 March 1927, p. 308.

57 Stepney MCW Committee Minutes, 19 Feb. 1929, p. 63.

58 Stepney MCW Committee Minutes, 14 April 1931, p. 38.

10

COMMUNITIES, 'CARING', AND INSTITUTIONS

Apartheid and child care in Cape Town since 1948[1]

Sandra Burman and Patricia van der Spuy

I

Apartheid was introduced into South Africa in 1948, with the advent of the National Party government. Many Nationalists were Nazi sympathizers during the war, and apartheid – literally, 'separateness' – proved to be an experiment in social engineering so nakedly racist that it aimed to introduce racial criteria into every aspect of social policy, and to ensure that even the most intimate aspects of family life conformed to the requirement of separation of the 'races'. Since February 1990, when the State President announced that apartheid would be dismantled, the policy has been increasingly viewed both within and outside the country as an aberration which will vanish without trace. Our concern is to examine the extent to which the suppositions underlying this view are borne out by fact, focusing on child care as a crucial area for the development of society. Were the social policies introduced by the Nationalists totally new, and how effectively were they actually implemented? This chapter discusses preliminary work on these issues, concentrating on various attitudes towards caring for children not provided for within the family, and therefore most dependent on state or other non-familial care and provision.[2] Given the dearth of secondary material on this topic, the investigation was limited to Cape Town, the earliest, and one of the three largest, cities in South Africa.

Apartheid was not imposed onto a society free from racial classification and discrimination. From the establishment of Cape Town as the Dutch East India Company's victualling station in

1652, distinctions had been drawn between the Dutch and other, darker-skinned people.[3] Racial discrimination was initially contained within regulations controlling labour and, later, public health. By the time that the National Party came to power in 1948, the inhabitants of South Africa were divided into four categories: 'European', 'Asiatic', 'Native' (referred to below as 'African'), and 'Coloured'. Apartheid legislation built on and refined these categories. In Cape Town and the surrounding area, the aim above all was to make provision for a plentiful supply of labour while preventing African families from settling there, and to ensure (as in the rest of the country) that Whites maintained their position at the top of the power structure by remaining 'pure-blooded' and therefore distinguishable. It is against this background that the fragmented story of care for children outside the family must be seen.

II

The children about whom we are writing are those defined by the Children's Acts between 1937 and 1983 as 'in need of care'. They are sometimes referred to as 'unwanted children', but this is probably less often true than in the case of wealthier societies where financial assistance for the poor is more readily available. Many of the children who were placed in foster homes or institutions during the apartheid era were there because growing family disintegration (which increased in all sectors of the society, though at different rates) had left mothers unable to cope financially and often emotionally with the needs of a family, though far from wishing to discard their children. Unfortunately, a high proportion of such children were never reunited residentially with their families, and we therefore include them as children without families.

Where children were indeed unwanted, some of the reasons were unique to an apartheid society, although historical precedents can no doubt be found both in and outside South Africa. The ramifications of apartheid legislation were numerous and, presumably, not always foreseen, least of all in the area of family life. For example, where a child was born as a result of a transgression of the Immorality Act (prohibiting sexual intercourse between Europeans – or Whites – and other ethnic groups), the child would constitute evidence of the crime which it would be

240

difficult to refute, especially if the mother were the White party. Should a complaint be laid – and there were many instances of neighbours, husbands, or boyfriends doing so – the evidence of the child's existence would almost certainly result in jail sentences of at least six months for its parents. Such children were likely to be unwanted.[4]

Or take the rather more ambiguous – and convoluted – case of children living on the streets of Cape Town. Case histories vary, but such factors as apartheid laws on labour and Group Areas played an important role. For example, domestic servants living on their employers' premises in a Group Area from which the former were excluded were eventually prohibited from having any child, including a baby, live with them in the servant's quarters. Repeated police raids – in White Group Areas at least – attempted to enforce this.[5] The penalties were prison sentences for the servant, *de facto* for the child if no other care were immediately available, and increasingly punitive fines for the employer. In these circumstances it became essential for 'live-in' domestic servants, where possible, to send the child to live with any available relatives or friends in the rural areas or the appropriate townships of the city, however unsuitable they might be. A prevalent myth among non-Africans held that such 'placements' were not an unusual hardship for African children in particular. It is true that there was a long tradition among Xhosa families of sending children to live with grandparents as soon as they were old enough to be of help,[6] and that the extended form of Xhosa families originally made absorption of non- or distantly related children much easier and more common than in nuclear families. However, the introduction of pass laws, citizenship restrictions, the Coloured Labour Preference Area policy (which provided that no African in the Western Cape could be given a job if a Coloured person were available for it), standardized small houses for urban Africans, and a housing system that required a male household head all severely restricted the choice of possible care-givers. Many children were placed with unsuitable people and chose to run away rather than remain there. Similarly, as African marriage and family life disintegrated under the impact of the migrant labour system (which forced families of men working in the cities to remain in – or leave for – the rural areas), illegitimacy figures for Africans spiralled upwards from the 1960s. This resulted in an increase in the number of African children taking to the streets of Cape Town and surrounding areas rather than remaining in homes in which they faced violence and abuse. We have no record of White children becoming street children in the same way, presumably because there were many more institutional facilities for White children, and because the police would have ensured that they did not remain on the streets.

Within the limits set by the apartheid state, the facilities provided and the choices made by parents and children all determined whether children would be raised by members of their families or not. In what follows we explore the options where familial care was not available to the child: institutional care, fostering outside the child's family, and adoption.

III

When apartheid was introduced, the legislation governing children's homes was the Children's Act, No. 31 of 1937, which contained no explicit provisions for homes to be racially segregated. However, the first half of the twentieth century had seen a trend in Cape Town and the country as a whole towards racial segregation of welfare institutions and state intervention in the provision of welfare services, including institutional care.[7] It was noted that in Cape Town, where in 1939 there were apparently 103 private or semi-private organizations,

> the position . . . is far more favourable to the Non-European population than in the country at large. A survey of the principal welfare organizations of the Union [of South Africa] conducted in 1938 . . . showed that 75 per cent. of the 400 organizations investigated restricted themselves to work among Europeans and 8 per cent. to work among Non-Europeans.[8]

Act 40 of 1947 represented the initial apartheid interference in the organization and administration of voluntary welfare services by the state, whereby provision was made for the centralization and registration of welfare organizations. The National Welfare Board was established and organizations had ninety days in which to register; only registered organizations were permitted to raise funds or were eligible for state subsidies.[9] In this way the state could control the 'racial' composition of children's homes. In 1948 there were approximately twenty voluntary homes in Cape Town, most of which were segregated.[10] There were also two Places of Safety and Detention: Bonnytoun for Coloured children and Tenterton for White children. These were under the control of the Department of Social Welfare. Despite the government's avowed intention to segregate institutions, Bonnytoun, founded in 1942, was forced to accommodate African children until the late 1960s, when a Place of Safety was established for African children.

Although none of the Children's Acts enforced the segregation of children's homes, the apartheid laws and regulations, including the 1955 Registration of Separate Amenities Ordinance, together with ministerial powers of discretion, allowed the respective ministers to decide which institutions could be registered and certified. No 'Non-White' children were cared for in White institutions, although some Coloured homes did accept African children. Moreover, the state attempted to enforce segregated *administration* of welfare services – a more problematic step in a city where the voluntary welfare organizations had a history of philanthropy from 'Europeans'. In 1957 the Department of Native Affairs 'advised local authorities and all organizations providing services to Africans that it would *not* approve the control of social welfare or recreational services for Africans by voluntary White bodies or by mixed committees'.[11] Historically, Africans' rights to live in Cape Town had never been recognized, and the term 'Non-European' in Cape Town generally referred to Coloured rather than African. It is not surprising, therefore, to note that when institutional child care was officially segregated along racial lines, no provision was made for Africans. Influx control and the prohibition of 'mixed' administration of social welfare services militated against such provision being made in the apartheid era. In 1966, the principle of 'separate administrative control' was extended to voluntary services for Coloured people.[12]

Financial need forced many voluntary organizations to register, including both religious and secular associations. Between 1948 and 1960, when a new Children's Act came into effect, no new homes were established in the city. According to Helm's *Cape Town Directory* of 1959, ten homes existed for mainly Whites, nine being provided by religious and one by a secular organization. There were also six homes for Coloured children, including a Muslim orphanage. In addition to Helm's list there existed a Lutheran establishment for White children, the Schweizer Institut Deutsche Weisenheim, and, in emergencies, homes for unmarried mothers

243

tended to take infants in need of care. No children's homes existed in Cape Town at this time for neglected or abandoned African children. In 1968 a registered children's home was opened in the African township of Guguletu (formerly Nyanga West), but it never operated as such; from the outset it was used as a Place of Safety and Detention, where juveniles could be held pending court cases. In the early 1980s a Place of Safety was established in the African township of Langa, which provided temporary care for young children who were to be fostered or adopted. By 1984 the Guguletu Place of Safety had closed down, leaving only one institutional home for African children in need of care in Cape Town. If these children were not fostered or adopted, the welfare services had no alternative but to send them to institutions in other parts of the country.

The amount of institutional care for children altered very little over the entire period, despite increased need for such homes.[13] Part of the dearth of children's homes in Cape Town was due to an attitude shared by both the state and many sections of the community. Throughout the period under review, leading members of both religious and pro-apartheid groups in Cape Town believed that the best care for children could be, and should be, provided within 'the family', one of the few concepts not defined in apartheid legislation. Therefore, children's homes were meant to provide *temporary* care. Practically all children's homes, only excluding Places of Safety and Detention, were under the control of religious bodies. The Roman Catholic Church and Protestant churches provided 70 per cent of White and 80 per cent of Coloured homes in 1960.[14] The Dutch Reformed Church ran two homes for White children in the city, as well as a home for unmarried White women which was registered under the Children's Act and in exceptional circumstances provided care for neglected White girls.[15] However, despite a need for more homes and the Dutch Reformed Church's belief that 'the family', the cornerstone of the Afrikaner 'volk' (nation), was in danger of disintegration, it established no new children's homes in this period. The 'Jeugkommissie van Algemene Sinode' of 1966 argued that institutional care was a last resort for children who could not be contained within the family; it was better to place orphaned and neglected children in foster, rather than institutional, care because it allowed the child to learn about the importance of the family. It was felt necessary to encourage members of the Church to provide foster care for such children.[16] This belief was shared by the Muslim and Hindu communities.[17] Indeed, children's homes were discouraged, if not prohibited, by Islam, because it was believed that parents should care for their children.[18] No registered children's homes were run by the Muslim or Hindu communities of Cape Town, although Muslims made sporadic use of a building in which to care for children.[19] In the 1970s this building was apparently converted into a Muslim orphanage, but due to a scandal involving child abuse, it was closed, and then became the Bruce Duncan Children's Home, a Place of Safety for Coloured children.[20]

As a consequence of the perceived need for the family to provide for children 'in need of care', the emphasis of voluntary child welfare provision was on feeding schemes and day-care services, rather than institutional care. Mathews reported that a 'major thrust in pre-school care' for Coloured children occurred in the late 1960s, which she suggests may be attributable to the 'large scale entry of women into wage labour during the 1950s and 1960s'.[21] Along with a belief in the centrality of familial care is the belief in the role of the mother as primary care-provider. Child care provision tended to cater for the needs of children whose mothers worked outside the home and therefore could not care for them during the day, rather than for children who had no home to which to return.

Another major factor in determining the provision of children's homes in Cape Town was the differential allocations in the national budgets to apartheid-defined groups. Similarly, given the ratio of wealth in the different sections of the population, and the tendency for each community to provide first for its own group, it is not unexpected that there should have been many more privately funded homes for Whites than for Coloureds or, even more so, for Africans. But this provides only part of the picture, for during the period under discussion apartheid measures had other crucial but more indirect effects on the demand for such homes, with very different consequences for Coloured people, Indians, and Africans.

For the Coloured communities (including Indians), the years from 1961 constituted a period of catastrophic upheaval, as all Coloured families living in areas proclaimed as White Group Areas were moved from their homes to new housing estates in newly proclaimed Coloured Group Areas on the outskirts of the city. Often the small size of the new houses forced extended families to split into nuclear families, and old established communities which had grown up over many decades were scattered through-out the new housing. No attempt was made in housing allocation to keep extended families or communities together. Others were removed under slum clearance legislation, which was used in conjunction with the Group Areas Act but did not place a legal responsibility on the government to provide alternative housing. The result was an escalation in squatting throughout the Cape Peninsula and on vacant land on the outskirts of the Cape Town metropolitan area, to the extent that by the late 1970s approximately a quarter of the Coloured population were squatters.[22] Apart from such effects as swiftly escalating crime rates, the moves meant that new buildings had to be found for children's homes.

Within the Indian community in particular, the effects of the Group Areas Act were accentuated by the result of forcing almost all Indians into Group Areas separate from the rest of the so-called Coloured community. Strong family bonds prevented the development of squatting, but the smallness of Indian suburbs led to great overcrowding and financial hardship. As Indians were largely traders and small shopkeepers, the call for which was obviously limited within one area, many were forced to change their occupation. Women, who before had served first in the shops of their natal families, and then those of their husbands, were forced out into factory jobs, with increasing changes in attitudes and marital patterns. The community lost much of its cohesion, dividing between those who were able to continue trading, and those who perforce moved into factory and similar work.[23] Community institutions faltered, and there was very little provision for children in need of care. No children's homes or reformatories catered for Indian children in Cape Town; if no form of foster or adoptive care could be provided, the children had to be sent to Natal, the province where South Africa's largest Indian community lived.[24]

For Africans, apartheid had yet other effects. In Cape Town, the only city where the Coloured Labour Preference Area policy was in force, African families were increasingly excluded and most jobs for Africans (other than domestic work) were for men. It was almost impossible for women to get permits for factory work, and they were excluded from nursing in provincial hospitals. There

246

were few schools for Africans – in 1959 no government schools for Africans at all, only one community high school, twenty-one community primary schools and two private Church schools.[25]

For Langa location, which had been established as a 'model in housing and planning', and where originally 'great stress was laid on providing married quarters', it was decided in 1956 that in future only single male accommodation would be built.[26] Men were accommodated in single men's hostels from which women were officially excluded, although it proved impossible to enforce this in practice. By the late 1970s official housing ratios indicated that 79 per cent of all African workers legally living in Cape Town were meant to be there *without* their families.[27] It was therefore felt that there was little need to provide for the requirements of women or children. Indeed, the myth existed that there were almost no Africans resident in the city on any long-term basis,[28] although a 1977 survey of one of the larger of the mushrooming illegal squatter camps, Crossroads, revealed that about 85 per cent of households contained two-parent families. However, while some 50 per cent of the heads of households (all males) had a legal right to be in the Cape Town area, only 9.3 per cent of the women were there legally. Similar proportions were found in the Unibell squatter camp which sprang up in 1976.[29] Despite frequent raids by the police and deportations of such women and children, census figures for the Cape Town area showed that in 1960 there were 14,231 African women in Cape Town and 23,912 children, 8,674 of whom were under the age of 5. By 1970 the figures had risen to 18,794, 36,831, and 10,310 respectively.[30] Yet government attitudes and measures precluded any possibility of children's homes.

Indeed, both sets of policies described above – the Group Areas removals and the ramifications of the pass and labour laws for Africans – actually drastically increased the need for children's homes. Such indices of family disruption as divorce/separation rates and illegitimate birth rates appear to have escalated as apartheid measures took effect in both Coloured and African communities, although defective statistics make this difficult to document except from anecdotal information gleaned from interviews with experienced community workers and religious leaders.

Where homes were unavailable or regarded as a last resort, the question arose of what alternative forms of child care were available to children outside their families. These may be listed as fostering – formal and informal – and adoption.

IV

By 1948, legislation controlling adoption and fostering was in force, but while officially the same for all adoptions and fostering placements in South Africa, it in fact applied very differently to the different groups that comprised Cape Town. The relevant legislation had been put in place by the Children's Act, No. 31 of 1937, which had replaced much of the earlier child protection legislation as well as the first South African act on adoption.[31] The underlying policy embodied in the 1937 Act was of state supervision, but foster care or adoption between people regarded as of different racial or religious groups was not explicitly prohibited. This was obviously completely unacceptable to the new apartheid government, but without the introduction of new legislation, racial conditions could be imported into adoption by the use of such sections as 2(e), which required that the proposed adoption serve the interests and conduce to the welfare of the child. Moreover, as apartheid legislation accumulated and hardened both the law and attitudes, foster or adoptive parents of children of a different population group were increasingly liable to persecution from neighbours and prosecution under the Group Areas Act.

From the government's point of view, however, adequate attention to these considerations was not always ensured, and stronger measures were eventually introduced in a new Children's Act, No. 33 of 1960. This provided that before granting an adoption order, a children's court had to have regard, *inter alia*, to the religious and cultural background, ethnological grouping, and nationality of the child. However, subsequent court cases elicited the interpretation that these were merely factors to be considered by the court and did not prevent the adoption of a child belonging to one population group by a person belonging to another.[32]

Not unexpectedly, the next act on fostering and adoption, the Child Care Act, No. 74 of 1983, carried the explicit prohibition of a child's being placed in the custody of or being adopted 'by any whose classification in terms of the Population Registration Act, 1950 (Act No. 30 of 1950), is not the same as that of the child, except where such person is the parent or guardian of the child'. The implementation of the Act was delayed, and it eventually came into effect in February 1987, by which time the dismantling of apartheid had already begun. However, as the operative law, the racial provisions remained in full effect until partially vitiated by the Population Registration Act Repeal Act, No. 114 of 1991, after which new babies were no longer classified and assigned to 'population groups'. Older children, however, retained their racial classification and thus continued to be affected by the 1983 legislation.

Throughout most of the apartheid period, parallel with the child care legislation was the possibility of a customary law adoption in the case of Africans, as customary law exists as a recognized system of law, albeit subsidiary to the South African state's Roman-Dutch law and statute. However, customary law adoption was generally used only to supply an heir for an otherwise heirless branch of a family or 'house', and was rare, although fostering was very common. In 1952 the question came up for decision as to whether the statutory provisions governing adoption overrode customary law, and the court held that they did not in the case of the institution of an heir, as a custom peculiar to Africans.[33] While we should not discount the possibility that this type of adoption was used in Cape Town during the apartheid period, no mention of it has been found in archival, legal, or interview sources. It is more likely to have been used in rural areas. In so far as it was practised, it arguably became illegal in 1987 (when the 1983 Act came into effect),[34] but such illegality in the eyes of the state would not necessarily have prevented its continued use, and informal fostering, without state supervision, has continued to be a very common form of coping with children without families.

Many other factors have played a role in the differential use of adoption in different sections of the population. One has obviously been the supply of babies for adoption by each population group. Illegitimate births, the most common source of such children, have increased for all groups throughout the period, but at different times and at differing rates. In 1955, for example, the Medical Officer of Health for Cape Town reported that 2.65 per cent of all births of babies classified as European and 23.66 per cent of non-European were illegitimate.[35] By 1965 the figures had risen to 4.6 per cent for Whites and 27 per cent for Non-Whites.[36] In 1989–90, the last year for which detailed illegitimacy statistics for Cape Town are available, the figures were 19.6 per cent for Whites, 44 per cent for Coloureds, 7.3 per cent for Asians, and 69.8 per cent for Africans. The total of illegitimate births as a percentage of total live births was 45.7 at the last count.[37]

From the point of view of fostering and adoption, the rise in the relatively low proportion of White illegitimate births has been offset by an increase in the number of mothers of illegitimate children who have kept their offspring, as both religious control and the stigma of illegitimacy have declined. Greater economic resources and child care assistance for single mothers have further encouraged this trend. One of the results of the change has been the continuation of long waiting lists of White couples wanting to adopt. In contrast, there is no waiting period for Coloured couples wishing to adopt, except for Muslims, there being relatively few Muslim babies available; Muslim girls are usually more strictly supervised and illegitimate babies tend to be absorbed into the family and privately adopted for religious and status reasons. The greatest surplus of children waiting to be adopted is among the African community.

The number of children available for adoption has also been influenced by the extent of poverty within different groups at different times, as well as the alternative sources of child care available to mothers in desperate straits. While the record of child support payments by children's fathers has been dismal in all groups,[38] White mothers, the population group least likely to be able to turn to family help, could usually resort to temporary placements in homes, when necessary, and in more recent years have also been more likely to be able to cope with the aid of the better day care available to them. Coloured and African mothers would most commonly use the extended family or friends where these were available, but the disruptions of urbanization, Group Areas removals, migrant labour, and – for Africans – pass legislation, have all tended to make resort to the family increasingly difficult. As official facilities for African children in particular were non-existent for much of the first thirty years of the apartheid era, the outlook was bleak for the child of a mother unable to cope and without informal assistance on which she could call. Even after official Places of Safety were established, facilities were grossly inadequate. At the Nonzamo Place of Safety in Langa, for example, the thirty places available were too few, according to a nursing sister there in 1984, to provide for all the children who were abandoned or so grossly neglected that they were removed to the home. Whenever the home was full, the staff were forced to refuse to accept children brought in by social workers. Many of the children's parents were alcoholics; some were in hospital, others in jail. Between three and five children were brought in every month, with the number greatly increasing at Christmas. If the children were not adopted within three months, they were either placed in foster care, if a foster home could be found, or sent to a children's home for Africans – all of which were in other parts of the country.[39] Given this situation, it is not surprising that the hospitals have found themselves in the last few years faced with an increasing number of African children abandoned there after birth or admission for sickness, most recently many AIDS babies.[40]

The demand for adoptive children was influenced by similar factors to the supply. Smaller housing, greater poverty, and the greater need for education that came with urbanization all tended to limit the demand as industrialization and apartheid took their toll, especially among the Coloured and African populations. These considerations were, to some extent, counteracted by the continued importance of certain cultural considerations, such as the unacceptability among Africans in particular of being childless. A woman's status derived from her motherhood to a large extent, and among the most poverty-stricken who were childless, there was also frequently a desire to adopt a child to care for them in their old age.[41]

On the other hand, there were also certain cultural and religious taboos which militated against adoption rather than fostering. Among Africans, adoption of children from outside the family was not regarded as desirable, since such children could not call on, sacrifice to, or otherwise propitiate, the family ancestors when this was required. Such rites as initiation for boys (which involves the ancestors) were generally observed among the Xhosa throughout the period under discussion, but an adopted boy could not be catered for by his adoptive family. Similarly, a belief in misfortune being due to ancestor displeasure, which required propitiation, was also widespread. As a result, adoption was frowned on, although by the 1980s this appeared to be changing: some informants spoke of it as still operative, while a nursing sister involved daily with adoptive parents believed it to have disappeared.[42]

Among Muslims, adoption was frowned on for religious reasons, since in Islamic law an adopted child may not inherit on intestacy from the adoptive parents, while a foster child can still inherit from its natal family. A factor of a somewhat different order in diminishing Muslim adoptions was the provision observed by some adoption agencies that a child would not be placed with a Muslim couple unless they had been married in court rather than only by Muslim rites (as is the case with a high proportion of the Muslims in Cape Town).[43] Among the Indian community, babies for adoption were usually imported from Durban, rather than the adoption of Cape Town babies taking place. This was in response to the wishes of adoptive parents, who feared that, given the smallness of the Cape Town community, they might 'bump into the natural mother somewhere along the line'. Unwanted Indian babies from Cape Town were either sent to orphanages in Natal or fostered.[44]

Where adoptive parents could not be found for children who were available for adoption, many of the children were placed in foster homes, which all South Africa's welfare departments preferred to institutions. Attitudes to fostering appeared to differ between different groups. Social workers in the Indian community, for example, stressed the reluctance of people to take in foster children, given lack of space in overcrowded homes and, according to at least one informant, ignorance of what was expected of them. Wherever possible, members of the extended family were asked to provide foster care. In contrast, both the Coloured and African communities had such long histories of informal fostering that the question of role expectations did not arise. Moreover, although space became an increasing problem in both the latter communities, the need for supplementary income by those who were likely to be asked to foster children was so great that even the low foster grants available were a major inducement to take in foster children on those terms. Foster grants were available – at differential rates for each population group – throughout the apartheid period.

Although no statistics are available, anecdotal evidence indicates that informal fostering also continued at a high rate in both African and Coloured communities, most of the children being relatives, but with a number, especially in the African community, being unrelated. Many life histories we have collected indicate that abandoned children were much more readily absorbed into African families than was the case with other population groups – to the extent that it was not uncommon to find cases of Coloured women who left their babies with African care-givers and then vanished, with the result that the children were raised as Africans, speaking Xhosa as their first language, and with the girls marrying African men. There are many descriptions, starting in the nineteenth century, of the enjoyment Africans appeared to derive from their children, and the value they attached to them,[45] and this is borne out by many comments in our interviews in the 1980s, when interviewees spoke scathingly of the coldness of White people, even to their own children. However, when one of the nursing sisters at the Nonzama Place of Safety in Langa was interviewed in 1984, the picture was beginning to change.[46] Babies in the home had been found abandoned – by railway police who had found them in railway stations, by social workers who had found them on the streets, or – most shocking of all in a community where grandparent child care is the norm[47] – by grandparents no longer able to afford to keep them. Since then, workers with 'strollers' – homeless children living on the streets – have found that the number of African children 'strolling' has increased noticeably since approximately 1989, from about 10 per cent to some 30 per cent. They attribute this to rapidly escalating African urbanization in Cape Town since the abolition of the pass laws in 1986,[48] interacting with increasing rural poverty as over-crowding and drought conditions take their toll. But urban poverty too has been increasing as the economy rapidly declines and inflation rises; the impression of workers in the Cape Town shelter for strollers is that most Africans are now generally so poor that they cannot afford to absorb children into their families as they once did.[49]

V

How far, then, did apartheid change the situation regarding child care for children outside the family in Cape Town, rather than merely continue existing practices? In the first place, although White children were already cared for in separate institutions, apartheid led to the segregation of children classified as Coloured, Indian, and African into separate children's homes, and with access to facilities, of very different standards. Each population group was increasingly controlled by different bureaucracies under separate departments, until it became virtually impossible for a child in need of care to obtain it from anywhere other than those classified as of its own group. Racial as well as religious considerations placed increasing limits on who could become adoptive parents, while fostering across the colour line became virtually impossible as Group Areas legislation was implemented, making it illegal and increasingly difficult for a child of one population group to live in the area of another. Group Areas removals and pass laws broke up extended families and limited the size of houses, making fostering more difficult in both Coloured and African families. The combination of the Coloured Labour Preference Area and the pass laws also removed many potential foster families and rendered remaining ones so poor that eventually the informal fostering system began to disintegrate too.

In the light of current political changes, it must be asked how far these effects of apartheid can be reversed, so that the irreversible may be recognized as permanent, and provision made accordingly. While the new South African government has sought to abolish apartheid bureaucracy and provisions, the social and economic ills and disparities caused by apartheid will take several generations to banish on the most optimistic scenarios, and urbanization is likely to continue for many years yet. For child care, these trends combine with probably the most damaging and long-lasting bequest of apartheid – the disintegrative effect it has had on the families of those not classified as White. The predominant consequence has been that a far greater number of children not only no longer have a secure home base, but very possibly will not find one with a foster or adoptive family, especially if current worldwide trends of placing children within their communities prevail. While a foster home may well remain the best option if it is available, it is evident that the vision of the all-welcoming African family in particular no longer accords with much of the reality of Cape Town, even if the myth of its existence continues both within the African community and outside it. The growing number of abandoned and abused African children, and even some evidence of an increase in infanticide,[50] make it clear that for the immediate future at least, institutional homes must be provided as a safety net for *all* children in South Africa. Moreover, a sharp increase in the number of orphans as a result of AIDS is projected.[51] It is to be hoped that with a higher proportion of all sections of the South African population involved in the same institutions, greater financial provision, sympathetic planning, and tighter supervision will eliminate the type of scandals that have plagued some in the past.[52] If good institutional homes are not provided to supplement fostering and adoption, it seems probable that the number of street children will continue to grow and that this phenomenon will eventually embrace children of all sections of the population, as measures which have protected Whites are eliminated. While there may well be a temptation to recall days where foster homes were plentiful and to seek such a solution as less expensive for a country which faces the heavy expense of economic reconstruction, the long-term costs of seriously neglecting the needs of a section of the country's children are likely to be far greater than the immediate saving. Moreover, if South Africa is to build a more humane and less violent society after the era of apartheid, it cannot afford to economize on this aspect of post-apartheid reconstruction.

NOTES

1 The research for this paper was sponsored by the Human Sciences Research Council, the University of Cape Town Research Committee, the Wingate Foundation, and the Save the Children Fund, UK, to all of whom we are most grateful. Our thanks, too, to Professor Christopher Saunders and Dr Elizabeth van Heyningen for comments on an earlier draft, and to Claire Fiddian-Green and Lydia Maier for research assistance. Factual information in what follows is correct as of July 1994.

2 Besides the normal archival and library sources, much of the information for this article was derived from interviews conducted over the past twelve years for a series of contemporary research projects on divorce and illegitimacy in South Africa. As many of the interviews were granted on condition that the identities of the interviewees would be kept confidential, their names have not been included in the references.

3 South African historiography has been marked by debates on the origins of racism, and the relative importance of race and class in the shaping of the country's history. See C. Saunders, *The Making of the South African Past: Major Historians on Race and Class* (Cape Town, 1988).

4 For an example of a White baby having been abandoned by a Coloured mother, see Cape Archives 1/WBG 1/1/1/134, Case B 11223/1966, *The State v Freda van der Merwe*, 31 January 1967.

5 S. Burman, 'The Interaction of Family Law and Legislation for Urban Africans in South Africa', *Acta Juridica* (1984), pp. 96–7.

6 P. Mayer and I. Mayer, *Townsmen or Tribesmen: Conservatism and the Process of Urbanisation in a South African City*, 2nd edn (Cape Town, 1971), pp. 273ff.

7 See S. Burman and M. Naude, 'Bearing a Bastard: the Social Consequences of Illegitimacy in Cape Town, 1896–1939', *Journal of Southern African Studies* 3 (1991), pp. 396–8, for a description of institutions caring for illegitimate children, in particular in the years from 1895 to 1939.

8 E. Batson, 'The Social Services: Discrimination and Counteraction', *Race Relations* 7 (1940), p. 21.

9 Welfare Organizations Act, No. 40 of 1947, sections 3 and 6.

10 There is no published directory for Cape Town in 1948. These figures have therefore been extrapolated from O. J. M. Wagner, *Social Work in Cape Town* (Cape Town, *c.* 1939), and B. Helm's *A Cape Town Directory of Social Welfare* (Cape Town, 1959).

11 South African Institute of Race Relations, *A Survey of Race Relations in South Africa, 1958/59* (Johannesburg, 1960), p. 288.

12 Consolidated Circular No. 29 of 1966. See also *A Survey of Race Relations in South Africa, 1966* (Johannesburg, 1967), pp. 288–9.

13 The Theron Commission Report of 1976 stated that there were ten institutions for Coloured children in the Cape Peninsula, catering for 604 children. There was such a shortage of accommodation for Coloured children that many were sent to the ten homes in the Northern Cape, eight of which were run by the Roman Catholic Church (*Commission of Inquiry into Matters Relating to the Coloured Population Group* (Cape Town, 1976): Paragraphs 11.12 and 11.125).

14 The Theron Commission, Paragraph 11.126, stated that of the thirty-four Coloured children's homes in South Africa, thirty-one were run by the Christian church: five by Nederduitse Gereformeerd Sendingkerk, nine by the Anglican and fifteen by the Roman Catholic Church. The report does not state who ran the remaining two homes.

15 Interview with a social worker at Magdalena Huis, Parow, 10 May 1990.

16 Nederlandse Gereformeerd Kerk, 'Jeugkommissie van Algemene Sinode' (n. p., 1966), paragraph 1.52.

17 See, e.g., *Muslim News* (Cape Town), 11 Dec. 1981, p. 2.

18 Interview with a social worker, 9 April 1986, concerning a Muslim children's home in Durban. Much resistance was experienced from the religious community, despite the fact that the home took only Muslims, including African Muslims. The same views were expressed in an interview with a social worker in the Muslim community in Cape Town, 19 June 1992.

19 Helm, *A Cape Town Directory*, lists one Muslim orphanage for 1958, but it does not appear to have been registered. Our statements regarding Muslim institutional care are tentative, pending the completion of our research.

20 Interview, 19 June 1992.

21 C. Mathews, 'Childcare in Cape Town: an Investigation of the Childcare Problem in "Coloured" Working Class Families', Hons. thesis (Cape Town, 1983).

22 J. Western, *Outcast Cape Town* (London, 1981), p. 279.

23 Interviews with two leading professional men of the Indian community, 7 Jan. 1983 and 13 April 1983.

24 Interview with social worker, 9 Feb. 1989.

25 Helm, *A Cape Town Directory*, Appendix E. Community schools were state-aided, whereas private schools were not.

26 M. Wilson and A. Mafeje, *Langa* (Cape Town, 1963), p. 4.

27 Western, *Outcast Cape Town*, p. 292.

28 In 1968 a proclamation defined all African workers in Cape Town as one-year contract labourers (Western, *Outcast Cape Town*, p. 292).

29 Western, *Outcast Cape Town*, pp. 297–8.

30 1960 Census, Report 02–02–01; 1970 Census, Report 02–05–13. In 1970 the ratio of adult African women to men was 1 : 3.5 and that of children (aged 0–19 years) to adults was 1 : 5.

31 The Adoption of Children Act, No. 25 of 1923.

32 *Joffin v Commissioner of Child Welfare, Springs* 1964 (2) SA 506 (T); *S v Kommissaris van Kindersorg*, 1967 (4) SA 66 (SWA); *S v M* 1968 (1) PH M3 (SWA); *C v Commissioner of Child Welfare, Wynberg* 1970 (2) SA 76 (C); *Ex parte Kommissaris van Kindersorg, Boksburg: In re NL* 1979 (2) SA 432 (T).

33 *Zibi* 1952 NAC 167 (S).

34 Bennett argues that the statutory adoption provisions in the Child Care Act of 1983 supersede customary law on adoption, as a result of the imperative language of the Act (which was the same in the 1937 and 1960 Acts), read together with section 27 (a new provision which makes it clear that the Act was intended to be applied to Africans). T. W. Bennett, *A Sourcebook of African Customary Law for Southern Africa* (Kenwyn, 1991), p. 377.

35 City of Cape Town Health Department, *Annual Report of the Medical Officer of Health*, 1954–55.

36 *Annual Report of the Medical Officer of Health*, 1965.

37 *Annual Report of the Medical Officer of Health*, 1989–90. Research has shown that the figures are for children who are born outside any form of marriage, and nearly all to single mothers who are not living in stable relationships. See S. Burman, 'The Category of the Illegitimate in South Africa', in S. Burman and E. Preston-Whyte (eds), *Questionable Issue: Illegitimacy in South Africa* (Cape Town, 1992), pp. 121–35.

38 S. Burman and S. Berger, 'When Family Support Fails: the Problems of Maintenance Payments in South Africa', *South African Journal on Human Rights* (July 1988), pp. 194–203 (November 1988), pp. 334–54; and S. B. Burman, 'Maintaining the Single-Parent Family in South Africa: Law and Reality', in M. T. Meulders-Klein and J. Eekelaar (eds), *Family, State and Individual Economic Security* (Brussels, 1988), pp. 507–32.

39 Interview with a nursing sister at the home, 27 Nov. 1984.

40 Interviews with social workers at Red Cross Children's Hospital, 4 Dec. 1989 and 26 Dec. 1990. For a sample of newspaper articles, see *Cape Times*, 12 Sept. 1984; 2 Oct. 1984; 8 Jan. 1987; and 20 Feb. 1987.

41 However, research in the 1980s showed that as the economy deteriorated and the high rate of African unemployment became even higher, pensioners' children actually frequently lived off their

parent's pension rather than supported the parent, at least as regards financial assistance (S. Burman, 'Law versus Reality: the Interaction of Community Obligations to and by the Black Elderly in South Africa', in J. Eekelaar and D. Pearl (eds), *An Aging World: Dilemmas and Challenges for Law and Social Policy* (Oxford, 1989), pp. 216–21.

42 E.g. interview with nursing sister at the Nonzamo Place of Safety, 27 Nov. 1984; interview with an adoption officer attached to a children's home in Cape Town, 8 May 1990.

43 Interview with adoption officer, 8 May 1990. According to South African law, marriages must be solemnized by a marriage officer, and at the time of writing no imam in Cape Town is one, as the requirements for taking up such an office include an undertaking to uphold the laws of the land, which exclude polygamous marriages. Religious and political objections to such a provision have prevented the Cape Town imams from becoming marriage officers.

44 Interviews with social workers in the House of Delegates Welfare Department, Jan. and Feb. 1989.

45 E.g. E. Casalis, *My Life in Basutoland* (London, 1889), pp. 179–80; and M. Hunter, *Reaction to Conquest: Effects of Contacts with Europeans on the Pondo of South Africa* (London, 1961), p. 164. See also C. Molteno, M. Kibel, and M. Roberts, 'Childhood Health in South Africa', in S. Burman and P. Reynolds (eds), *Growing Up in a Divided Society: The Contexts of Childhood in South Africa* (Evanston, IL, 1986), p. 52.

46 Interview, 27 Nov. 1984.

47 See, e.g., Burman, 'Law versus Reality'.

48 The Abolition of Influx Control Act, No. 68 of 1986.

49 Interview with the head of The Homestead, 13 June 1992.

50 For instance, the *Cape Times*, 16 Jan. 1988, reported on the discovery of a day-old baby who had been buried alive. In September of the same year, the mother, another woman, and a man were charged with the murder of the baby (*Cape Times*, 15 Sept. 1988). See also *Cape Times*, 9 Oct. 1988, and *Cape Times*, 13 Oct. 1988, where it was noted that there had been six cases that year of new-born babies abandoned or buried. Although the impression reflected in the media is that infanticide and abandonment increased in the 1980s, further research into criminal and other primary records is required in order to validate this. Unfortunately many of the criminal records in the State Archives have been 'weeded', so that a full record no longer remains. For examples of reports of abandonment in the 1990s, see, e.g., *Cape Times*, 29 Mar. and 12 Dec. 1990, and *Argus*, 24 July 1991.

51 See, e.g., A. H. Lategan, 'NEPI Preschool Working Group: Final Report', n. p., 10 Mar. 1991, p. 3.

52 See, e.g., *Cape Times*, 16 Mar. 1991, where it was reported that 180 children in a Place of Safety had been horribly abused.

11

DEMOGRAPHIC CONDITIONS, MICROSIMULATION, AND FAMILY SUPPORT FOR THE ELDERLY

Past, present and future in China[1]

Zhongwei Zhao

China has experienced great demographic changes during the last few decades. Because of the improvement in people's living standards and public health, mortality has declined considerably. Before 1950 the crude death rate was very high, around 35 per thousand or even higher; during the 1950s it decreased dramatically to under 15 per thousand; by the mid-1960s it had fallen further, to below 10 per thousand, and has stayed at this low level since. According to the 1990 census the crude death rate was 6.3 per thousand during the previous year. As a direct result of this mortality decline Chinese people now live much longer than before, and life expectancy at birth has increased from about 35 years in the late 1940s to about 70 years in the early 1990s.[2] Another significant demographic change is China's unprecedented fertility decline, which has been generated, to a large extent, by the nationwide family planning campaign. High fertility was widespread in China until the late 1960s. During the 1950s and 1960s the crude birth rate was higher than 30 per thousand in most years, and China experienced her most rapid population expansion. Since the early 1970s, however, fertility has dropped considerably. The 'total fertility rate'[3] has fallen from around 6 in the late 1960s to about 2 at present – which is lower than the level of population replacement.[4]

According to these figures China has already moved from the combination of fertility and mortality typical of a less developed country to being close to the typical profile of a more developed country. The so-called demographic transition has been completed in China in less than forty years. This is much faster than that observed in Europe, where the transition started first, and is perhaps the fastest ever recorded. Such radical developments have considerably altered the age composition of the Chinese population. On one hand the proportion of old people has noticeably increased, and on the other the proportion of young people has rapidly fallen. Such changes are most likely to accelerate in the coming decades, and they have caused increasing concern about how China will support her huge population of the elderly in the next century.

There has been a widespread notion that, in the past, old people in China were always supported by their families, particularly by their sons. Partly because of such a belief, the rapid demographic change, especially the rapid change in the age structure of the Chinese population, has also created some panic. People worry that because of the considerable reduction in the number of children and in the complexity of the Chinese family, which itself is partly a result of decreasing fertility, the long tradition of family support of the elderly may collapse in the ageing society of the future.

The feasibility of old people's being supported by their families is first of all determined by demographic conditions, although it is also affected by political and legal systems, socio-economic development and cultural traditions. In discussing whether the elderly could be supported by their family members or other relatives, we should first examine their kinship networks or the availability of kin. The number and type of living kin available to an individual is primarily determined by demographic factors, i.e. fertility, mortality, and nuptiality. Birth and marriage will increase the number and the type of kin, while death will decrease them. For the same reason, the feasibility of the elderly's living in a household with a complex structure and being supported by their children is also, at least partly, determined by whether certain demographic conditions can be satisfied; and how long such an arrangement will last depends upon the length of time during which these conditions can be maintained. In a population in which each couple has only one child – as for example under the family planning regime that is now observed in many parts of China – even if all married children remain in the households of the parents of either the husband or the wife, around 50 per cent of the parents may not be able to live with their married children and form complex households. Similarly, in a population with high levels of celibacy, divorce, or mortality, a high frequency of 'incomplete' or 'broken' families is likely. For these reasons, examining demographic conditions and changes in the availability of kin is important in the investigation of family support for the elderly.

Before 1950 demographic conditions in China were characterized by high mortality, fairly high fertility, early age at marriage, universal marriage for women, and a high proportion of men marrying.[5] Under such a demographic regime, was the situation of family support for the elderly really as ideal as that described in many stories? How many old people could have lived in large multi-generational households and been supported by their children? Given the considerable demographic changes recorded during the last half century, how does the contemporary Chinese kinship network differ from those existing in the past? Finally, is the rapid fertility decline observable in China since the early 1970s really going to cause great difficulties with family support for the elderly or even lead to the collapse of the traditional support system in the coming century? These issues, which are undoubtedly of great interest to social scientists and of great importance to policy-makers, will be examined in this paper by the use of computer microsimulation.

Computer simulation is a technique whereby computers are used to mimic 'reality' under 'experimental' conditions. A simulation is normally carried out through the following procedures. Firstly, according to the issue to be tackled, an algorithm is constructed which specifies the operations to be performed by computers in generating the outcome. Secondly, on the basis of such an algorithm, a computer program is written. Finally, the input parameters required are selected and the program is run to produce simulation results.

The simulation system used in this study is called CAMSIM, which has been invented by James E. Smith. In simulating the kin of each person, the system starts with an individual who is designated as 'ego' and treated as a central figure in generating his (or her) kin set.[6] At birth such an ego will be assigned an age at death according to the life table distribution of ages at death, then other events such as marriage and fertility will be simulated according to the predetermined probability governed by the input parameters. If the ego is scheduled to marry, a spouse of the appropriate gender and age will be created by the system. After that, if they are scheduled to have a baby, a child of appropriate gender will be simulated. When the simulation of the life history of ego has been completed, the system will, by using a similar method to allocate the demographic events due to occur to his (or her) relatives, simulate ego's descendant kin forward and ascendant kin backward.[7] After this has been done, detailed records of all these simulated people will be kept for later data analysis and the system will start to simulate the second ego and his (or her) kin set. By repeating the same procedure, a model population with a certain number of egos and their kin can be created. The kin composition of these egos can then be examined at any time selected by the researcher. This simulation approach introduces substantial computational efficiencies and enables easy movement forward and backward in time when the kin of each ego is simulated; but it also leads to some limitations. The egos simulated by CAMSIM, for example, can be seen only as a group of persons of the same birth cohort or generation, but not an entire population of a certain time. Furthermore, the current version of the system is still not able to simulate rapid demographic changes and their influences in a single simulation run. Since this paper is not about computer microsimulation itself, detailed discussion of these issues will not be presented here.[8]

In spite of its limitations, the simulation result produced by CAMSIM is useful in demonstrating what kinship networks would be like if the demographic conditions specified in a given simulation remained constant, and how kinship networks would change in response to a change in demographic conditions. Theoretically, questions of this kind can be studied through empirical research, but in practice the data which allow these questions to be examined are extremely difficult to obtain. This is particularly the case in historical research. Family reconstitution can provide some insights into the kinship network of the past, but problems arise when we lose track of those who moved out of the reconstituted parish and those who lived elsewhere.[9] The kinship structure constructed through family reconstitution is, therefore, hardly complete. Chinese genealogies generally provide better information on inter-generation linkage and on the ascending and descending kin of an individual, but female kin and kin of the female side are frequently found to have been excluded from such records.[10] For these reasons, detailed quantitative studies of historical kinship networks are rather limited. Fortunately, computer microsimulation has aided developments that overcome these problems. By linking demographic conditions and various types of kin available to each individual at different stages of the life course, it has provided an important tool for the study of kinship networks.

In this exercise, three simulations have been carried out under different demographic conditions, and each simulated population consists of 500 male egos and their kin. In the first simulation the input parameters are similar to the demographic rates recorded in China around 1930 and represent a high fertility and high mortality regime.[11] In the second, the parameters are close to the demographic conditions of the mid-1960s, and they represent a regime with high fertility, relatively low mortality, and rapid population growth. In the third, the mortality rates and marriage patterns are close to those observed in the 1980s and early 1990s, and the fertility parameters are deliberately set at a relatively low level – the simulated 'total fertility rate' is about 2 and the net reproduction rate 0.92 – in order to investigate the influence of below-replacement-level fertility. This regime, therefore, is characterized by low mortality and low fertility. The major demographic indicators derived from the three simulated populations are summarized in Table 11.1. In this table and also in the following discussion, the three simulations are referred to as simulation one, two, and three.

Before presenting the results of the simulation, the following points need to be addressed. Although a considerable amount of work has been done to make the CAMSIM system more realistic, the simulated demographic process is still much simpler than the

Table 11.1 Demographic rates in three simulated populations

Simulations	Life expectancy at birth		Reproduction rate		Intrinsic growth rate	Mean age at marriage	
	Females	Males	Gross	Net	(%)	Females	Males
One	25.0	25.2	2.68	1.08	0.3	18.0	19.5
Two	65.5	61.2	2.92	2.61	3.4	19.8	20.1
Three	72.7	68.5	0.95	0.92	–0.4	22.0	22.5

actual demographic process observed in any population, and the simulation outcome is not equivalent to those obtained from survey or census data. In a real world, variations in kinship networks and in demographic regimes are affected by many complicated factors. When a population is surveyed and its changes are recorded, all the factors which cause these changes are effectively taken into account. In contrast, a computer simulation can take into account only those factors which have been explicitly included in the simulation process. Therefore, strictly speaking, computer simulation does not simulate reality, but rather the implications of certain specified conditions. Nevertheless, the simulation result has provided us with some important points of reference in the study of kinship networks of the past and has shed light on possible future changes in kin composition.

In Figures 11.1 to 11.4, the mean numbers of surviving parents, spouses, siblings, and children for the male population, and the proportions of male egos without surviving kin of these types are presented graphically. All these data are derived from the three simulated populations.

The mean number of surviving parents and the proportion of males having no surviving parents are displayed in Figure 11.1, both by age of egos. The graphs show that under the three different demographic regimes, the mean number of surviving parents each ego would have and the proportion of males having no surviving parents vary considerably. Under the high mortality applied in simulation one, which is similar to that recorded in China around 1930, the mean number of surviving parents decreases very quickly, and the proportion of males without surviving parents increases quickly. For example, at age 25 each ego, on average, has only 1 surviving parent, and those without surviving parents account for about a quarter. At age 50 the mean number of surviving parents is only 0.1 of a person, and the proportion having no surviving parents is nearly 90 per cent. In contrast, under the low mortality conditions applied in simulations two and three, many more people could share lifetime with their parents, and for a much longer period. For example, under the mortality similar to that observed in the 1980s and the early 1990s, each ego would have 1.9 surviving parents at age 25 and nobody would have lost both of their parents. At age 50, each ego would still have one surviving parent and those without surviving parents are only about a quarter.

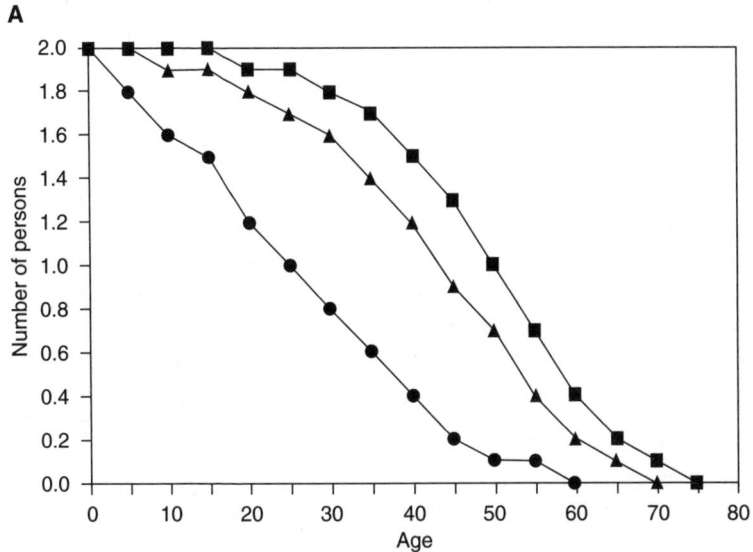

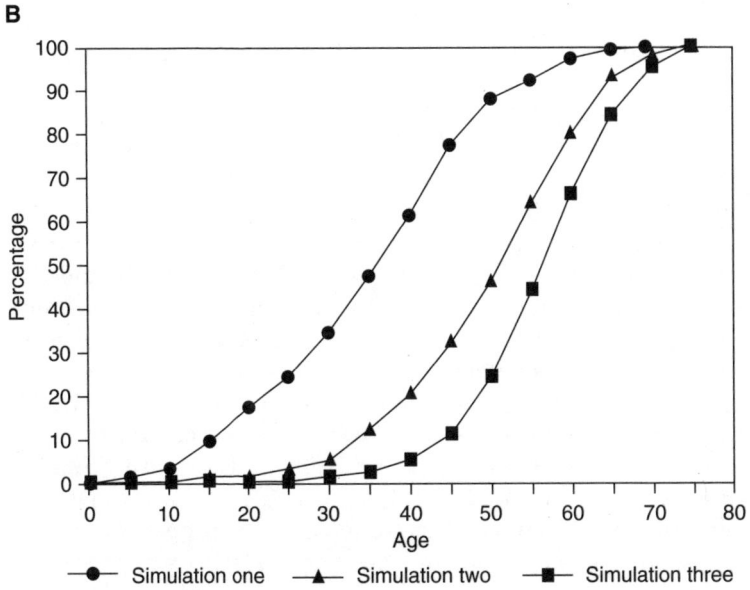

Figure 11.1 (a) Mean number of surviving parents by age of male ego
(b) Percentage of males with no surviving parent by age

Figure 11.2 maps the mean number of surviving spouses and the proportion of men having no surviving spouses. The graphs further illustrate the impact of mortality on changes in kinship networks, although the differences between these graphs (especially at lower ages) are also related to variations in marriage patterns. As indicated by simulation one, under the severe mortality, the proportion of men without surviving spouses is considerably higher from age 30 and widowhood arrives very early for many people. At age 50, for instance, about 40 per cent of men would have no surviving spouse. Under the demographic regime which is similar to that existing in contemporary China, as suggested by simulation three, people marry later than they did in the past, but because of the improvement in mortality from age 30 onward the proportion of men with living spouses and the mean number of surviving spouses are considerably higher. According to this simulation, for example, even at age 60, the number of men without surviving spouses is less than 10 per cent. It is quite obvious that, with low mortality, people could live with their spouses for a much longer time.

When the mean number of surviving siblings and the proportion of male egos having no surviving siblings (see Figure 11.3) are examined, the following points stand out. According to simulation two, under the demographic conditions similar to those existing in China in the mid-1960s – high fertility and relatively low mortality – the proportion of egos having no surviving siblings is extremely low and the mean number of surviving siblings is very high. From ages 10 to 60, almost everyone would have at least one surviving sibling and each ego, on average, would have more than four surviving siblings. In contrast, under the low fertility and low mortality similar to those observed in the 1980s and early 1990s, the proportion having no siblings is notably higher, and the mean number of siblings notably lower; but because of the low mortality both figures remain at the same level for a very long time. Under the demographic conditions similar to those recorded in China around 1930, the high fertility inevitably leads to a great number of births, but because of the high mortality the mean number of surviving siblings is not very high and the proportion having no surviving siblings is not low. As suggested by the graphs, starting from age 20, the mean number of surviving siblings declines and the proportion of egos without surviving siblings increases rapidly. Under such a demographic regime, the mean number of surviving

A

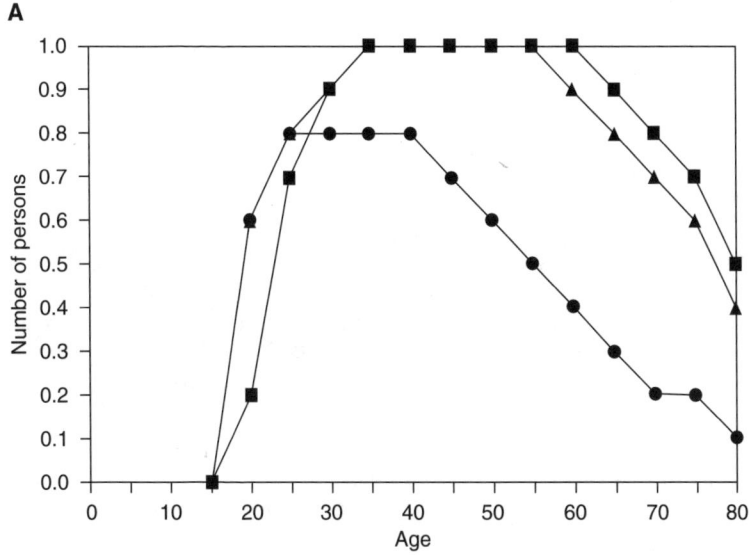

B

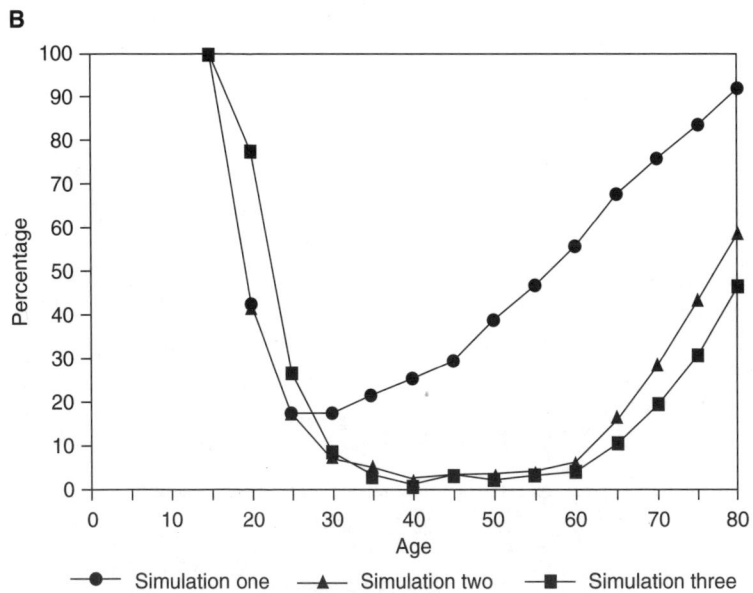

Simulation one ── Simulation two ── Simulation three

Figure 11.2 (a) Mean number of surviving spouses by age of male ego
(b) Percentage of males with no surviving spouse by age

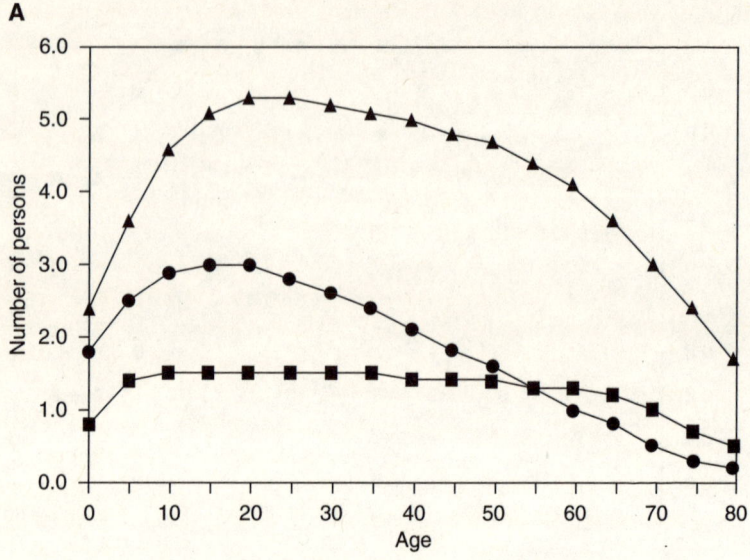

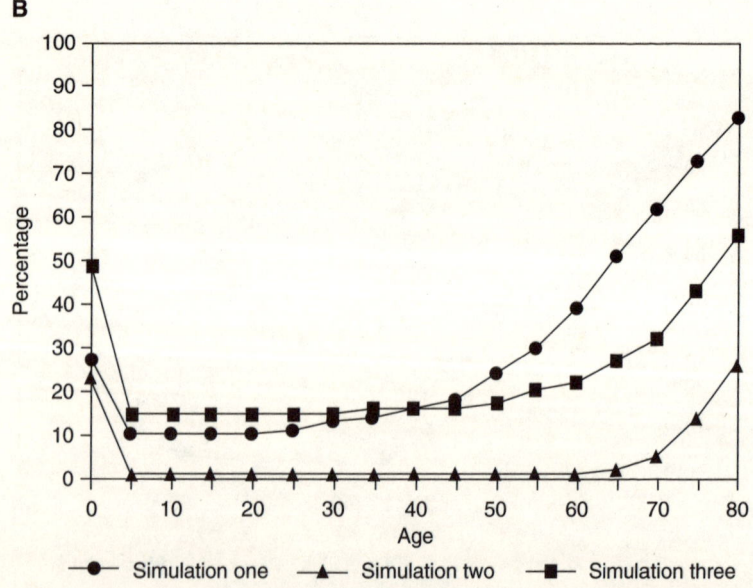

Figure 11.3 (a) Mean number of surviving siblings by age of male ego
(b) Percentage of males with no surviving siblings by age

siblings of a person aged 60 or above is even lower, and the chance of that person having no surviving siblings is much higher than that under the low fertility regime applied in simulation three.

Finally, let us look at the mean number of surviving children and the proportion of male egos having no surviving children (see Figure 11.4). The combined influence of the high fertility and relatively low mortality is evidently revealed by simulation two. This simulation suggests that under the given demographic conditions, the proportion of males having surviving children and the mean number of their surviving children would rise rapidly when egos are aged between 20 and 40. After the latter age, those having no surviving children constitute about 10 per cent and the mean number of surviving children is about 5. Under the demographic regime specified in simulation three, people marry and give birth at a slightly older age, and for this reason the rapid increase in the proportion of male egos having children comes three or four years later. Because of the low fertility, the mean number of surviving children is much lower in comparison to that suggested by simulation two. However, according to the third simulation, the proportion of people having no surviving children is rather similar to that of the second. This obviously arises from the fact that in contemporary China, although fertility is low, a very high proportion of married couples still have at least one child. Results produced by simulation one are particularly noteworthy. These results show that under the high mortality and the high fertility, which are close to those observed around 1930, the mean number of surviving children is not very high and at most of the specified ages it is only between 2 and 3. More notably, from age 30 onward, the proportion of male egos without surviving children is much higher than those indicated by the other two simulations.

So far, we have briefly examined the impact on kinship networks of three different demographic regimes. Because of limitations of space, only the proportion of males who have no surviving parents, spouses, siblings, and children, and the mean numbers of these kin have been provided in this paper. However, changes in the kinship network of females have also been examined in the exercise and the results have confirmed the findings presented earlier. In addition, changes in some other types of kin such as uncles and aunts, nephews and nieces, grandparents and grandchildren have been simulated, and they have shown a trend which is similar to those reported above.

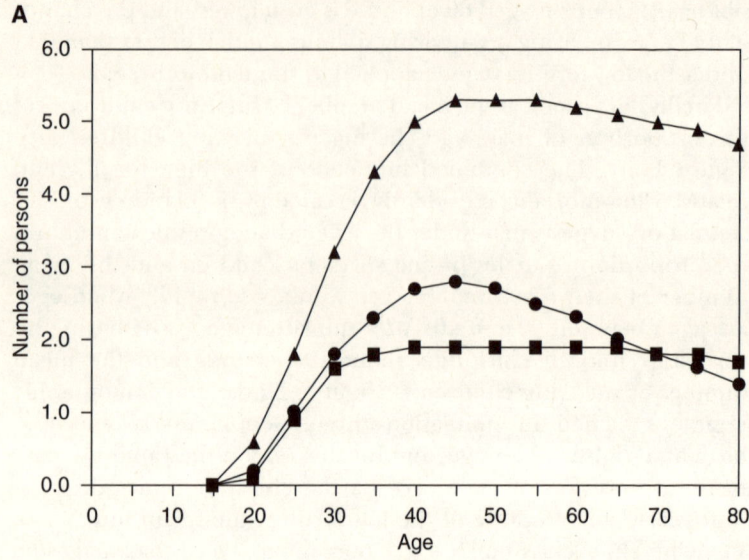

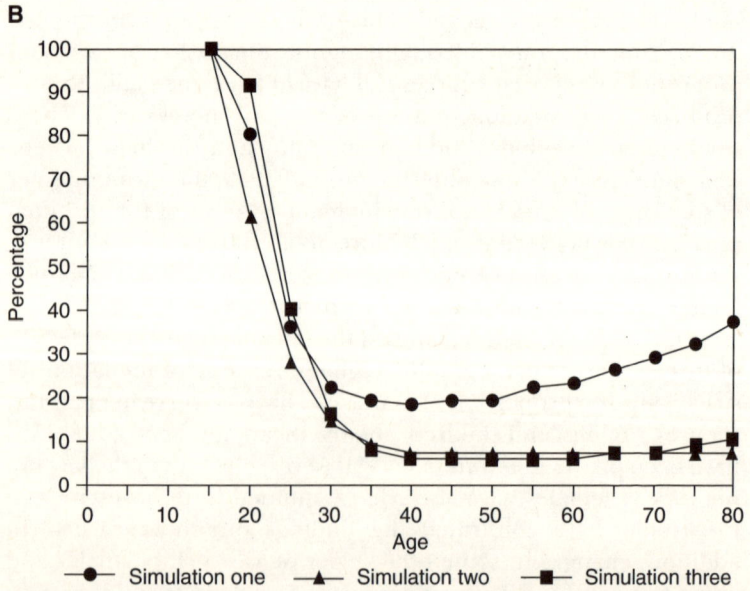

Figure 11.4 (a) Mean number of surviving children by age of male ego
(b) Percentage of males with no surviving children by age

As has been said, certain assumptions used in the simulation may not be very realistic and some of the demographic parameters put into the system may not be exactly the same as those observed in either the past or the present. For these reasons, the simulated population differs from any recorded population. The simulated population, for example, has gone through a stable demographic regime, while in reality an observed population, either a birth cohort or a group of people of a certain area, would have experienced changing demographic conditions. These may lessen the credibility of the simulation results, but the importance of the simulation study and its outcomes should not be neglected. The simulation results reported above are obviously very important in expanding our understanding of kinship networks, household composition and their interrelationship with demographic conditions, and the following lessons can be learned from this exercise.

In China in the past, the formation of complex kinship networks and extended families was severely constrained by high mortality. The 'demographic feasibility' of family support for the elderly, therefore, might not have been as high as people normally expected.

According to Barclay and his colleagues, the crude birth rate was 41.2 per thousand for Chinese farmers between 1929 and 1931. Life expectancy at birth was about 25 years for both males and females. Mean age at first marriage was 17.5 years for women and 21.3 for men.[12] Under similar demographic conditions, the annual population growth rate would be around 3 per thousand. This is higher than the average population growth rate recorded before 1500, and close to that recorded between 1500 and 1900.[13]

Under such a demographic regime, the number of living kin available to each individual, as indicated by the simulation results, is not very high but only moderate. Because of the high mortality, a fairly large proportion of people would have had no surviving sons when they reached old age. Although the extended family, consisting of an elderly couple and their married as well as unmarried sons, was widely held to be the ideal, and living arrangements of this kind have been widely seen as the primary source of family support for the elderly, support from their immediate family, particularly their sons, was simply not available for a considerable number of people.

In Table 11.2, the simulated male egos are divided into four groups – men having neither spouses nor children surviving; men with no married sons but with surviving spouses, daughters or unmarried sons; men with one married son; and finally men with at least two married sons. The figures show that under the high fertility and high mortality similar to those found in China around 1930, the probability of a person forming an extended family including one or two married sons is not high. At age 50, only 13 per cent of males could live with two or more married sons, and at ages 60 to 70 those having two or more married sons are only about a quarter. At these specified ages, those who could live with at least one married son account for 47 to 58 per cent. These figures are not only considerably lower than those suggested by simulation two, but also lower than those produced by simulation three which is characterized by low fertility and low mortality. The results of the first simulation also show that under the high mortality – although fertility is high as well – the proportion of egos without a married son, particularly those having neither surviving spouses nor children, is very high. At age 50, for example, 16 per cent of them would have neither spouses nor children, and it rises to more than a quarter when egos reach age 70.

In the Chinese past, people might have preferred to form large multi-generational households and the younger generation was widely expected to take responsibility for supporting their old parents, but many people, perhaps even the majority, might not

Table 11.2 Percentages of males having the given number of married sons

Age	Simulation	2+ married sons	1 married son	No married sons	No spouse or child
	one	12.8	34.0	37.4	15.8
50	two	46.4	28.0	23.8	1.8
	three	14.2	33.0	51.6	1.2
	one	27.8	30.6	21.2	20.4
60	two	67.4	20.8	9.6	2.2
	three	24.4	38.2	36.2	1.2
	one	23.8	29.2	20.2	26.8
70	two	70.4	18.0	8.6	3.0
	three	24.2	38.4	35.0	2.4

have been able to live in households of such a type for a long time because of the constraint imposed by mortality. As I have shown in other studies, under similar demographic conditions the proportion of those who could share lifetime with their sons and grandsons was not very high, and the period during which the elderly could live with their children and grandchildren and enjoy their support was not very long. Under such demographic conditions, even if each individual followed family formation rules requiring all males to live with their parents and grandparents when possible, nearly 60 per cent of those who reached age 70 would have spent more than 20 years in simple family households. A substantial part (40 per cent) of those aged 60 or 70 would have been found living in households with a simple structure.[14]

It is important to realize that in China, as in many other countries, the improvement in mortality is only a 'new' development which has been recorded for less than a hundred years, or even less than fifty. Before then, demographic conditions might always have been typified by high mortality. As has been indicated by the simulation outcomes, under high mortality conditions, the proportion of old people who could get support from their children might be even lower than that under the low fertility regime we are experiencing now. In some historical Chinese populations, for instance, although many people were found living in complex households with their children and grandchildren, the proportion of single-person households was not low, owing to a relatively high celibacy rate among the male population and high mortality.[15] For those who lived alone or who had no immediate kin to support them, help from other sources could have played an important role. Hence, before we say that old people were supported by their families or their sons, we should avoid simplifying a complex situation or idealizing the past.

During the 1950s and 1960s, apart from the period between 1959 and 1962, China experienced a relatively low mortality and a high fertility, which considerably increased the density of Chinese kinship networks.[16] The traditional ideal that many people survive to very old age and are supported by their sons, which perhaps had never been widely achieved in the past, has become a reality only under such modern demographic conditions.

The results of the second simulation (see Table 11.2) suggest that if the given demographic conditions are maintained, the proportion of male egos who can live with one or two married sons will rise sharply and the percentage of those having no married sons will be very low. Compared with the results of the first simulation, the proportion of men with two or more married sons will have more than doubled. Under the demographic conditions specified in simulation two, nearly half of the male egos would have two or more married sons at age 50 and more than two-thirds at ages 60 and 70. Those who have at least one married son will be close to 90 per cent when egos reach ages 60 and 70. At age 50, the number of males who have no married sons is not high and accounts for about 25 per cent. However, this is not because they have no sons at all, but because their sons are still unmarried.

These simulation results are in agreement with recent empirical research. As I have reported in another paper, because of the mortality decline and the high fertility of the 1950s and 1960s, the density of kinship networks is very high in the contemporary Chinese population. Table 11.3 presents the mean numbers of surviving kin of some selected types by people's age and all the statistics are derived from a survey conducted in three villages in the Beijing area during the winter of 1989.[17]

Unlike the simulated population, the one living in the three villages experienced changing demographic conditions. Before the mid-1960s, especially during the crisis period of the early 1960s, they were likely to have experienced a demographic regime under which mortality was more severe than that observed in the simulated population. For this reason, the mean number of their surviving siblings and the mean number of their surviving children are smaller than those indicated by the second simulation. For those under age 55, the lower number of children also arises from the fact that they have been subject to the nationwide family planning campaign and their family size has been effectively limited. Even so, the mean number of surviving children and that

Table 11.3 Mean numbers of surviving kin of specified type by age of ego

Age	30–34	35–39	40–44	45–49	50–54	55–59	60–64	65–69	70+
Spouses	0.98	0.99	0.97	0.98	0.96	0.89	0.82	0.62	0.49
Brothers	1.93	1.94	1.61	1.52	1.31	1.08	0.99	0.76	0.54
Sisters	1.70	1.57	1.62	1.35	0.98	1.03	0.82	0.65	0.46
Sons	0.67	0.86	1.22	1.51	1.83	2.15	2.44	2.28	1.86
Daughters	0.52	0.74	1.05	1.41	1.79	2.07	1.97	1.93	1.66

of surviving siblings recorded in this population may still be much higher than those which were likely to be found in the past. In addition to the kin listed in the table, people also have a very high number of children-in-law, grandchildren, nephews and nieces, and kin of other kinds. According to these statistics, family support for the elderly may not be difficult in the near future. For instance, the average number of surviving children for people aged 40 and over is 3.5. Even if we assume all these people are currently married, each couple would still have 3.5 children.[18] Up to the year 2020 when people of the 40 to 44 age group reach 70 to 75, it will not be difficult for old people to get support from their children if the children are in a position to provide it. Indeed, as far as family support for the elderly, or the dependency ratio between the elderly and the population of working age is concerned, the next twenty-five years are likely to be the best time in Chinese history – at least from a demographic point of view.

Since the early 1970s China has been experiencing another dramatic demographic change which is characterized by rapid fertility decline. This change has already had, and will continue to have, a significant effect on the availability of kin and, in turn, on household formation and family support for the elderly. As indicated by both the computer simulation and empirical research, Chinese kinship networks are undergoing another significant change.

The figures in Table 11.3 show that in comparison with those age 40 and over, the mean number of children for those under this age is very low. Accordingly, the mean number of siblings of their children will be very small. If the current low fertility is maintained or declines further, the mean number of children and siblings for these people (as well as for future generations) is likely to be maintained at these low levels or to show a further decrease. The lateral extension in Chinese kinship networks will soon be replaced by vertical extension. Current complex Chinese kinship networks will become simpler in the next century.

Because of the above changes, the probability of an elderly person's living with more than one married son, or the probability of a person's forming a joint family will be notably lessened. As has been indicated (see Table 11.2, p. 272), under the low fertility used in the third simulation the proportion of people who could live with two, or more than two, married sons is considerably lower, and the proportion having no married sons among those aged

60 and 70 is noticeably higher than that produced by the second simulation. Compared with the current situation, family support for the elderly will become difficult in the future. However, when these results are compared with those of simulation one, the following points are noteworthy. In spite of the fact that the 'total fertility rate' in the third simulation is only less than two-fifths of that in the first, the outcome of the third simulation shows that the proportion of those having at least one married son is even higher and the proportion having neither spouse nor children is considerably lower. These are primarily caused by the improvement in mortality. These results suggest that under such demographic conditions, the feasibility of an elderly person's residing with one or two married sons might be even greater than that under the demographic regime which typified China half a century ago.

Although the simulation results show that in comparison to the past, family support for old people seems unlikely to be very difficult in the future, we should not be too optimistic about the rapid ageing of the population or its socio-economic consequences. Some population projections indicate that both the number and the proportion of old people will increase rapidly in China. By the year 2030, those aged 60 and over could reach 335 millions and make up 22 per cent of the whole population.[19] In some areas the pace of population ageing will be much faster and the proportion of old people will be much higher, because of the considerable regional variation in fertility. More noticeably, the number and the proportion of the very old have increased and will continue to increase at an even faster rate. In some countries where better data on the oldest old are available, for example, though the increase in the size of total population has been fairly small during the period between 1950 and 1990, 'the number of octogenarians has grown 4-fold, that of nonagenarians 8-fold and that of centenarians more than 20-fold'.[20] A similar process is most likely to be found in China. During this rapid ageing of the population, we will inevitably meet many difficulties which humanity has never experienced before. To have an increasing number of people reaching a higher age is of course itself a great success, but it also means that more and more people will live for a much longer period after their retirement if there is no change in the age at which people leave the work force. In the past a person of age 65 was almost certainly seen as one who ought to be supported by his (or her) family, but in the near future such a person is most likely to act as a help provider to his (or her) long-lived parents. Given the speed and the magnitude of these changes as well as their significant influences on China's future development, it is not unreasonable to say that at some time during the next century, perhaps after the year 2025, both family and state support for the elderly are likely to face a serious challenge.

NOTES

1 This research has been undertaken in the ESRC Cambridge Group for the History of Population and Social Structure, and the East–West Center of Hawaii. I would like to thank James Smith and Jim Oeppen for giving me access to the CAMSIM computer simulation system and helping me to apply it to Chinese data. I would also like to thank Peter Laslett, Richard Smith, Richard Wall, Kevin Schurer, and Chris Wilson for their invaluable comments. Some of the results presented in this paper were reported at the 'International Seminar on Consequences of Replacement and Below Replacement Level Fertility in East and Southeast Asia' held in Seoul in 1993.

2 For discussion of the high mortality before the 1950s and the mortality change thereafter, see Z. Zhai, 'An Adjustment of the 1990 Infant Mortality Rate and an Estimation of the Life Table', *Population Research* 2 (1993), pp. 9–16 (in Chinese); Population Census Office under State Council, *National Statistical Bureau Communiqué of Main Results of the 1990* Census (Beijing, 1990) (in Chinese); China Financial and Economic Publishing House, *New China's Population* (London, 1988); J. Banister, *China's Changing Population* (Stanford, 1987).

3 The average number of children that a woman would have if initial fertility conditions remained unchanged and she survived to age 50.

4 Z. Jiang, 'Fertility Policies in China: Performance and Prospects', unpublished paper presented to the International Seminar on Consequences of Replacement and Below Replacement Level Fertility in East and Southeast Asia, Seoul, 1993; G. Feeney and J. Yuan, 'Below Replacement Fertility in China? A Close Look at Recent Evidence', *Population Studies* 48 (1994), pp. 381–94; B. Gu, 'China's Population Programme: from the 1970s to the 1990s', *China Population Newsletter* 7 (1990), pp. 1–2 (in Chinese).

5 For further discussion of demographic conditions in Chinese history, see Z. Zhao, 'Household and Kinship in Recent and Very Recent Chinese History', Ph.D. thesis (Cambridge, 1993).

6 A kin set is defined by J. Smith as 'a set of all of those people who at any time occupy any relevant kinship position relative to ego. A relative kinship position is simply one that the modeller decides for his or her purpose'. J. Smith, 'The Computer Simulation of Kin Sets and Kin Counts', in J. Bongaarts, T. K. Burch and K. W. Wachter (eds), *Family Demography: Methods and Their Application* (Oxford, 1987), pp. 249–66.

7 The types of kin generated by the simulation system can be decided by researchers according to their own purposes.

8 For further discussions of computer simulation and particularly of the CAMSIM system, see J. Smith, 'The Computer Simulation of Kin Sets and Kin Counts'; J. Smith and J. Oeppen, 'Estimating Numbers of Kin in Historical England Using Demographic Microsimulation', in D. Reher and R. Schofield (eds), *Old and New Methods in Historical Demography* (Oxford, 1993), pp. 413–25.

9 Family reconstitution is a method invented by the French demographer L. Henry in the 1950s. This method has been widely used, particularly in Europe, in the study of population history. For further details see E. A. Wrigley, 'Family Reconstitution', in Wrigley (ed.), *An Introduction to English Historical Demography* (London, 1966), pp. 96–159.

10 For Chinese genealogies and their under-registration problems see J. M. Meskill, 'The Chinese Genealogy as a Research Source', in M. Freedman (ed.), *Family and Kinship in Chinese Society* (Stanford, 1970), pp. 139–61; Z. Zhao, 'Demographic Conditions and Multi-generation Households in Chinese History: Results from Genealogical Research and Microsimulation', *Population Studies* 48 (1994), pp. 413–25.

11 The mortality rates used in the first simulation are very high. However, under this high mortality and high fertility, the average annual population growth rate is still around 3 per thousand, which is not low for a historical population. In order to estimate the influence of changing mortality, this set of mortality rates has also been replaced by lower rates in the exercise and this has slightly increased the number and the type of kin available to each individual. Such changes, however, generally have no influence on the conclusions reached in the following discussion.

12 G. W. Barclay, A. J. Coale, M. A. Stoto and T. J. Trussell, 'A Reassessment of the Demography of Traditional Rural China', *Population Index* 42 (1976), pp. 606–35.

13 According to W. Zhao and S. Xie, *Population History of China* (Beijing, 1988) (in Chinese), for example, the Chinese population was about 93 million in 1500 and 406 million in 1911. If this was the case, the average annual population growth rate would be 3.6 per thousand.

14 Z. Zhao, 'Demographic Conditions and Household Formation in Chinese History: a Simulation Study', unpublished paper presented at the Conference on Asian Population History, Taipei, 1996.

15 J. Lee and J. Gjerde report that in 1801 in Chinese villages near Shenyang the proportion of single-person households was slightly higher than 12 per cent. J. Lee and J. Gjerde, 'Comparative Household Morphology of Stem, Joint and Nuclear Household Systems: Norway, China and the United States', *Continuity and Change* 1 (1986), pp. 89–111.

16 During the period between 1959 and 1962, because of the economic crisis and famine, fertility was relatively low and mortality was very high in China. For demographic changes during this period, see

X. Peng, 'Demographic Consequences of the Great Leap Forward in China's Provinces', *Population and Development Review* 13 (1987), pp. 639–70.

17 For further discussion of this survey and its findings see Z. Zhao, 'Demographic Transition and Changes in Chinese Kinship Networks', unpublished paper presented at the American Sociological Association Annual Meeting, 1994.

18 As a measure of the density of kinship networks, this paper frequently uses the mean number of kin, which has been calculated by dividing the total number of kin of a given type into the total number of people being surveyed. Because an individual may occupy several kin positions (e.g. a woman can be recorded as mother, wife, and daughter) or may be recorded as kin of a certain type more than once (e.g. a man can be recorded as a son for both his mother and his father), such a measure indicates only that each person on average has a certain number of kin relations of a given type. It should not be confused with other measures, for example the dependency ratio.

19 C. Wu and P. Du, 'Recognition of the Ageing Trend of China's Population', *Population Science of China* 3 (1992), pp. 1–5 (in Chinese).

20 V. Kannisto, *Development of Oldest–Old Mortality, 1950–1990: Evidence from 28 Developed Countries* (Odense, 1994).

INDEX

Guguletu 244
guilds 75

Hadleigh, Suffolk 10–11, 14, 25, 73ff.
Hadley, Middlesex 157
Hajnal, John 45ff., 91
Halesowen 42, 46
Hammersmith 186
Hampstead 220ff.
Hampstead Council for Social Welfare 225
Hanwell 155
Hardington, Somerset 156
health visitors 222
Hedley Committee Report (1929) 207
Helm 243
Henderson, John and Wall, Richard 8, 60n, 61n
Hertford 166
Hesiod 55
Hindus 245
historical demography 176
Horsham 182
Hospital Plan (1962) 2
hospitals 4, 11, 12–13, 25, 26, 27, 29, 71, 73, 82, 94–8, 108n, 111, 126–50, 187; governors 134; patrons/subscribers 97–8, 126ff., 138–46, 146n, 147n, 148n, 149n; statutes 128; voluntary 12, 126ff.; workhouse infirmary 134; see also patients
household 51; complexity 32; composition 271; formation 46, 58, 104, 168; joint 48–50; medicine 22, 23, 29; multi-generational 272; pauper 40, 41, 92; size 31, 50, 92; see also family
House of Correction 83
housing, cheap 234
Hoxton 155
Huddersfield Infirmary 140
Humber 188
Huntingdonshire 130

Iceland 58, 59

Ignatieff, Michael 177
Iliffe, John 49
illegitimacy 162, 166, 242, 249–50, 256n, 257n
illness 12, 74, 76, 77, 78, 79, 96, 100, 116, 121–2, 133, 143; chronic 143
Immorality Act 240
incurables 97–8
India 50
individualism 42
infanticide 254
infant mortality 220, 228
infant welfare centres 222
infirm, the 72, 73
inflation 73
insanity see mentally ill and disabled
institutions 1, 5, 7, 12, 14, 15, 27, 74, 79, 90, 93, 98, 115, 198, 106–7n, 172n, 176–7, 201, 204–5, 242, 243
Interdepartmental Committee on Physical Deterioration (1904) 219–20
Ipswich 74
Ireland 158; post-famine 186
Irish Catholics, immigrants 234; residents 236
Islam, early 58
Islamic law 251

Japanese village 50, 168
'Jeugkommissie van Algemene Sinode' (1966) 244
Johnson, Paul 5
Judaism 25, 112, 124n

Kensington 15, 220ff.
Kenya 48, 67
Kettering 133
Keynesian economic management 3
Keynsham, near Bristol 131
kin, affinal 33; ascending 263; descending 263
kin availability 5, 47, 190, 261–77 see also demographic change
Kingsthorpe, Northants 130, 132